Millennia of Language Cha

Were Stone-Age languages really more complex tl
Was Basque actually once spoken over all of Westei   . .ɪe Welsh-speaking slaves truly responsible for the loss of English morphology? This latest collection of Peter Trudgill's most seminal articles explores these questions and more. Focused around the theme of sociolinguistics and language change across deep historical millennia (the Palaeolithic era to the Early Middle Ages), the essays explore topics in historical linguistics, dialectology, sociolinguistics, language change, linguistic typology, geolinguistics, and language contact phenomena. This collection will be indispensable to academic specialists and graduate students with an interest in the sociolinguistic aspects of historical linguistics.

PETER TRUDGILL is a world-renowned theoretical dialectologist, with Honorary Doctorates from the Universities of Uppsala, East Anglia, La Trobe, British Colombia, and Patras. Recent publications include *Dialect Matters: Respecting Vernacular Language* (2016) and *Investigations in Sociohistorical Linguistics* (2010).

Millennia of Language Change
Sociolinguistic Studies in Deep Historical Linguistics

PETER TRUDGILL
University of Fribourg, Switzerland

CAMBRIDGE
UNIVERSITY PRESS

CAMBRIDGE
UNIVERSITY PRESS

University Printing House, Cambridge CB2 8BS, United Kingdom

One Liberty Plaza, 20th Floor, New York, NY 10006, USA

477 Williamstown Road, Port Melbourne, VIC 3207, Australia

314–321, 3rd Floor, Plot 3, Splendor Forum, Jasola District Centre,
New Delhi – 110025, India

79 Anson Road, #06–04/06, Singapore 079906

Cambridge University Press is part of the University of Cambridge.

It furthers the University's mission by disseminating knowledge in the pursuit of
education, learning, and research at the highest international levels of excellence.

www.cambridge.org
Information on this title: www.cambridge.org/9781108477390
DOI: 10.1017/9781108769754

First published 2020

Printed in the United Kingdom by TJ International Ltd. Padstow Cornwall

A catalogue record for this publication is available from the British Library.

Library of Congress Cataloging-in-Publication Data
Names: Trudgill, Peter, author.
Title: Millennia of language change : sociolinguistic studies in deep historical linguistics /
Peter Trudgill.
Description: 1. | New York : Cambridge University Press, 2020. | Includes bibliographical
references and index.
Identifiers: LCCN 2019046532 (print) | LCCN 2019046533 (ebook) | ISBN 9781108477390
(hardback) | ISBN 9781108769754 (ebook)
Subjects: LCSH: Historical linguistics. | Linguistic change. | Sociolinguistics.
Classification: LCC P140 .T78 2020 (print) | LCC P140 (ebook) | DDC 306.44–dc23
LC record available at https://lccn.loc.gov/2019046532
LC ebook record available at https://lccn.loc.gov/2019046533

ISBN 978-1-108-47739-0 Hardback
ISBN 978-1-108-70864-7 Paperback

For Jim Milroy, in memoriam

Contents

Acknowledgements

I am very grateful indeed for help with the current book and the original articles which – now revised, updated and expanded – make up the chapters of this book to: Anders Ahlqvist, Alexandra Aikhenvald, Lieselotte Anderwald, Enam Al-Wer, Torben Arboe, Peter Arkadiev, Sigbjørn Berge, Raphael Berthele, Kurt Braunmüller, David Britain, Rik De Busser, Magdalena Charzynska-Wójcik, Juan Manuel Hernandez Campoy, Andrew Carstairs-McCarthy, Bernard Comrie, Östen Dahl, Gunther De Vogelaer, Bob Dixon, Bridget Drinka, Andreas Dufter, Martin Durrell, Nick Evans, Jan Terje Faarlund, Małgorzata Fabiszak, Paul Fletcher, Michael Fortescue, Michael Garman, Patrick Griffiths, Jean Hannah, Ray Harlow, Dagmar Haumann, Jack Hawkins, Raymond Hickey, Jarich Hoekstra, Jan Hognestad, Kristine Horner, David Hornsby, Neil Jacobs, Ernst Håkon Jahr, Mark Janse, Paul Johnston, Mike Jones, Brian Joseph, Paul Kerswill, Jacques Van Keymeulen, Juhani Klemola, Kristin Killie, Paul Kiparsky, Gerry Knowles, Martin Kümmel, Tony Lodge, Angelika Lutz, Jim Mallory, John McWhorter, Christian Mair, Marianne Mithun, John Nerbonne, Agnete Nesse, Daniel Nettle, Terttu Nevalainen, Hans Frede Nielsen, Helge Omdal, Andy Pawley, Inge Lise Pedersen, Karen Margrethe Pedersen, Gro-Renée Rambø, Gertrud Reershemius, Elisa Roma, Jürg Schwyter, Peter Siemund, J. C. Smith, Philip Stickler, Sali Tagliamonte, Hildegard Tristram, Edward Vajda, Wim Vandenbussche, Theo Vennemann, Alastair Walker, Martijn Wieling, Roland Willemyns, David Willis, Ilse Wischer and Justyna Wubs-Mrozewicz.

Prologue: the Long View

We do not know for certain how old human language, as we understand it, is. Lieberman (2008: 359) argues for a date in the Upper Palaeolithic around 50,000 BC as the 'start-point for *fully* human linguistic capacity' [my italics]. Dixon (1997: 2) mentions 100,000 years as a possibility for the age of human language. Evans (2010: 14) suggests that language dates back to 'long before' 150,000 years ago. Foley (1997: 73) says that 'language, as we know it, was born about 200,000 years ago'. And Dediu and Levinson (2013) argue, on the basis of their supposition that Neanderthals and Denisovans also had language (a possibility specifically excluded by Lieberman, and others), that it might even be 500,000 years. Whatever the answer may be, however, we are at least justified in describing human language as having been with us for 'a very long time indeed'.

One of the points that I try to make in this book is that there are a number of linguistic phenomena which we can only fully understand by recognising (with Dahl, 2004) that some linguistic features take a very long time indeed to develop; and that there are other features which can be fully understood only by looking back at linguistic situations and events that occurred a very long time ago indeed.

Until relatively recently, historical linguistic research did not typically probe too far into the prehistoric linguistic past, not least because of the constraints which were imposed by the comparative method. But increasingly scholars are thinking back into the Neolithic, Mesolithic and Palaeolithic. For example, papers on the American-Siberian Dene-Yenisean connection in Kari and Potter (2010), following pioneering research by Edward Vajda (2010a, 2010b), discuss dates as far back as 14,000 BC; and Fortescue, in his *Language Relations across the Bering Strait: Reappraising the Archaeological and Linguistic Evidence* (1998), similarly discusses remote linguistic scenarios. So do the contributors to Bengtson (ed.) (2008) *In Hot Pursuit of Language in Prehistory*. Foley likewise goes back many millennia in his discussion of a possible genetic relationship between Australian languages and the Eastern Highlands languages of New Guinea (1986: 269ff.). And the language of hunter-gatherers – albeit mainly contemporary hunter-gatherers – is the subject of Güldemann et al. (2019).

In any case, whether we are talking about 100 millennia, 200 millennia or 500 millennia of human language history, it is clear that nearly all of the linguistic past took place in Old Stone Age societies; and that nearly all the rest of the linguistic past took place in New Stone Age societies. And even the New Stone Age did not see too much: if the earliest date for the beginning of the Neolithic anywhere in the world was around 10,000 BC, then human languages were spoken during the Palaeolithic and Mesolithic periods for 90 per cent to 98 per cent of their history, depending on whether we go with Dixon or Dediu and Levinson. And if the earliest date for the end of the Neolithic anywhere in the world was around 4000 BC, then human languages were spoken in stone-age communities – neolithic and pre-neolithic combined – for 96 per cent to 99 per cent of their history. Post-stone-age societies have therefore had, in comparison, rather little of human language history; and so it makes sense for linguistic scientists to ponder over the issue of what stone-age languages were like.

Someone who has done some pondering is Comrie (1992). He hypothesises, in his paper 'Before complexity', that there must have been an earlier language state which was 'typologically distinct from attested languages' in that it was 'less complex' than attested languages. He makes a very persuasive case. He points out that there is a widespread belief amongst linguists that certain linguistic phenomena always develop from earlier linguistic states which those phenomena are absent from. For example, it is accepted that so-called tone languages such as Chinese acquired tone through tonogenesis. This is a process whereby pitch begins to be used contrastively where it was not so used before (i.e., phonetically conditioned non-contrastive pitch differences become contrastive through the loss of some conditioning environment). 'We have solid evidence for the origin of tonal phenomena in nontonal phenomena: all tonal oppositions in language have nontonal origins' (Comrie 1992: 207). Word tones have frequently appeared under the influence of the laryngeal articulations of adjacent consonants (see Haudricourrt 1954). Kingston (2011) shows the following tonogenesis path for the modern Vietnamese monosyllable *pa:*

*pa >   pa [high level tone]
*pas >   pa [high falling]
*ba >   pa [low level]
*bas >   pa [low falling]

We can therefore assume with some degree of certainty that the very earliest prehistoric languages were not tone languages.

Two other absentees from these earliest of languages will have been nasal vowels and morphophonemic alternations. It is widely agreed that contrastive nasal vowels always arise from earlier sequences of oral vowel plus nasal consonant, where the vowel first becomes allophonically nasalised and then the nasal consonant is lost, as with French *vin* /vɛ̃/ from Latin *vīnum*. Given that this is the case, we can assume that the very earliest languages did not have nasal vowels. Similarly, morphophonemic alternations such as English *mouse–mice* always arise from earlier states where there were no such alternations. In the specific case of *mouse–mice*, the earlier pre-umlaut stage consisted of singular *mūs* versus plural *mūsiz*. We can therefore similarly suppose that the world's earliest languages had no such alternations.

In my own work, I have suggested that insights into the nature of prehistoric languages may be gained from work in sociolinguistic typology, a theme I will take up at greater length in Chapter 1 of this book, 'Prehistoric Sociolinguistics and the Uniformitarian Hypothesis: What Were Stone-Age Languages Like'. The point is that there are many obvious respects in which the structure of palaeolithic, mesolithic and neolithic societies was very different from the structure of contemporary societies; and that this social fact might be reflected in certain aspects of the structures of these languages, as a sociolinguistic fact. The demographies of stone-age societies were very different from those of the modern age. Communities then were very small: Mailhammer (2011: 672) suggests that people lived in groups of 25 to 100 during the final stages of the European Palaeolithic. Because of that, social network structures would have been dense, and there would have been large amounts of communally shared information. There were also far fewer communities. Hassan (1981), as quoted by Nettle (1999: 102), reckons that the human population of the entire world 70,000 years ago was 1,200,000 – about the same size as modern Prague or Adelaide. Biraben (1979) suggests an even lower figure of 500,000 for 40,000 BP [Before Present]. Such estimates are obviously subject to large margins of error, but, in any case, the average density of population in the inhabited parts of the globe at that time was very low indeed compared to today. It would of course be an error to imagine a scenario in which the population of Prague was spread out evenly across the entire globe, because obviously there would have been uninhabited zones as well as particular concentrations in different areas. But this thought experiment does make the point that, in the Middle Palaeolithic, there would have been a much lower degree of intergroup contact than today, and therefore a much lower degree of language contact. And even by the Mesolithic period, population density was still astonishingly low by modern standards: Mallory (2013) reports research indicating that the population of Ireland in the Mesolithic – which in Ireland lasted from c. 8000 BC to c. 4000 BC – was about 3,000, or about 0.04 people per square kilometre (i.e., 25 square kilometres (c. 10 square miles) per person), with comparable figures for elsewhere in the British Isles including, for example, a possible total population of 800 for Wales.

A number of other distinguished linguists have also been pondering over various different aspects of linguistic prehistory. Vennemann (2010a), for example, has argued that the first important language-contact events which have significance for modern western European languages took place a very long time ago indeed: his story begins way back in prehistory at the end of the last Ice Age, so perhaps around 8000 BC. The scenario which Vennemann outlines goes as follows: during the last glacial period, the only area of western Europe where human habitation was possible was the Franco-Cantabrian Refugium. This was an area which stretched from the Asturias region, in northern Spain, to Provence in southern France (Gamble 1986). As the Ice Age was ending, there was a gradual repopulation of the northwestern part of the European continent, as the ice receded. This repopulation, as climatic conditions became more favourable, took off from southern France, the only area north of the Great Divide – the barrier which was posed to easy movement and migration by the Pyrenees and the Alps – where human habitation had been possible during the glacial period.

Vennemann's theory is exciting and 'provocative' (Baldi & Page 2006: 2184), and is also quite naturally highly controversial. I cannot do justice to his extensive argumentation and linguistic exemplification here, but Vennemann hypothesises that the people who were involved in this Mesolithic migration out of the Franco-Cantabrian Refugium were speakers of Vasconic – a language from which modern Basque, the only language truly indigenous to western Europe, is descended. In time, Vasconic came to be spoken in 'almost all of western, central, and northern Europe' (Vennemann 2010: 388). Eventually, there must have been, one supposes, a number of Vasconic varieties in western Europe: Mailhammer (2011) writes that it was only when Europe was repopulated, mainly from the continent's south-west, that people and languages were given space to go off in separate ways. Mailhammer then supposes that this state of affairs continued for a few thousand years until the arrival of the Indo-European languages. In other words, the first significant language contact events which subsequently took place in western Europe, and which have present-day relevance, were those which occurred, during the late Neolithic and/or early Bronze Age, between Vasconic and the languages of the first Indo-European speakers, as these arrived from the east.

In this book, albeit from a mainly sociolinguistic perspective, I follow Comrie and Vennemann in attempting to take a long view of language change processes, their genesis and their consequences. In Chapter 3 'First-Millennium England: a Tale of Two Copulas', I note an attempt to account for aspects of the structures of certain modern western European languages in terms of a form of inheritance from Proto-Vasconic, which might perhaps ultimately go very far back in time. According to Vennemann, the Urheimat – the 'cradle' or primeval home of Vasconic – lay very close to the current modern Basque homeland, and dates back to maybe 12,000 BC.

Less remote in time, but still a matter of a distance of many millennia, was the genesis of the Proto-Eskaleut (Eskimo-Aleut) language, which seems to have arisen around the Bering Strait perhaps five millennia ago (Fortescue, 1998; Fortescue & Vajda, fc.). And it does indeed seem to be necessary to go back a very long way, as I do in Chapter 2 'From Ancient Greek to Comanche: on Many Millennia of Complexification', in order to account for the degree of complexity demonstrated by the polysynthetic languages which descend from Proto-Eskaleut. This proto-language (which Dumond (1987) dates to some time between 4000 and 2000 BC) has been suggested by Bergsland (1986) to have begun to separate into Eskimo and Aleut around 1000 BC. And, according to Fortescue (1998) and Fortescue and Vajda (fc.), Proto-Eskaleut itself can be argued to descend from Proto-Uralo-Siberian, which dates back to 8000–6000 BC.

The Native American Indian language Comanche, which is another of the topics treated in Chapter 2, is a member of the Numic language branch of the Uto-Aztecan family, with the Proto-Uto-Aztecan family being thought to have come into being in what is now southern Arizona, southern New Mexico, northern Sonora and northern Chihuahua, in around 3000 BC. The development of certain of the characteristics of this language, too, will be argued in Chapter 2 to be comprehensible only if a very long view is taken.

The same is also true of data I present in Chapter 2 from Klamath, a language which has sadly been extinct since 2006, but which was formerly spoken in the USA around the shores of Klamath Lake in southern Oregon and northern California. This language, along with Nez Perce, Molala and Sahaptian, has been argued to be a member of a probable or possible Plateau Penutian family of languages spoken on the Columbian Plateau of eastern Washington state and north-central Oregon. The status of any broader 'Penutian' language family is a matter of some considerable doubt, dispute and discussion (see DeLancey & Golla 1997; Shipley 1980), but for the Plateau Penutian family (Berman 1996) there is some evidence, according to Cressman (1956), for continuous occupation of the Klamath Lakes region dating back to about 5000 BC.

The Austronesian language family is the main focus of Chapter 6 'Deep into the Pacific: the Austronesian Migrations and the Linguistic Consequences of Isolation'. The homeland of the Proto-Austronesian language has been securely located to the island of Formosa/Taiwan (Blust 2009), and is generally dated to approximately 4000–3500 BC (Nichols 1997; Greenhill et al. 2010). In Chapter 6, I take a long view of Austronesian languages geographically as well as chronologically, given that a number of rather impressive phonological developments occurred in this language family as its speakers, over periods of several millennia, gradually spread from Formosa out across the thousands of square kilometres of the Pacific Ocean.

It is also relatively easy to take a very long view of Greek. The 3,500 (albeit not entirely unbroken) years of written records we have of Greek (Horrocks 2010) quite naturally invite a long view of its history. Proto-Greek has been located by Georgiev (1981) to northwestern Greece and southern North Macedonia and Albania (as Indo-European speakers spread southwards into the Balkans) and to a date of around 2500 BC. Various aspects of Greek language history are discussed at some length here in Chapter 2, as well as in Chapter 7 'The Hellenistic Koiné 320 BC to 550 AD and Its Medieval and Early Modern Congeners'.

The Celtic languages appear to descend from a proto-language which was located in Central Europe around 1300 BC. The Proto-Celts are often identified with the archaeological Urnfield culture dated 1300 BC–750 BC and located in an area stretching from western Hungary through what is now Austria and southern Germany to eastern France. According to MacAulay (1992: 1):

The earliest named Celts (in Greek and Latin sources) are associated with two major Central European Iron Age cultures, the Hallstatt, dated to the seventh century BC, and La Tène, dated to the fifth century BC. The archaeological evidence suggests a cultural continuity backwards through the late Bronze Age Urnfield Culture *with no material evidence that the Celts were newcomers to the region.* [my italics]

The Celtic languages come into the discussion in a major way in Chapters 3 and 4 of this book, where I argue that the structure of English may well have been influenced by speakers of Celtic languages as a result of language contact situations which occurred, not only in Britain in historical times, but also in continental Europe before – and in some cases long before – the arrival of Germanic-speaking peoples on the island of Britain.

Proto-Finnic has been argued to date to around 1000 BC (Sammallahti 1977: 131–3), with its speakers having been situated in the zone around the shores of the Gulf of Finland, between Finland and Estonia (Itkonen 1983). Finnic appears in these pages in Chapter 2, where I discuss millennia-long developments in Finnic including phenomena associated with the putative 'morphological cycle'. Finnic descends from Proto-Uralic, which dates back to 4000 BC (Nichols 1997) and quite possibly beyond that to Proto-Uralo-Siberian (see above), as judiciously argued by Fortescue (1998).

This book itself is written in a tongue that is a member of the Germanic language family, which is treated in a number of places in this book: in Chapter 4 'The First Three-Thousand Years: Contact in Prehistoric and Early Historic English'; in Chapter 5 'Verner's Law, Germanic Dialects, and the English Dialect "Default Singulars"'; and in Chapter 8 'Indo-European Feminines: Contact, Diffusion and Gender Loss around the North Sea'. The Urheimat of Germanic is thought to have been located, perhaps around 2000 BC, in southern Scandinavia; but the developments involved in Verner's Law, having occurred some time after 2000 BC, are still having consequences in modern Germanic dialects today, three or four thousand years later, as I show in Chapter 5. And in Chapter 8, I discuss how and why feminine grammatical gender, having arisen as a new grammatical category in Proto-Indo-European perhaps 6,000 years ago, has now disappeared – or is in the process of doing so – in Germanic languages spoken all around the shores of the North Sea.

1 Prehistoric Sociolinguistics and the Uniformitarian Hypothesis: What Were Stone-Age Languages Like?

Introduction

One of the fundamental bases of modern historical linguistics is the *uniformitarian principle*. This principle states that *knowledge of processes that operated in the past can be inferred by observing ongoing processes in the present*.

The notion of uniformitarianism can be credited to British scientists, beginning with the work of the Scottish geologist James Hutton, who lived from 1726 to 1797. This was extended in the thinking of another Scot, John Playfair (b. 1748). And it became widely known as a result of the work of yet another Scot, Charles Lyell, in his 1830 work, *Principles of geology*. The actual term *uniformitarianism* itself, however, was coined by his English contemporary William Whewell. The extension of the concept into linguistics has been chronicled by Thomas Craig Christy (1983). But the attention that many linguists have paid to the term is due to Labov's *Sociolinguistic patterns* (1972).

The way Labov expresses it, the uniformitarian principle implies that language structures in the past must have been subject to exactly the same constraints as language structures in the present; and that the mechanisms of linguistic change that operate around us today are precisely the same as those which operated even in the remote past. According to Labov, this leads us to the methodological principle of *using the present to explain the past*: we cannot try to explain past linguistic states and changes in language by resorting to explanations that would not work for modern linguistic systems. For example, we cannot happily reconstruct a Proto-Indo-European consonantal system which would be typologically bizarre and unexpected from a twenty-first-century point of view.

In this chapter, I present a sociolinguistic-typological perspective on this issue, where by 'sociolinguistic typology' I mean a form of linguistic typology which is sociolinguistically informed and which investigates the extent to which it is possible to produce sociolinguistic explanations for why a particular language variety is like it is in structural terms. This work is based on the assumption that there is a possibility that certain aspects of social structure may be capable of having an influence on certain aspects of language structure (Trudgill 2011). I argue that, insofar as the characteristics of individual human languages are due to the nature of the human language faculty, there cannot be any questioning of the uniformitarian principle. We have to assume that the nature of the human language faculty is the same the world over, and that it has been like that ever since humans became fully human.

But there is a caveat to this principle.

This is that it seems rather clear that some of the characteristics of individual human languages are due to social factors. These social factors, as I have argued at length in Trudgill (2011), include the following:

degree of language contact
type of language contact
degree of social stability
community size
density of social networks
amount of communally shared information

If such social factors can have an influence on language structure, then the common faculty of the human mind will produce different types of language structure in different societies, in different places, at different moments in human history. And that will mean that the linguistic present might not altogether be like the linguistic past; which would in turn mean that the methodology of using the present to explain the past could be less useful as a principle and a technique the further back in time we go.

Palaeolithic and neolithic societies can be characterised as face-to-face societies, as opposed to the at-a-distance societies which most modern humans inhabit today. Hymes (1974: 50) writes of 'cheek-by-jowl communities'. And Givón (1979: 287) uses the term 'societies of intimates'. Until the domestication of plants and animals, our ancestors were all hunter-gatherers. They belonged to societies which were very different from 'societies of strangers' (Givón 1984: 249) – the large, complex human groups which began to develop around 10,000 BC and which most of us live in today. According to Givón, for nearly all of human history, human beings lived in societies which were stable; small in size; culturally uniform; of restricted territorial distribution (with a radius of no more than 20 miles/30 kilometres); and with dense social networks. My thesis is that such societies provided a social matrix which allowed linguistic phenomena to develop which are most unlikely to arise today in our own modern at-a-distance societies – a fact which we should take into consideration when extrapolating from the linguistic present to the linguistic past.

In modern times, population size and geographical mobility have increased very dramatically, so that we have seen larger and larger language communities, and more and more language contact. It has become much less common to find languages and dialects spoken in low-contact, isolated communities with tightly knit social networks. So my sociolinguistic-typological perspective leads me to ask:

to what extent can we really suppose that what is true of human languages today was also true of human languages in the remote past? And to the extent that it is not, where does that leave the uniformitarian principle?

I suggest that it leaves us needing to be somewhat cautious about extrapolating from the present to the past as far as certain features of language structure are concerned.[1] Labov, in his discussion of the uniformitarian principle, warns us that we must be 'wary of extrapolating backward in time to neolithic pre-urban societies' (Labov 1994: 23). And clearly this admonition becomes even more forceful in any consideration of palaeolithic societies. I now, therefore, proceed to an examination of a number of such caution-inducing features.

Caution-Inducing Features

Linguistic Features Due to Arbitrary Human Invention

One phenomenon of this type is a category of linguistic changes which we can characterise, following Blust (2012), as being the result of 'arbitrary human invention'. The sort of phenomenon Blust is referring to is illustrated in his account of vowel metathesis in Hawu, an Austronesian language from the Indonesian Lesser Sunda Islands. Blust calls it 'the first case of regular vowel metathesis ever reported'. In Hawu, vowels in adjacent syllables have metathesised according to a regular pattern. The metathesis did not occur unless the original first vowel of the pair was closer or more fronted than the second, and the two vowels were separated by a consonant. But if those conditions were fulfilled, it happened without exception. Then, once the metathesis had occurred, the vowel which was now in first position was centralised to schwa. Examples include:

uma > əmu 'house'
iru > əri 'to pull'
pira > pəri 'how much?'

Blust writes:

[I]f Hawu vowel metathesis is a product of universal phonetic predispositions, there is no obvious reason why phenomena similar to it have not been reported in other languages. By accepting the premise that the optimal explanation for a linguistic or cultural trait is inescapably tied to its geographical distribution, we are clearly forced to seriously consider some cases [of sound change] as products of arbitrary human invention. (2012: 230)

---

[1] And perhaps even more so about predicting what human languages will be like in the future – if we wanted to do that.

As Blust said in an earlier discussion of 'bizarre' sound changes in Austronesian languages, 'speakers may sometimes engage in a conscious, arbitrary manipulation of linguistic symbols' (2005: 264). In other words, the only way he can think of explaining some phonological changes in Austronesian languages is to suppose that speakers produced these sound changes deliberately – they did it consciously and on purpose. One such change is the Proto-Manus prenasalised alveolar trill which, extraordinarily, becomes an aspirated voiceless velar plosive in Drehet, one of the languages spoken on the Admiralty Island of Manus in Papua New Guinea (2005: 226).

In case we feel a bit sceptical about linguistic change being indulged in by speakers deliberately, Blust refers us to Laycock's description of a change in the Uisai dialect of Buin on Bougainville: all masculine nouns have become feminine, and all feminines have become masculine. Laycock says 'there is no accepted mechanism for linguistic change which can cause a flip-flop of this kind and magnitude', so we have to assume that

at some stage in the past, some influential speaker of the Uisai dialect announced that from now on his people were not to speak like the rest of the Buin. Once the change was adopted, it would become the natural speech of the community within one or two generations. (1982: 36)

A similar arbitrary switch in a nominal classification system is described by Schadeberg (1981) for the Kordofanian language Laro/Laru. He reports Stevenson (1956: 99) as saying that 'the Laro story is that this was done deliberately to confuse their neighbours'. And Nettle (1999: 138) has written about the possible role of individuals: 'if a group consists of just a few hundred people, the idiosyncrasies of one very influential individual can spread through it very easily'.

The moral would seem to be that, the further we look back into the linguistic past, the more we should be on the alert for such features. Arbitrarily invented sound changes and gender switches are not the sort of developments which are likely to succeed as linguistic changes in most contemporary societies of strangers. But in the remote linguistic past they could well have been more common than they are now.

Historical linguistic reconstructions involving unlikely seeming phonological or grammatical developments should perhaps not necessarily always be rejected out of hand if there can be a possibility of their having been introduced intentionally.

Linguistic Features Due to Non-Anonymity

A second example of a linguistic phenomenon that could only have developed in a face-to-face society comes from the work of Uri Tadmor (2015). Tadmor is the first linguist to have worked on Onya Darat, a West Malayo-Polynesian (Austronesian) language which is spoken in the interior of southwestern Indonesian Borneo. According to Tadmor, the Onya Darat personal pronoun system distinguishes between singular, dual and plural; and it also has an exclusive vs. inclusive distinction in the first-person dual and plural. But, remarkably, it also has another very unusual grammatical category: generational affiliation.

The way it works is that the singular pronouns indicate the generational affiliation of the referent vis-à-vis the speaker, with the two-way distinction of forms being between pronouns for members of the same or a younger generation, on the one hand, and pronouns for members of an older generation, on the other. The dual and plural pronouns work differently. They indicate generational relationships, with the distinction being between pronouns for members of the same generation and those for a different generation – except that the first-person dual and plural inclusive pronouns don't do this.

As an example, the third-person forms are as follows:

singular ≤	*iyo*	(s)he [same or younger generation than speaker]
singular >	*idoh*	(s)he [older generation than speaker]
dual =	*doduh*	they two [same generation as each other]
dual ≠	*damaaq*	they two [different generations from each other]
plural =	*diyen*	they [same generation as each other]
plural ≠	*denaq*	they [different generations from each other]

So if a woman was talking about her granddaughter and her great-granddaughter, she would have to say *damaaq* 'they (dual)', but if she was talking about her two granddaughters she would have to say *doduh* 'they (dual)'. Obviously, a system like this can only work in a society where everybody knows everybody else: generation does not necessarily match with age – your nephew might perfectly well be older than you. A speaker actually has to know the generational affiliation of absolutely everybody in the community to be able to use the correct pronoun. This system, Tadmor says, always used to work very well, because every village consisted of a single longhouse. A newly established village would have maybe six families, an older village perhaps sixty – but all the inhabitants of the village lived in the same house and knew each other well (Tadmor 2015). Sadly, destructive logging of the forest habitat has now more or less wrecked this traditional way of life; the long-houses are disappearing – and the pronoun system is disappearing with them. This feature is quite possibly unique amongst the languages of the modern world, but it is worth considering the possibility that perhaps, in the remote past, it was not.

Linguistic Features Due to Non-Optimality

Nettle (1999) points to a further interesting possibility concerning small language communities which is relevant when thinking about languages in prehistory. He considers the issue of word order in the typology of the world's languages and points out that languages with canonical object-initial constituent order are exceedingly rare. Until relatively recently, in fact, this order was widely believed to be non-existent, in spite of the fact that it had been reported by, for example, Beauvoir (1915).[2] Most linguists became aware of the possibility only with the publication of Derbyshire's paper (1977) on OVS order in the Amazonian language Hixkaryana.

Nettle also points out that all OVS and OSV languages are spoken by small or very small numbers of speakers. His suggestion is that this is not a coincidence, and he has an explanation for this. He accounts for both the rarity of object-initial order, and for the small numbers of speakers in communities speaking languages which have it, by using an argument from statistics. In population genetics, the effects of random change are known to be greater when the population is small. 'This is because the probability of a slightly deleterious variant becoming fixed in a population is inversely related to the population size. The smaller the community, the greater the stochastic chance of changes in gene frequency' (Nettle 1999: 139). Nettle hypothesises that the same is true of linguistic communities, and of linguistic features. Then, importantly, he suggests that non-optimal word orders are 'more likely to be found in small communities than in large ones, since these would be more vulnerable to drift away from optimal states' (1999: 139).

As to what might be 'non-optimal' about object-initial order, Givón (1984: section 7.3) argues that SOV is in some sense the basic order – and indeed the earliest pattern to be found in human language – and is favoured by factors to do with the role of the position of agent/topic and goal/object in the origins of human communication; he also argues that diachronic development to SVO, VSO or VOS, where this has occurred, has been favoured for reasons of a discourse-pragmatic nature (1984, section 7.11). OVS and OSV, however, are not favoured by either factor. And there is, in fact, a considerable body of more recent work indicating that there is a strong default tendency for listeners to perceive the first noun phrase in a construction as being the agent, something which obviously disfavours object-initial order (Primus 1999; Bornkessel 2002; Demiral et al. 2008; Wang et al. 2009; Hawkins 2012).

At earlier periods of human history, there were a higher proportion of small communities than there are today, and it is therefore not entirely unreasonable to suppose that there might have been more object-initial languages in the world. This is at least a possibility we should be alert to when considering the remote linguistic past.

Linguistic Features Due to Dense Social Networks

Wohlgemuth (2010: 271) writes that, although 'one cannot establish direct correlations other than the rather vague implication that rare characteristics

---

[2] As pointed out to me by Harald Hammarström.

can be found with clearly more than chance frequency in languages which have a small speaker community', it is still true that 'there are significant differences between the rarity index distributions of small languages versus the huge sample of WALS languages'.

Andersen (1988) has made what I would like to argue is a related observation, proposing a sociolinguistic correlate of the development of marked as opposed to unmarked sound changes. He points to unusual sound changes in dialects which 'are located in peripheral dialect areas, away from major avenues of interdialectal communication', and his hypothesis is that 'there is a connection between the limited socio-spatial function of a dialect, its relative closeness, and its ability to sustain *exorbitant phonetic developments*' (1988: 70, my italics). Andersen argues that 'dialects that serve predominantly local functions are more prone to elaborate phonetic detail rules than dialects with a wider sphere of use'.

Andersen cites, as an example of a sound change which would seem to fall into the category of 'unusual', an 'unprovoked fortition' which strikes many historical linguists as odd. This is a – significantly – historically unconnected series of developments of parasitic velar consonants out of high or mid vowels, in several isolated areas of Europe. It has occurred in dialects of a number of languages, including Romansch, Provençal, Danish, German and Flemish – changes which are absent from metropolitan varieties and less isolated varieties of the same languages. The Danish dialects Andersen cites are spoken in out-of-the-way places including 'the extreme western, most isolated parts of Funen and Jutland' (1988: 70). Examples include *bi* [bik] 'bee'; *missil* [misigl] 'missile'; *hel* [hekl] 'whole' (Nissen 1945; Nielsen 1947; Søndergaard 1970).

Such unprovoked fortitions generally do seem to be confined to small communities in geographically remote and/or peripheral areas. In Romansch, for instance, parasitic consonants occur in three separate and non-contiguous dialects – suggesting independent development – in the upper reaches of three separate river basins, namely the Inn, the Albula, and the Oberhalbstein branch of the Rhine. And this appears to be true elsewhere in the world also (Mortensen 2012).

How can we account for Wohlgemuth's observations about unusual features; and Andersen's observations about unusual changes?[3] One line of reasoning might be as follows. Grace writes:

A language exists in the people who speak it, but people do not live very long, and the language goes on much longer. This continuity is achieved by the recruitment of new speakers, but it is not a perfect continuity. Children (or adults) learning a language learn it from people who already speak it, but these teachers exercise considerably less than total control over the learning process. (1990: 126)

---

[3] It does not follow, of course, that unusual changes will necessarily give rise to unusual features.

We can accept that no 'teachers' exercise total control over intergenerational transmission, but Grace's perspective also allows us to suppose that 'teachers' in some societies may have more control than in others. This will be due to differences in social network structure. Small stable societies are much more likely than larger societies to have dense social networks with strong social ties.

There is therefore the possibility that small, tightly knit communities are better able to encourage the preservation of norms, and the continued adherence to norms from one generation to another, with concomitant relatively slow rates of linguistic change (Trudgill 2011a). But, though linguistic change will tend to be slower, when changes do occur there is a greater chance that they will be of a marked type. Not only are small communities more able to have a decelerating effect on the rate of change, they are also more able, because of their network structures, to push through, enforce and sustain linguistic changes which would have a much smaller chance of success in larger, more fluid communities – namely changes of a relatively marked, complex type. (There is no suggestion that this is done overtly, however: the mechanism responsible will be the frequency and density of face-to-face interaction.)

If this is correct, then it may well be that *innovations* of a marked type occur with roughly equal frequency in all types of community, but that it is simply the case that these innovations are more likely, perhaps much more likely, to succeed and become established as linguistic *changes* (i.e., innovations which are accepted and become permanent) in communities with tighter networks.

If we accept that this type of social structure was more common in prehistory than today, then there might have been more linguistically marked rarissima – very rare linguistic features – of the type discussed in Wohlgemuth and Cysouw (2010), as well as more marked changes in prehistory also. We should be prepared, as we go back in time, to discover more changes which are 'exorbitant', and more features which are marked, rare or very rare.

Linguistic Features Due to Communally Shared Information

Another characteristic of face-to-face societies is that they have large amounts of communally shared information. Givón calls it 'informational homogeneity' (Givón 1979: 297).

Kay (1976) argues that this factor has linguistic consequences. He says that:

in small, homogeneous speech communities there is a maximum of shared background between speakers, which is the stuff on which deixis depends. As society evolves toward complexity and the speech community becomes less homogeneous, speakers share less background information, and so one would need to build more of the message into what was actually said. (1976: 18)

Keenan (1976), too, suggests that deictic systems are better developed in smaller than in larger communities. And Perkins (1995) has demonstrated that there is indeed a correlation between community complexity and the number of deictic markers in a community's language.

One example of the extensive development of deixis is provided by large personal pronoun systems. These are clearly 'cross-linguistically dispensable phenomena' (Dahl 2004): Finnish makes do with six personal pronouns while !Ora has thirty-one: Siewierska (2004: 111) wrote that !Ora had the fullest pronoun paradigm she has ever seen. !Ora is a Khoekhoe language which *Ethnologue* showed to have fifty speakers in 1972 and which is now extinct. The thirty-one-pronoun system distinguished between male, female and common gender in the first and second as well as third persons; it had dual number, and contrasted exclusive and inclusive in the dual and plural. Perhaps, we can hypothesise, such systems were more common in prehistory than they are today.

The same can also be hypothesised for large systems of grammatical evidentiality. Aikhenvald's work has indicated that 'complex evidential systems, in their vast majority, are confined to languages with smallish numbers of speakers, spoken in small, traditional societies' (2004: 355). She also provides an excellent explanatory insight:

being specific in one's information source appears to correlate with the size of a community. In a small community everyone keeps an eye on everyone else, and the more precise one is in indicating how information was acquired, the less the danger of gossip, accusation, and so on. No wonder that most languages with highly complex evidential systems are spoken by small communities. (2004: 359)

There is good reason, then, to believe that highly developed evidential systems may be a linguistic feature particularly strongly associated with small face-to-face societies. And it may very well be, therefore, that they were commonplace in prehistoric languages.

In general, we can suppose that elaborate deictic systems and extensive evidential systems were more fully developed in prehistory than is usually the case with contemporary languages.

Conclusion

In considering languages and language relationships in prehistory then, it is as well to consider the sociolinguistics as well as the linguistics, as Nichols (2007: 176) has done, suggesting, for example, that language contact 'may well have been rare in prehistory'. Given that the development of large, fluid high-contact communities is mainly a post-neolithic phenomenon, then a sociolinguistic-typological perspective suggests that the dominant standard modern languages in the world today are not likely to be very typical of how languages have been for most of human history.

It is true that Bickel and Nichols (2020) have suggested that 'there is no significant typological difference between [contemporary] hunter-gatherer and other languages'. But this hardly seems relevant for the argument I am putting forward here, because their methodology – extracting data from very large databases such as WALS and examining all the variables for which there were enough responses across languages – did not permit them to look at rarissima such as generation-based pronominal systems or highly developed evidential systems; or at surprising linguistic changes such as gender reversal and unprovoked fortitions.

There is also another interesting problem for typology. Lots of attention has been paid to the sampling of the world's languages for typological purposes. It is agreed that we have to avoid *areal* bias in constructing samples, so that languages in one part of the world are not overrepresented; and that it is also vital to avoid *genetic* bias, so that certain language families are not overrepresented (e.g., Dryer 1989; Song 2001: 1.5.3–1.5.4). But there would also now seem to be a problem of *chronological* bias. This problem is insuperable. There is obviously no way we can make a genuine sample of all the languages that have ever existed. And if modern languages are not, as a whole and on average, typical of how languages have been for most of human existence, then a representative modern sample will not in fact be representative.

But it might help if we simply bear in mind that, while we have to assume that the uniformitarian hypothesis is basically correct, it is nevertheless – if there actually are social determinants of linguistic structure as I suppose throughout this book – not entirely unproblematic.

2 From Ancient Greek to Comanche: on Many Millennia of Complexification

Nettle (1999: 138) has written that 'no relationships of grammatical typology to structure or social organisation have been convincingly demonstrated', but that 'it seems quite plausible that some such relationship could exist', although 'the question has received little rigorous scholarly attention'. It is precisely this question which sociolinguistic typology is intended to devote scholarly attention to.

The term *sociolinguistic typology*, as noted in the Prologue and in Chapter 1, refers to research which attempts to apply sociolinguistic data and insights to the study of the typology of the world's languages. The goal is to investigate whether, and to what extent, the typological characteristics of the world's languages are influenced by social structure and social organisation – by the sociolinguistic characteristics of the communities in which they are spoken.

To this end, in Trudgill (2011) I isolated a number of different social parameters which, when taken in combination, shed light on the social determinants of linguistic structure. As already mentioned in Chapter 1, I considered different types of community with respect to the roles of community size, social network structure, social stability, contact with other communities and shared information.

The issue of *how* and *why* there should be links between linguistic and social structure was also investigated. Specifically, I attempted to answer the *how*-and-*why* question by examining different types of linguistic change because linguistic structures at any given moment are to a considerable extent the result of the changes which have produced them. And it emerged from this work, as it has from other writings in sociolinguistic typology (Trudgill 1983; Andersen 1988; Thurston 1989; Grace 1990; Ross 1997; Nettle 1999; Nettle & Romaine 2000; Wray & Grace 2007; Sinnemäki 2009; Lupyan & Dale 2010), that the most significant consequence of these social factors for linguistic structure has to do with issues concerning phonological, morphophonological and morphological simplicity as opposed to complexity.

Case Study: Dutch

As an illustration of the linguistic consequences that social factors may have for linguistic structure, let us begin by observing linguistic changes which have taken place in varieties of the Dutch language over the last few centuries.

The Southern African language Afrikaans, which is historically a variety of Dutch, provides a good starting point. Compared to European varieties of Dutch, Afrikaans has many innovations. For example, it has totally lost grammatical gender: 'gender in the noun had virtually disappeared by 1797' (Roberge 1995: 78) – about 150 years after the first Dutch settlement of the Cape. The modern Afrikaans system is now one of natural gender in which the definite article *die* applies to all nouns, singular and plural (and the indefinite article is *'n* [ə]) (Donaldson 1994), for example:

die man 'the man'   *die vrouw* 'the woman' *die huis* 'the house'.

Afrikaans has also lost all person-marking on verbs; and the infinitive is identical with the single finite present-tense form.

Contrast this with the metropolitan varieties of the north of the Netherlandic-speaking area of Europe, including Northern Standard Dutch, where grammatical gender has not been lost, and where person-marking on verbs survives. However, while these varieties have not lost grammatical gender as such, they have merged feminine and masculine into a common gender (see also Chapter 8), so Northern Standard Dutch has the definite article forms *de* (common gender – masc./fem.) and *het* (neut.).

On the other hand, the dialects of the Flemish south of the Netherlandic-speaking area have retained the three original genders (De Vogelaer 2009). These Netherlandic dialects of Belgium and the southern Netherlands have *den* (masc.), *de* (fem.) and *'t* (neut.), with corresponding differences of adjectival agreement (Taeldeman 2005: 62):

	'the thin farmer'	'the thin farmer's wife'
Flemish	*den dunnen boer*	*de dunne boerin*
Standard Dutch	*de dunne boer*	*de dunne boerin*
cf. Afrikaans	*die maer boer*	*die maer boervrou*

Two further interesting points can be noted about varieties of Flemish. First, in French Flanders – the Dutch-speaking area of northern France – the Romance Picard dialects of the region have exercised considerable grammatical influence on the local dialects of West Flemish. In the Flemish of France we find conjunctions such as *puisque dat* 'since', *parce que* 'because' and *soit* 'that is'; and prepositions such as *à force van* 'by dint of' and *grâce van* 'thanks to' (Ryckeboer 2002: 30). Moreover, 'the Flemish dialect in France also shows syntactic characteristics that reflect . . . the age-old influence of French', including the 'extra-position of some adverbial complements and even inherent complements' – these are 'very common in French Flemish' (Ryckeboer 2002: 37). Second, certain of the Flemish dialects of Belgium have a number of innovations which are, however, of a very different type from those exhibited by Afrikaans. De Vogelaer (2004: 191) notes, for example, that in many East Flemish dialects, subject tripling occurs as an innovation. In the first-person plural, a verb can take a preverbal pronoun as well as two post-verbal pronouns. The three pronominal forms of 'we' are *wij*, *we* [weak form] and *me* [clitic form]. De Vogelaer cites as an example:

We   zulle-me   wij   dat   doen.
we   shall-we   we   that   do
'We shall do that.'

Another rather extraordinary development also involving grammatical agreement is that certain Flemish dialects have developed a highly unusual system of person agreement on the words corresponding to English *yes* and *no*, which he refers to as 'answer particles' (De Vogelaer 2005: 35):

Zullen we gaan? Jom.	'Shall we go? Yes [1pl.].'
Heb je dat gedaan? Jok.	'Have you done it? Yes [1sg.].'
Is het warm vandaag? Jot.	'Is it warm today? Yes [3sg.].'

This person-marking is obligatory – all instances of *jo* 'yes' have to be marked for person, with *jot* being the default unless a clear plural or first-person or second-person subject is involved. Contrast this with Afrikaans, where agreement for person has been lost even on verbs.

Third, some of these Flemish dialects have also developed another interesting rarissimum which also has to do with grammatical agreement: person-marking on complementisers. In a construction such as

Ze   zegg-en   da-n=ze   naar Brussel   gaa-n.
They say-3pl   that-3pl =they   to   Brussels   go-3pl
'They say that they are going to Brussels.'

the form *da*, corresponding to the English complementiser *that*, compulsorily takes the third-person plural marker *-(e)n*, which also occurs in *zeggen* and *gaan* (De Vogelaer & van der Auwera 2010).

Explanations

Typically, few explanations are proffered by linguistic typologists as to why a particular language has a particular configuration of linguistic features rather than some other. Typological commonalities between languages may be described as being due to genetic factors – it is not a surprise if languages which are related to one another resemble one another because of commonly inherited features. And geography is also alluded to – it is no surprise if languages which are spoken in the same geographical region have linguistic similarities as a result of the geographical diffusion of linguistic forms, which gives rise to areal features.

Work in sociolinguistic typology, however, attempts to develop insights about the linguistic-typological characteristics of particular languages which go beyond the genetic and the areal into the social. As far as the varieties of Dutch just discussed are concerned, for example, the similarities between them – to the point that they are all, to different degrees, mutually intelligible – are clearly due to their very close genetic relationship, as well as, with the exception of Afrikaans, to the fact that they are spoken in the same geographical region of Europe. But what about the differences? What, in particular, about the different typological directions they have taken during the last few centuries?

A sociolinguistic-typological approach to these facts about Dutch suggests that light can be shed on the different types of processes which these different dialects have been subject to by examining the social backgrounds against which these changes took place. It is clear that we can refer to the changes which have occurred in Afrikaans as *simplification* (Trudgill 2011). Roberge (1995) accounts for this simplification in terms of Afrikaans' history of contact with indigenous, and other, languages in southern Africa. There were 'three groups primarily responsible for the formation of Afrikaans – European settlers (from 1652), the indigenous Khoekhoe, and enslaved peoples of Africa and Asia (from 1658)' (Roberge 1995: 68). Afrikaans underwent *simplification* as a result of *language contact* of an extent which has not been experienced by other varieties of Dutch. It is also vital to note that this language contact was necessarily of a very particular type. Contact can give rise to two very different types of linguistic outcome, depending on what kind of contact it is. Contact leads to simplification only if it involves large-scale second-language learning specifically by adults and adolescents who are beyond the critical period for language acquisition (Trudgill 2011). In the words of Dahl (2004: 40): when it comes to learning difficulty, 'the distinction between first and second language acquisition is evident'. Adults are typically not good language learners: when it comes to acquiring linguistic complexity 'human children indeed seem to have an advantage compared to . . . adult members of their own species' (Dahl 2004: 294). In learning a second language – particularly in informal, untutored learning situations – adults will therefore typically fail to acquire features which are *L2 difficult* (Dahl 2004). These are complex and/or redundant features like irregularity, syntactic agreement and grammatical gender.

If we now turn to northern varieties of European Dutch, we recall that simplification has also occurred here but to a much lesser extent. This can with some confidence be ascribed to adult dialect contact, which characteristically also gives rise to simplification, though to a smaller extent than language contact (Trudgill 1986). One likely explanation for the simplification in the northern Netherlands, as compared to the southern Dutch-speaking area, is the considerable amount of in-migration that occurred from other Dutch-speaking dialect areas during the period of rapid population expansion in the now highly urbanised north of the Netherlands after the surrender of Antwerp in 1585, and to further in-migration during the Dutch Golden Age of the seventeenth century (Geerts 1966; Trudgill 2013).

The Flemish dialects of the south of the Netherlandic-speaking area, on the other hand, demonstrate neither the extreme simplification of Afrikaans nor the more moderate simplification of northern metropolitan Dutch. This is, rather obviously, due to the fact that they have not experienced adult language contact or dialect contact on anything like the same scale.

The importance of *type of language contact* in producing linguistic-typological outcomes becomes clear when we note that contact can also lead to complexification, as in the case of French Flemish where complexity has increased as a result of *additive borrowing*. The Dutch/Flemish spoken in France and along the border has borrowed grammatical devices from French which it now possesses in addition to original Dutch features retained from an earlier time: Nichols (1992: 192) says that contact between 'languages fosters complexity, or, put differently, diversity among neighbouring languages fosters complexity in each of the languages'. But this has to be a different type of contact. Long-term contact between communities where small children become bilingual provides a social matrix where languages can become more complex by acquiring phonological and grammatical features from other languages, as speakers transfer them from one of their languages to the other. A good illustration of this kind of phenomenon can be seen from the work of Aikhenvald in Amazonia. Tariana, spoken in the Vaupés river basin area of northwest Amazonia on the borders of Brazil and Colombia, is the only member of the Arawak language family in the region, and has been in long-term contact with languages of the Tucano language family. There are many signs of Tucano influence on Tariana, some of which has produced additive complexification. For example, 'Tariana is one of the very few Arawak languages with case marking for core syntactic functions ... it developed the case marking under Tucano influence' (Aikhenvald 2003: 3). And Tariana has also acquired an extensive evidential system under the influence of Tucano.

Finally, complexification is by no means always the result of additive borrowing due to child bilingualism. Intriguingly, it can also result from spontaneous, internally generated complexification as illustrated by Flemish subject tripling and person-marking on answer particles and complementisers, where additional redundancy and therefore L2-difficulty – there is more for learners to learn and to remember to do – have been acquired. I have argued (Trudgill 2011) that it is in smaller varieties with low-levels of adult language/dialect contact, and dense social networks (Milroy 1980) that this type of complexification is most likely to occur.[1] It is not a coincidence that this complexification has occurred in Flemish dialects rather than in urban standard Dutch.[2]

---

[1] Dense social networks are found in communities where it is common for everybody to know everybody else, and where, for example, your neighbour and your second cousin and your workmate may be one and the same person.

[2] For an account of how this increase in redundancy may well have occurred, see Weiss (2015).

Simplification and Complexification

The term *complexification* as used above takes as its point of departure the notion of *simplification* as this has been understood in pidgin and creole studies. The different facets of simplification, which are typically the result of adult language contact and which are found at their most extreme in pidgins, are *regularisation, loss of redundancy* and *increase in transparency* (Mühlhäusler 1977).

Complexification simply consists of the opposite processes. Linguistic complexity can be equated with higher levels of L2 difficulty (Trudgill 2011), as referred to in connection with Afrikaans, and is typically produced by:

– greater irregularity
– higher levels of syntagmatic redundancy, i.e., repetition of information such as in grammatical agreement
– increased use of morphological categories
– higher levels of allomorphy
– a greater degree of fusion.

Both repetition of information and the employment of morphological categories are instances of redundancy, and both allomorphy and fusion are instances of opacity (as opposed to transparency).

Attempts to develop a sociolinguistic take on linguistic typology are not an entirely recent phenomenon[3]: earlier attempts to develop this kind of perspective also often focussed on simplicity and complexity, and also acknowledged the role of adult nonnative learners in producing simplification. Madvig (1857), as cited in Jespersen (1922: 324), pointed out that simplification in linguistic structure makes languages easier to learn 'for foreigners'. Vogt (1948: 39) also wrote that 'we can often note that a language loses formal distinctions in circumstances which make it rather natural to hypothesise that they result from foreign influence' [my translation].[4]

It was at one time widely felt that the diachronic move from complex to simpler structures in, for example, the Indo-European languages had something quasi-inevitable about it. Schlegel (1846) pointed to what Faarlund (2005: 1149) calls 'the well-known drift from a synthetic to an analytic type'. And Jespersen (1894, 1922) referred to inflectional languages as typically 'ancient', encumbered with morphological baggage, and described analytic languages as being streamlined and typically 'modern'. Linguists have even been tempted to regard this as a kind diachronic universal: there has been 'a traditional intuition of evolutionary direction ... we prefer morphological complexity to decrease' (Lass 1997: 253).

---

[3] Works in this tradition include Schlegel (1846), Madvig (1857), Jespersen (1894), Gabelentz (1901), Sapir (1912), Jakobson (1929), Whorf (1956) and Hymes (1974).

[4] 'On observe souvent qu'une langue ... perd des distinctions formelles, dans des circonstances qui rendent l'hypothese d'influence étrangère assez naturelle.'

But, as Lass says, this 'traditional intuition' is wrong: it is not supported by the evidence.

In fact, a sociolinguistic-typological perspective suggests that, while earlier linguists may have 'been right when they pointed to a kind of evolutionary trend in linguistic change', this was 'for demographic and sociolinguistic rather than straightforward linguistic reasons' (Trudgill 1983: 107). Linguistic simplification has been going on for the last 2,000 years, but this makes it a very new phenomenon in the scale of the whole of human linguistic history, and one which is due to a dramatic increase in the population of the world and a resultant increase in adult language contact: although language contact has been 'responsible for much reduction in morphology in Europe over the last two millennia', it was probably 'rare in prehistory' (Nichols 2007: 176).

The fact is, as we have already noted, nearly all of the linguistic past took place in Palaeolithic and Mesolithic societies, and nearly all the rest of the linguistic past took place in Neolithic societies. As we also have discussed, demography in those times was very different and communities were small. The sort of sociolinguistic conditions which produced Afrikaans and northern Metropolitan Dutch did not exist in the Mesolithic but they have been very much on the increase in modern times, a trend we can quite reasonably expect to continue, with a subsequent increase in linguistic simplification.

The sort of complexification seen in the increase in redundancy in Flemish dialects is also likely to become increasingly rare: 'the surface structures of languages spoken in small cheek-by-jowl communities so often are markedly complex, and the surface structures of languages spoken over wider areas less so' (Hymes 1974: 50). Such cheek-by-jowl 'societies of intimates' (Givon 1979), which were the norm for at least 98 per cent of human history (Trudgill 2020), are now becoming increasingly uncommon. Since it is these communities which are the most *hospitable to complexity development*, we can suppose that linguistic complexity is increasingly less likely to develop spontaneously (Trudgill 2011).[5]

Complexity Development

This raises the question as to why societies of intimates should be hospitable to linguistic complexity development in a way that 'societies of strangers' (Givon & Young 2002) are not. Let us consider this from the point of view of two indisputably complex language types, those which are often termed *polysynthetic* (or *highly synthetic*), and those which are generally known as *highly inflecting and fusional*.

We can consider these language types from the perspective of two of Kusters's (2003: 21) simplicity principles. The Economy Principle states that 'as few semantic

---

[5] I am grateful to Jim Blevins for suggesting this term.

categories or category combinations as possible should be expressed morphologically'. The Transparency Principle requires that 'the relation between form and meaning is as transparent as possible'. The combined role of divergence from the economy and transparency principles in producing complexity reflects Sapir's well-known (1921) typological taxonomy. According to Sapir, the morphological typology of languages can be considered along two dimensions: the degree of word-internal complexity and the transparency of word-internal boundaries – Kusters's principles of economy and transparency obviously derive directly from this dichotomy.

Sapir's first dimension concerns the number of morphemes per word, producing a continuum ranging from very analytic languages, with only one or very few morphemes per word; through synthetic languages, such as inflecting languages, which have more than that; to polysynthetic languages, which have many.

The second dimension, transparency, leads to the well-known classification of languages into three major types: isolating, agglutinating and fusional. Isolating languages are necessarily also totally analytic. But when we come to agglutinating and fusional languages, the two parameters can diverge. Polysynthetic and inflecting languages can both be more or less agglutinating and/or more or less fusional (see Aikhenvald 2007).

For Kusters, the highest level of transparency or analyticity is when 'every single meaning is expressed in a separate form' (2003: 21). One aspect of such 'separateness' is the extent to which morphemes are clearly separable or segmentable, as in strongly agglutinating languages, or not, as in fusional languages which 'have internally complex words which cannot easily be segmented into an exhaustive and non-overlapping string of formatives' (Anderson 1985: 8). Other things being equal, the more non-segmentability a language has, the more complex it will be. Languages which are fusional *and* highly inflecting or polysynthetic would therefore seem to present the greatest degree of linguistic complexity possible.

As far as polysynthetic languages are concerned, there can be no doubting their complexity, which has been variously described as 'daunting' (Fortescue 1992: 243), 'startling' (Aronoff 1994: 89), 'legendary' (Rice 1999: 392), 'exuberant' (Evans & Sasse 2002: 3), 'spectacular' (ibid.: 5), 'baroque' (Wier 2006: 221), 'rich' (McDonough & Sussman 2006: 1) and 'unusual' (Korotkova & Lander 2010: 299).

These languages have, by definition, a much greater use of morphological categories than other languages, and depart enormously from Kusters's Economy Principle: Sadock (2003: 3) tells us that West Greenlandic has a thousand inflectional affixes. And polysynthetic languages also have very many morphemes per word: in the Athabaskan language Tanaina, 'the verbal morphology consists of stem preceded by nearly 20 prefix positions' (Mithun 1999: 363).

So polysynthetic languages are more or less complex to the extent that they have:

- a (very) large stock of bound morphemes
- a (very) large number of morphemes per word, as well as
- large amounts of fusion.

Chiricahua Apache, for instance, is a polysynthetic language with a large stock of bound morphemes and large numbers of morphemes per word; and it also has a high degree of fusion conflating several units into non-analysable portmanteau morphemes (Aikhenvald 2007). In fact, most Athabaskan languages are fusional as well as polysynthetic, with 'notoriously complex fusional morphology' (Poulson 2011). Aikhenvald (2007: 8) cites Hoijer's (1945: 14) example:

/hàṅʔàːh/
out.of-2subj+impf-handle.a.round.object+impf
'you take a round object (out of enclosed space)'

Here /hàː-/ is 'out of an enclosed space', /-ṅ-/ is the disjunct imperfective second person subject pronoun, and /-ʔàːh/ is the momentaneous imperfective stem 'to handle a round object', where 'imperfective' and 'second person subject' are combined in one morph, as are also 'handle a round object' and 'imperfective'.

Highly inflecting fusional languages are also widely considered to be extremely complex. Ancient Greek has extensive grammatical agreement; four morphologically marked moods on the verb (indicative, imperative, subjunctive and optative); three morphologically marked voices (active, middle and passive); three morphologically marked persons (first, second and third); and three morphologically marked numbers (singular, dual and plural). Together with the fact that verbs typically have four main tense-aspects (present, future, perfect and aorist), this leads to a situation where a verb will normally have 275-plus forms – not to mention the fact that there are a number of different conjugations, and many irregularities as well.

Inflecting languages will thus be complex to the extent that they have:

- a (very) large amount of inflectional morphology
- a (very) large amount of grammatical agreement, as well as
- large amounts of fusion.

Both polysynthetic and inflecting fusional languages will also be more or less complex to the extent that they have:

- large amounts of allomorphy: the more conjugational and inflectional paradigms a fusional inflecting language has, for example, the more complex it will be
- large amounts of irregularity: the more irregularity a language has, the more complex it will be.

The Sociolinguistic Matrix

Scholars writing on polysynthetic languages generally assume that they became polysynthetic out of some earlier non-polysynthetic state, and that their poly-synthesis is the result of complexifying linguistic changes: 'the morphology of these languages was surely not always so complex', and they 'may have reached their present typological extremity from far less synthetic origins reflecting a middle-of-the-road agglutinative type quite familiar in northern Eurasia' (Fortescue 2002: 257). For sociolinguistic-typological purposes, we therefore have to consider the conditions under which these languages underwent simplicity-principle-defying changes, leading to a growth in the stock of bound morphemes, a growth in the number of morphemes per word, and the development of fusion and irregularity.

Scholars working on highly inflectional fusional languages similarly assume that they became so out of an earlier state in which they were less complex. Hodge (1970) argues that agglutinating languages may become less agglutinating and more fusional over time. And Dahl writes that 'fusional structures depend diachronically upon agglutinating ones' (2004: 184). We have to consider how these languages, too, have undergone simplicity-principle-defying changes.

The sociolinguistic-typological question which arises is this: what are the socio-linguistic conditions which are hospitable to the type of linguistic changes which produce the complexification associated with the growth of highly inflecting fusional languages like Ancient Greek, and of fusional polysynthetic languages like Apache?

Some of the linguistic changes we will need to consider are likely to be, to use Aronoff's term, rather startling. What does it take, for example, for a language to develop a bound morpheme such as Comanche /tsi-/ meaning 'with a sharp point, with the finger' (Charney 1993: 121)? What does it take to produce a growth of affixes such that the Oregon/California Penutian language Klamath has acquired twenty-five morphological position classes on the verb (DeLancey 1991)? What does it take for West Greenlandic to have developed so many fusional processes that about one-eighth of Sadock's (2003) grammar of the language is devoted to them? What does it take for a language to develop so much irregularity that de Reuse, in his pedagogical grammar of San Carlos Apache, at one point abandons all hope:

The ways in which the subject prefixes combine with prefixes preceding it and with prefixes following it and/or with the verb stem are very complex. There are rules that you can learn in order to properly insert a subject prefix inside a verb, but . . . you are better off memorising the paradigms with the subject prefixes inserted, rather than trying to learn a long list of complex rules. Having explained why we are not discussing the subject prefixes . . . . (2006: 202)

And what does it take for a language like Ancient Greek to develop a system where all nouns, adjectives, pronouns, articles, numerals and verbs are inflected and – with three main different major declensions – which has massive allomorphy? What does it take to develop not only three numbers and three genders but also five morphologically marked cases, such that the definite article has thirty-six different forms?

We can begin by considering the growth in the inventory of bound morphemes in polysynthetic languages like Klamath and Greenlandic: what are the sociolinguistic conditions, for instance, which would be hospitable to the development of the Comanche bound morpheme /tsi-/ 'with a sharp point'? Instrumental affixes of this type are widespread in certain areas of North America (Mithun 1999: 118ff.), with some languages having very large inventories. But the question as to what it takes, sociolinguistically, to produce such inventories needs to be answered, initially, by examining the linguistics. Mithun writes (1999: 123) that 'the origins of most of these instrumental affixes are no longer recoverable, but in a few languages resemblances can still be perceived between them and noun or verb roots', and 'the prefixes apparently developed from the initial roots of noun-verb and verb-verb compounds'. For some morphemes, such as 'with a sharp point', recovery is possible. Proto-Uto Aztecan *ci-a 'rose', which is perhaps built on a term meaning 'thorn', is hypothesised to be the metonymic source of the Proto-Numic instrumental *ci- 'with the point of a long object' – which corresponds to modern Comanche /tsi-/ 'with a sharp point, with the finger' (Charney 1993: 121).

For inflecting languages like Ancient Greek, Comrie (1980) gives us an insight into how highly inflectional fusional languages develop. He illustrates, from Buriat Mongolian, how person endings on verbs have descended from original personal pronouns. The subject agreement suffixes -b (first person) and -š (second person) 'clearly derive from the independent pronouns bi- "I" and ši- "you" found in Buriat and other Mongolian languages' (Comrie 1992: 209). Comrie further discusses the development of case endings in the Finnic languages via the trajectory: noun > postposition > clitic > suffix > case ending. In the Balto-Finnic of the first millennium BC, the form kanssa was an independent noun meaning 'people' (Campbell 1997). In modern Finnish it has become a comitative postposition:

hyvä-n   poja-n   kanssa
good-gen   boy-gen   with
'with the good boy'

Its independent lexical status can be seen from the fact that there is no vowel harmony in constructions with kanssa. In the related language Vepsian, a further stage of development has occurred, and the corresponding form ka has become a bound comitative suffix:

lahse-ka 'with the child' lehmä-kä 'with the cow'

The bound status of the form can be seen in the vowel harmony alternation between *ka* and *kä*. In Karelian, the comitative form *kela* has become more than just a bound suffix because there is not only vowel harmony but also grammatical agreement within the noun phrase (i.e., -*kela* is repeated on both elements):

kolme-n-kela lapše-n-kela 'with three children'
three-gen-com child-gen-com
tütö-n-kelä 'with the girl'
child-gen-com

Finally, we may consider the sorts of processes that give rise to fusion. It is rather clear that 'many instances of fusional morphology can be traced back to earlier affixes whose segmental nature has been eroded' (Comrie 1992: 208). And the growth of fusional forms, where segmentability is gradually lost, can be illustrated by the way in which modern Estonian has developed rather further down the road away from agglutination than the closely related language Finnish. Compare these two paradigms in the two languages (Comrie 1989: 50):

	Finnish			Estonian	
	'leg'	'flag'	'leg'	'flag'	'leg'
nom.sg.	*jalka*	*lippu*	*jalg*	*lipp*	
gen.sg.	*jala-n*	*lipu-n*	*jala*	*lipu*	
part.sg.	*jalka-a*	*lippu-a*	*jalga*	*lippu*	
part.pl.	*jalko-j-a*	*lippu-j-a*	*jalgu*	*lippe*	

The Finnish word-forms are readily segmentable: -*j*- is the plural morpheme, -*n*- the genitive, and -*a* the partitive. The stem remains constant throughout, except for a small amount of allomorphy provided by the (predictable) alternation in the genitive singular between *k* and Ø in *jalka*, and *pp* and *p* in *lippu*. The Estonian paradigms are much less transparent. The forms are not readily segmentable – the separate partitive and plural morphemes have been fused, for instance; and the alternations, such as between partitive plural -*u* and -*e*, are unpredictable. Estonian has experienced changes which have had the complexifying effect of obscuring an originally more transparent morphological structure. As far as the mechanisms that were involved in this loss of transparency are concerned, it is clear that the changes involved were initially phonological in origin – all word-final segments have been lost in Estonian, for example. Dahl (2004: 179) stresses that phonological change is crucial in the development of fusional opacity: 'structural condensation would depend on phonological condensation – the fusion of two words into one is conditioned by their having been phonologically integrated' – so fusional forms develop in the first place out of the phonological fusing of agglutinating structures.

Answers

At least one of the answers, then, to all of these 'what-does-it-take?' questions – about polysynthesis, inflection and fusion (as well as irregularity and allomorphy) – would therefore appear rather clearly to be: *time*. As we saw earlier, Comrie points out that 'morphophonemic alternation is always assumed to have developed from the absence of morphophonemic alternation' (1992: 206), for example, the Germanic umlaut alternation of /mus – mys/ 'mouse – mice' from earlier /muːs – muːsi/. The existence of morphophonemic alternation in a language represents the development of complexity, over time, out of an earlier less complex state.

In fact, morphology as a whole represents a diachronic development out of an earlier morphology-free state[6]; and relative morphological complexity increases over time, too, along the isolating > agglutinating > fusional path: 'increasing complexity can often be shown to reflect a diachronic process' (Comrie 1992: 208). Following this reasoning, to develop from a language state with no or little morphology to a state where there is fully fledged fusional polysynthesis or inflection is likely to take a very long time indeed.

As far as growth in the stock of bound morphemes in highly inflecting and polysynthetic languages is concerned, Mithun (1999: 540) has it that Proto-Uto Aztecan languages 'are assumed to have diverged around 5,000 years ago', so we can say that there has been a grammaticalisation of nouns such as 'thorn' into a set of instrumental affixes such as 'with a sharp point' – which have added to the morphological complexity of the languages which have them – at some time during the last 5,000 years. Growth in the number of morphemes per word, too, appears even more clearly to require considerable periods of time to play out. This is illustrated in DeLancey's discussion (1991) of the affix-proliferation in the Penutian language Klamath, which as we have noted has twenty-five morphological position classes on the verb. DeLancey views the gradual chronological increase in the number of affixes per word in terms of 'chronological strata' (1991: 426) of suffix classes. This geological metaphor paints a picture of the accretion of morphological complexity in the language over considerable periods of time as more classes are added, and as more members are added to those classes. DeLancey (1991: 427) points to phonetic erosion over time as forms become more and more grammatical: some morphemes are of 'considerable antiquity' and their 'fairly minimal phonological profile ... is also consistent with the notion that they are of considerable age'. There are also differences between 'the various morphemes in these classes in the relative antiquity of their incorporation into the verb complex' (1991: 429). DeLancey sorts these into separate chronological strata: for example, in (aspectual) classes 17 to 22 (out of the twenty-five ordered positional classes), there is a clear gradient of lexical

---

[6] For a contrary view, see Dubé (2015).

specificity. The members of classes 15 to 19 all have broad meanings which are often associated with grammatical morphemes. Those of class 20 (except for *o:t*) ['while'], on the other hand, show more lexically specific senses, which tend to be less common cross-linguistically as grammatical categories. There is a similar gradient of phonological bulk: while none of the members of classes 15–19 has more than two consonants [e.g., *obg* 'durative'], and only one has more than three segments, five of the seven members of class 20 have both [e.g., *nannwi* 'at once']. Both of these suggest a greater degree of grammaticalisation for 15–19 and imply a more recent origin for class 20 (DeLancey 1991: 430). So more and more bound morphemes have been developed, and at the same time more and more categories have been created, gradually adding to the morpheme-per-word ratio – a very time-consuming process.

As far as fusion is concerned, in illustrations of the putative *morphological cycle* (Hodge 1970; Bynon 1977: 265; Dixon 1997), the cycle is often portrayed as a clock face, with purely isolating languages like Classical Chinese standing at, say, 4 o'clock, agglutinating at 8 o'clock and fusional at 12 o'clock. According to Dixon (1997), Proto-Finno-Ugric was perhaps at about 9 o'clock, while the modern languages in the family have moved to 10 or 11 o'clock, with Estonian having moved further than Finnish, as we have seen. Now, if Proto-Finnic was at 9 o'clock and modern Estonian is at 11 o'clock, we can obtain a suggestive chronological estimate of how long this kind of change takes. Proto-Finno-Ugric dates to c. 4000 BC (Campbell 1997). Even if modern Estonian has been at 11 o'clock for as long as 1,000 years, this means it took 5,000 years to 'travel' from 9 to 11; for a language to move from fully isolating to fully fusional (i.e., from 4 o'clock to 12), if the same trajectory speed was maintained, would take 20,000 years. I am not suggesting that this figure has any particular reality. It simply indicates that the development of a language like Ancient Greek out of an earlier agglutinating and an even earlier isolating state will need (tens of) thousands of years to take full effect, not least when we observe that Estonian is still a very far removed indeed from the extreme complexity of Ancient Greek.

Both polysynthesis and fusion are, then, to use Östen Dahl's insightful term, *mature linguistic phenomena*. Mature linguistic phenomena are linguistic features which 'imply a lengthy period of historical development' – they 'presuppose a non-trivial prehistory' (Dahl 2004: 2): 'linguistic phenomena have life cycles in the sense that they pass through a number of successive stages, during which they "mature", that is, acquire properties that would not otherwise be possible'.

This is also very much true of the inflectional structures of highly inflecting languages. Dahl confirms that 'reviewing the candidates for inclusion in the class of mature linguistic phenomena, we find that the most obvious one is inflectional morphology' (2004: 111); and he includes here also the presence of different inflectional classes. For Dahl, L2-difficult features such as irregularity, grammatical gender and syntactic agreement are also mature phenomena.

Now if, for the sake of argument, it did take something like five millennia for Estonian to travel from '9 o'clock' to '11 o'clock', we can ask: however long did it take for Ancient Greek to acquire the extreme complexity which it demonstrates when we first encounter it in the historical record? After all, as Smitherman and Barðdal (2009: 270) say, 'the assumption of an evolution of Proto-Indo-European from an isolating stage ... is hardly radical'. And from the structure of isolating languages to the structure of Ancient Greek is a very long way indeed.

Lehmann indicates that Proto-Indo-European had a considerably higher level of complexity than Pre-Indo-European. Pre-Indo-European appears to have lacked inflectional person-marking on verbs, for instance. Szemerényi (1990: 329), moreover, says that 'it has been usual' in Indo-European scholarship to see the personal endings on verbs, such as first-person singular *-m*, as having their origin in earlier personal pronouns (just as with Comrie's Mongolian example cited previously). This scenario 'is also valid for the 1st pl., where the original form of the pronoun was **mes*, and for the 1st dual, whose ending *-we(s)* similarly contains the pronoun'.

Many scholars also accept that an early stage of Indo-European 'had an inflectional system for nouns that was far simpler than that reconstructed on the basis of Sanskrit, Greek and other dialects', concluding that 'Pre-Indo-European had very few inflectional markers for nouns'; 'it is far more likely that the case system was gradually expanded rather than reduced in the late proto-language'. Note too that 'forms parallel to Latin ablatives are the bases of adverbs in Germanic' (Lehmann 1993: 223–6), with Melchert and Oettinger (2009) suggesting that certain of the case endings were actually still adverbs in Proto-Indo-European itself.

Shields (1987) similarly argues that, at an early stage of development, Indo-European possessed only two cases, nominative and objective, with the objective later bifurcating into accusative and oblique, which then formed the basis of the oblique cases – dative, instrumental, locative, ablative, and genitive – which we find in the historical record. This process involved 'the grammaticalization of deictic particles ... as case markers' such that the particles 'underwent fission with noun stems (cf. Fairbanks 1977) ... which led to the possibility of their being reanalyzed as genuine inflectional case markers' (Shields 1987: 37). And Szemerényi concurs that some of the oblique case endings were derived from adpositions: the ablative-dative plural and the instrumental plural in some Indo-European languages were formed out of **bh* (abl.-dat. Pl.: Skt. *pad-bhyas* Lat. *ped-ibus* < **ped-bh(y)os* ; inst.pl. Skt. *pad-bhis* Gk. *pop-phi* < **ped-bhis*) which 'was no doubt originally a postposition *bhi* (cf. Eng. *by*)' (Szemerényi 1996: 165). Fortson (2010: 118) also writes that Indo-European instrumental, dative and ablative plural case endings beginning with **bh-* and **m-* 'may have originally been postpositions or adverbs ultimately related to Eng. *by* and Germ. *mit*'. Drinka (2003) argues that even Proto-Indo-European itself does not represent the latest and highest point of historical complexity development: Ancient Greek and Sanskrit are in some respects more complex, having developed even further down the complexification road. Hittite, for example, has less complexity than Greek and Sanskrit because Anatolian split off from Indo-European before full complexity had developed: for example, 'in the [Hittite] noun there was no feminine gender distinct from the masculine. The verb showed no obvious trace of the aspectual contrast between "present" and "aorist" or of the "perfect" category at all' (Drinka 2003: 77). The subjunctive and optative moods were also missing (Melchert 2015). Greek and Indo-Iranian later went on to develop even further complexity (Drinka 2003).

So what about the timing of all this, and the claim I have made concerning very long periods of time? Anthony (2007: 100) suggests that Anatolian lost contact with the other Indo-European languages c. 4200 BC: 'the first identifiable migration out of the Pontic-Caspian steppes was a movement towards the east about 4200–3900 BCE that could represent the detachment of the Pre-Anatolian branch'. Anthony further suggests that Indo-Iranian and Greek, much of whose complexity (in the verbal paradigm, for instance) is shared 'as a later dialectal innovation in the south-east of the Indo-European area' (Szemerényi 1990: 377), lost contact with each other 'after 2500 BCE' (Anthony 2007: 57). If his suggestions are valid, this would indicate at least 1.5 millennia of complexity development to arrive from the Hittite to the Ancient Greek level of complexity. And Hittite was already, of course, a highly inflecting language, far removed from the isolating state hypothesised by Smitherman and Barðdal (2009) in accordance with Comrie's (1992) 'Before complexity' insight.

All this points to an answer to the 'however long?' question being many millennia rather than a few centuries, with Ancient Greek representing just one culmination of very many generations indeed of complexity development.

Hospitality to Complexity Development

But, obviously, time is not enough. We need also to consider what kind of social matrix is required to produce this kind of complexity-inducing development: in what kind of social conditions are we most likely to see the development over long periods of time – out of earlier more analytic ancestors – of highly fusional, inflecting languages like Ancient Greek and Sanskrit, and highly fusional polysynthetic languages like Apache and Greenlandic, with large degrees of irregularity?

A sociolinguistic-typological perspective suggests that processes which lead to an increase in complex forms are such that they must not only be allowed to run for long time periods, but that these periods must be uninterrupted by episodes of significant adult language contact. For example, irregularity takes many generations of uninterrupted linguistic change to develop, according to Dahl, because it makes for L2 difficulty. Highly irregular and non-transparent features are harder to learn and remember: they are 'cognitive irritants' (Carstairs-McCarthy 2010: 120);

and 'if Gothic, Latin and Greek burden the memory by the number of their flexional endings, they do so even more by the many irregularities in the formation of these endings' (Jespersen 1922: 332). Large amounts of irregularity will not survive adult language contact on a large scale.

Societal *isolation* and *stability* would therefore both seem to be crucial for complexity development. Only stable situations without contact will permit the undisturbed development of, for example, highly fusional morphology over the long periods of time required; high levels of adult language contact would lead to more transparent forms. So complexity is more likely to develop in relatively stable, low-contact communities (bearing in mind that 'stable' is not necessarily identical with 'sedentary'). It would seem that for complexity to increase, languages need to avoid periods of what Dixon (1997) has insightfully called *punctuation*. According to Dixon, any long period of stable equilibrium may be punctuated by factors which disturb it. 'It is likely most examples of punctuation stem from non-linguistic factors' (1997: 75), and Dixon cites a number of such factors. They include natural catastrophes such as floods, famines and epidemics, which will certainly produce instability. And they also include factors such as migration, invasion and colonisation, which will very often involve large-scale adult language contact. For internally generated complexifying developments to occur, and to keep on occurring, a state of equilibrium needs to be maintained without any such punctuating factors intervening.[7]

Absence of punctuation is also required for the maintenance of any complexity which has already been produced. This can be seen in Fortescue's discussion of simplification in Aleut. According to Fortescue, one is 'struck by certain ways in which Aleut seems closer to Uralic than Eskimo does' (1972: 267); but this is not because Aleut is conservative vis-à-vis Eskimo and has failed to acquire full complexity. Rather it is because of 'later restructuring in Aleut' (1972: 268): 'Aleut was undoubtedly once much more polysynthetic than it is today' (1972: 272).

As far as explanations for this simplifying restructuring are concerned, Fortescue cites external developments of the type discussed by Dixon as a factor, mentioning 'decimation by epidemic and geographical displacement at the hands of Russian fur traders during the early contact period', a clear instance of punctuation in Dixon's sense. However, this was probably too late to be the main cause of the loss of polysynthesis, according to Fortescue. Rather, 'a more likely – and long-lasting – source of influence on developments here was substratum and/or areal effects' (Fortescue 1972: 274). Relative simplicity compared to Eskimo therefore reflects

---

[7] Periods of equilibrium involving language contact of the child bilingualism type will also tend to lead to additive complexification: 'during periods of equilibrium, languages in contact will diffuse features between each other' (Dixon 1972: 70–1).

'not so much ancient retentions but the "undoing" of some of the processes which led up to polysynthesis in the family in the first place', a development which was 'spurred on' by effects which are clearly related to language contact (1972: 274).

So the apogee of linguistic complexity is reached by languages that are highly polysynthetic or highly inflecting, highly fusional and highly irregular. These are the languages which defy the economy principle and the transparency principle to the greatest extent. But they take a very long time indeed to develop, with no periods of punctuation being allowed to intervene.

Sociolinguistic factors other than stability and isolation are also involved in producing hospitality to complexity development, however. Not least amongst these is community size. Polysynthetic languages, for instance, can be found amongst many different language families and in many different areas of the world, including the Americas, northern Australia, Papua New Guinea and north-east Asia. Amongst them we find Iroquoian languages such as Mohawk and Cayuga; Eskimo-Aleut languages such as Yup'ik and Greenlandic; Athabaskan languages like Apachean; Caddoan languages such as Wichita; Tanoan languages like Tewa and Jemez; Gunwiniguan languages such as Bininj Gunwok, Ngalakgan, and Rembarrnga; Papuan Sepik languages like Yimas and Alamblak; the Chukotko-Kamchatkan language Chukchi; the Yeniseian language Ket; and isolates such as Ainu. But in spite of this broad genetic diversity, and this very wide geographical spread, a sociolinguist-typological perspective focuses on the rather striking fact that all these languages have two characteristics in common. First, all of them are spoken in relatively small communities: they nearly all have fewer, mostly very many fewer, than 10,000 speakers, with some exceptions such as Apache (16,000) and Greenlandic (50,000); and they are all spoken in traditional, non-industrialised rural tribal communities.

Complexity development is clearly favoured by *small community size*, and the concomitant *dense social networks* and large amounts of *communally shared information* (Trudgill 2011). This can be seen, first, from work by linguists on certain types of growth in the stock of bound morphemes in languages. Long-term grammaticalisation of morphological categories progresses to a much greater extent in small face-to-face societies of intimates with informational homogeneity (Givón 1979) than elsewhere. Suggestive work which gives us some insight into why this might be can be seen in Perkins (1980, 1995). Keenan (1976) suggests that large deictic systems are better developed in non-literate communities with fewer than 4,000 speakers than in larger communities (see further, Trudgill 2011). Perkins follows this up by arguing that deictics identify referents by linking them to the spatial-temporal axis of speech events. Persons, tenses, demonstratives, directionals and inclusive versus exclusive markers need the spatio-temporal context of their use to be available to listeners for the identification of the referents, so deictics can be more salient in smaller societies of intimates with larger amounts of shared information than in larger societies; and deictics are therefore more likely to occur in the inflectional systems of their languages than periphrastically. The more often deictic morphemes occur, the more likely they are to become grammaticalised into bound morphemes, which of course is crucial for the development of polysynthesis and inflection.

Secondly, community size would also appear to be relevant in terms of growth in other L2-difficult factors such as grammatical agreement and irregularisation. The insight of Grace (1990: 126) already quoted in Chapter 1 is relevant here. It will be recalled that he pointed out that children learning a language learn it from people who already speak it, but that those 'teachers' have much 'less than total control over the learning process'. The fact that there is no 'total control over the learning process' is very pertinent here. A sociolinguistic-typological approach suggests that, although it is clearly true that control is less than total, in small, stable, isolated communities control may be more nearly total than in others. In such communities, linguistic change tends to be slower than elsewhere (Trudgill 2011); but when it does occur, there is also a greater likelihood that changes which do occur it will be of a kind that will lead to greater complexity.

Innovations of a complexifying type probably occur with roughly equal frequency in all types of community, but such complexifying innovations are more likely to succeed and become established as permanent linguistic *changes* (i.e., innovations which are accepted and become permanent), in small, isolated communities. Irregularisation, for example, is less likely to succeed in larger societies where innovators as 'teachers' have less 'control' and influence: 'if a group consists of just a few hundred people, the idiosyncrasies of one very influential individual can spread through it very easily' (Nettle 1999: 138). As I also argued in Chapter 1, it is in small isolated communities that social network structures make for a greater likelihood of complex changes being enforced and maintained from generation to generation.[8]

The Influence of the Social Matrix

We can now conclude the following:

1. A language variety which is spoken in a high-contact community which is in short-term contact with other communities speaking different languages, in such a way that large amounts of adult second-language learning of the language variety occur – and under demographic and social conditions which are such that the simplification that results from the removal of linguistic L2-difficult features also becomes part of the speech of later generations of native speakers – will undergo simplification.
2. A language variety which is spoken in a high-contact community which has experienced considerable contact with other communities speaking other

---

[8] I am not suggesting that any of this occurs above the level of conscious awareness.

varieties which are mutually intelligible with it will also undergo a certain amount of simplification.

3. A language variety which is spoken in a low-contact community will not undergo simplification.

4. A language variety which is spoken in a high-contact community which is in long-term contact with other communities speaking different languages, in such a way that large amounts of child bilingualism occurs – and under demographic and social conditions that are such that linguistic features are transferred from the one language to the other and also become part of the speech of later generations of native speakers – will experience additive complexification, to the extent that new features do not replace but remain alongside already existing features.

5. Low-contact communities which are also stable and small in size, with dense social networks and large amounts of communally shared information, are hospitable to the development of spontaneous complexification. If such communities remain stable and isolated from adult language contact for very many generations, the complexification that can develop in their languages may be extreme, to the extent of producing polysynthetic or highly inflected fusional languages.

There is a natural tendency for languages to gradually become more complex over time. Over the centuries, they tend to add layer upon layer of complexity, as we have briefly seen illustrated here in terms of the stock of bound morphemes, morphemes per word, fusion, allomorphy and irregularity. Linguistic complexification is in an important sense more 'normal' than simplification. It is what quite naturally happens if languages are 'left alone'. In small cohesive communities with little or no contact, there is a tendency, although there appears to be no inevitability about it, for languages to accrue more and more complexity such as the growth of morphology and fusion.

But our discussion of millennia-long periods has also made it clear that the mature phenomena of which complexity consists depend for their development on lengthy periods of stability with no periods of punctuation due to significant episodes of social instability and adult language contact, such as that hypothesised by Fortescue (1992) to have led to a reduction in polysynthesis in Aleut. Mature phenomena are very vulnerable to being lost if high-contact situations develop: according to Dahl (2004: 207), mature phenomena 'are highly prone to being filtered out in suboptimal language acquisition', because 'there is a significant overlap' between them and 'those linguistic features which are most recalcitrant in second language learning' (2004: 286). And those features certainly include those found most profusely in fusional highly inflecting languages, and in fusional polysynthetic languages.

3 First-Millennium England: a Tale of Two Copulas[1]

The date of the arrival of Indo-European languages in Europe has not been established with any degree of certainty, and different scholars vary by some thousands of years in their estimates. According to Baldi and Page (2006), 4500 BC seems to be the earliest limit for the Indo-Europeanisation of Europe espoused by any historical linguist; and many other writers suppose that Indo-European-speaking migrants can first be associated with the archaeological Corded Ware culture which is not attested before around 3000 BC – and then only as far west as southern Poland (Mallory 1989). Baldi and Page (2006: 2194) further state that the 'traditional view of the settlement of the Celts places them in the British Isles no earlier than about 2000 BC'. Fortson (2010: 309) more cautiously says that the first identifiable Indo-Europeans who can actually be pinpointed archaeologically in western Europe are the Celts of the later stages of the Hallstatt culture of central Europe – as noted in the Prologue – who, according to him, then arrived in southeastern England at some point after 1000 BC.

If Vennemann's vision concerning prehistoric Europe is correct (see the Prologue), then there would have been long-term linguistic contact in mainland Europe between Vasconic and the incoming westward-moving Indo-European languages during at least the second and first millennia BC. Vennemann argues that there is considerable linguistic evidence for this contact, though this evidence has been vigorously disputed by a number of scholars, including the British Indo-Europeanist Peter Kitson (1996), and the American Basque scholar, Larry Trask (1995, 1997).

Vennemann's evidence is, however, interesting and, at the very least, thought provoking. It includes a number of what he argues to be Vasconic substratum features in the Indo-European languages of northwestern Europe which are, crucially, absent from other Indo-European languages spoken further east which would not have experienced this contact. As just one example, vigesimality (i.e., counting with twenty as a basic unit) was unknown in Proto-Indo-European, but it is found even today in Celtic and Romance languages, and in the Germanic language Danish as well as, crucially, in Basque. There are also vestiges in English, as in the word *score* 'twenty', and in German.

---

[1] With apologies to Eve Zyzik and Sue Gass, the authors of 'Epilogue: a tale of two copulas' (*Bilingualism: Language and Cognition* 11: 383–5, 2008), a paper I saw only after I had become hopelessly attached to the title I had already chosen for this chapter.

One of Vennemann's major substratum examples concerns the copula. According to Vennemann, Proto-Indo-European, like Proto-Germanic, had only one copula. The Proto-Celtic of, probably, 2000–1000 BC (Watkins 1998), on the other hand, has been reconstructed as having acquired a functional distinction between two different copulas, with meanings rather like those of modern Spanish and Portuguese where *estar* is non-habitual (or temporary) and *ser* is habitual (or permanent), as in Spanish *estar borracho* 'to be drunk' versus *ser borracho* 'to be a drunk' (de Bruyne 1995: 577).[2]

Lewis and Pedersen (1937: 317) write of Proto-Celtic that:

The paradigm of the verb 'to be' consists in Italo-Celtic of forms of the roots *es-and *bheu-. In Celtic a pres. stem *bhwi-, *bhwije-, derived from *bheu-, also appears. This latter present denotes either a praesens consuetudinale or a future … The root *es-stands only in the pres. and ipf. ind. in Celtic.

Consuetudinal is a term which is used by Celticists in the sense of 'habitual': Proto-Celtic thus had a formal distinction between a habitual and a non-habitual copula. And in modern times, there are in Irish two verbs 'to be' marking 'a distinction which bears some resemblance to, for example, Spanish' (Ó Siadhail 1989: 219).[3]

Vennemann ascribes the origins of this Proto-Celtic innovation to the substratum influence of Vasconic which, he hypothesises, at some stage prior to first contact with Indo-European had also developed two copulas. It is certainly the case that Modern Basque can be analysed as having two copulas (Trask 1997). According to Etxepare (2003: 365), the verb *egon* 'be in a location' is used to express transient properties, while 'standing properties are assigned through the verb *izan* "be"'. *Izan* is also used in equative sentences. Vennemann concedes, however, that the antiquity of this feature cannot be confirmed, as we have no records of Basque from before the 1500s.[4]

However, an important part of Vennemann's argument is that not only are there two-copula paradigms, based on Latin *esse* 'to be' and *stare* 'to stand', in Spanish, Catalan, and Portuguese/Galician, but also that there is no such paradigm at all in Romansch or in Rumanian. There was formerly perhaps also such a distinction in Old French (as we shall discuss). The point is, of course, that it was precisely in those areas of western Europe where Vennemann believes Vasconic was once found that these Italic and Celtic varieties developed their double copula systems. (It is

---

[2] The terms 'habitual' and 'non-habitual' which I use in this chapter obviously conceal a multiplicity of subtleties and differences between different languages.

[3] An important part of Vennemann's discussion has to do with Irish, and with Irish English. I do not, however, deal with Ireland (or indeed, in any detail, with Scotland) in this paper.

[4] Vennemann's argumentation is, of course, a good deal more substantial than what I have presented here. He discusses further lexical evidence for a Vasconic substratum in western Europe in, for example, Vennemann (2010b); and phonological evidence in Vennemann (2010a).

presumably an open question as to whether western Romance acquired the system directly from Vasconic or indirectly via Gaulish and other Celtic varieties.)

It is true that it is possible that Celtic and northwestern Romance innovated their two-copula systems independently. These are by no means the only languages in the world to have more than one copula. As Dixon (2010: 175) says 'some languages have more than one Copula verb'. But for many such languages the semantico-grammatical distinction is not the same as in the Celtic and Romance languages of Atlantic Europe, such as Spanish where '*ser* refers to a characteristic feature (a permanent state) whereas *estar* refers to a temporary state' (Dixon 2010: 175). According to Dixon, in most two-copula systems 'one [copula] will just refer to a state and the other to coming into a state, similar to *be* and *become* in English', citing the Nepalese Tibeto-Burman language Dolakha Newar as an example. Sneddon (2006: 98f.) describes Indonesian as having two such copulas; and Hedberg and Potter (2010) do the same for Thai. On the other hand, many languages of the world have no copula at all (Stassen 2008); while others may have three or more – the Papuan language Manambu (Aikhenvald 2008) has 'a goodly number of copula verbs' (Dixon 2010: 176). So the existence in the same geographical area of Europe of a two-copula system, with a distinction precisely and perhaps unusually between a habitual and a non-habitual copula, in members of three different language families, does seem to signal the possibility of some kind of contact-based explanation.

If Vennemann is right, this acquisition of a new grammatical distinction from another language (Vasconic) would be a typical example of additive complex-ification (Trudgill 2011, and see Chapter 2). The Celtic and Italic languages in question had now acquired an additional morphologically expressed grammatical category. The acquisition of grammatical categories from one language by another implies a long-term, co-territorial contact situation between social groups involving childhood bilingualism. As Mithun (1999: 314) says, 'strong linguistic areas are typically characterised by large numbers of small linguistic communities on good social terms. Their members are in frequent contact and often become multilingual.'

Vennemann himself argues that this is the kind of development that typically occurs as a result of language shift (cf. Thomason & Kaufman 1988). Indeed it is, but I do not agree that language shift is necessarily involved – long term contact and bilingualism with language maintenance rather than shift will have the exactly the same – and perhaps even more – complexification consequences, as in the case of *Sprachbünde*.

Latin-Celtic Contact in Lowland England

As we saw, Celts arrived in Britain sometime between 4500 BC and 1000 BC, bringing, again if Vennemann is right, their Vasconic-type two-copula system with them. However, the first actual instance of language contact we know anything about in Britain involving these Celts occurred long after their first arrival. This was in the England of the first millennium AD, when contact began between the, by then indigenous, British Celtic (Brittonic or Brythonic) language which appears to have been spoken over all of the island of Britain, on the one hand, and the Latin of the Roman colonists, who started arriving in AD 43, on the other – though Adams (2007: 577) adds that 'there are signs that British rulers had acquired some Latin before the conquest'. Similar Latin-Celtic contact had, of course, taken place earlier, nearby on the continent in what is now France, involving the Celtic language Gaulish: northern Gaul up to the English Channel was occupied by the Romans about ninety years before the colonisation of England.

How long this contact lasted in England is not entirely clear. Imperial government from Rome was withdrawn in 410, but Morris (1973: 30) argues that there is no reason to suppose that large numbers of people actually left the island because of this; and Roman civilisation 'lasted some thirty years more'. Indeed, it has been argued, albeit controversially,[5] that British Vulgar Latin continued to be spoken by Romanised Celts well after the beginning of the fifth-century Anglo-Saxon takeover, and, in fact, for long after that. For example, Jackson (1953) cites Pogatscher (1888) as believing that there were Latin speakers in England until about 600. And Schrijver goes further and talks of Latin lasting well into the 600s – he writes of 'large numbers of Latin-speaking refugees from the Lowland Zone entering the Highland Zone ... in the period between the fifth and seventh centuries' (Schrijver 2009: 195).

Under this scenario then, Latin-Celtic contact could have lasted for as long as 600 years in England. According to Schrijver (e.g., 2007), the linguistic consequences of this, possibly lengthy, Latin-Celtic contact were eventually to differ greatly as between the Lowland and Highland areas of the island of Britain, with the outcome in the Lowlands resembling the outcome in Gaul.[6] The Lowland Britain of the south and east was divided from the northern and western Highland area along a line which can be drawn approximately, starting in the south, from Dorchester via Bath, Gloucester, Wroxeter, Leicester, Lincoln and York to Corbridge and Carlisle.[7] That is, the boundary passes through Dorset, Somerset, Gloucestershire, Worcestershire, Shropshire, Staffordshire, Leicestershire, Nottinghamshire, Lincolnshire, Yorkshire, Durham and Northumberland, leaving on the Lowland side the whole of the English counties of Norfolk, Suffolk, Essex, Kent, Sussex, Hampshire, Cambridgeshire, Northamptonshire, Huntingdonshire, Bedfordshire, Hertfordshire, Middlesex, Surrey, Buckinghamshire, Oxfordshire, Berkshire, Warwickshire and Wiltshire.

---

[5] Adams (2007) is very sceptical, for instance.
[6] For the original presentation of this distinction, see Fox (1932).
[7] Peter Schrijver, personal communication (2008).

Schrijver (2002) argues that, during the course of the Roman occupation, the Lowland zone ceased to be monolingual Brittonic-speaking. Rather, as a consequence of Latin-Celtic bilingualism, a specifically British form of Vulgar Latin developed. Adams, too, says that 'there is evidence particularly in the curse tablets for the spread of Latin among the Celtic population' (Schrijver 2007: 622). According to Adams, at least some of these curse tablets from southern Britain, mainly published by Tomlin (e.g., 1988), 'emanate from a Romanised Celtic popula-tion which had not received any sort of literary education' and 'have traces of lower social dialects as they were spoken in Britain'.

This British Latin, Schrijver suggests, was extremely widely used by Celts as a native language or second-language lingua franca. Schrijver's argument for this is based on a detailed linguistic analysis which shows that Lowland Brittonic itself experienced considerable linguistic influence, notably phonological, from British Latin, suggesting that Latin was spoken in one way or another by a large propor-tion of the Lowland population.

Not a great deal is known about this British Vulgar Latin (Adams 2007; see also 2003); and much of what written Latin does survive seems to be 'Latin in Britain' rather than 'the Latin of Britain' (Adams 2007: 580), that is, it was written by Latin speakers who were outsiders and just happened to be visiting Britain – they might have been stationed there as soldiers, for example. One can speculate, however, about what the linguistic consequences of this contact with Brittonic would have been for the spoken Latin of Britain. One good guess is that the major linguistic consequences would have included simplification. Grammatical simplification in continental Vulgar Latin – loss of morphologically marked cases, for instance – has often been attributed to the influence of language-contact of the adult foreign-language learning type with indigenous languages, as can be supposed to have occurred in Britain also. Clackson and Horrocks (2007), for instance, have sug-gested of the Romance languages that it is possible to relate their change towards analyticity to the spread of Latin as a second language in the Roman Empire: 'given the choice between a synthetic construction with complex (and often irregular) morphology and an analytic construction which can be generalised across the board, language learners tend to prefer the latter option' (2007: 276).

There would also have been transfer: as we noted earlier, Adams (2007: 579) says that 'once Latin spread among the Celtic population it was bound to take on regional characteristics, given that it was by definition the second language of the locals and subject to interference from Celtic'. In England, according to Schrijver, this Latin-with-a-British-Celtic-substratum was a language which, if it had survived, would have ended up being very much like Old French; and indeed Schrijver links this spoken British Latin together with the Gallo-Romance precur-sor of Old French, labelling them both 'Northwestern Romance'.

Adams too (2007: 622) says recent discoveries and analyses show that the Latin of Gaul and Britain have a common 'northwestern character' and that certain Latin features which were 'found in Gaul are now attested in Britain as well' (2007: 596). This was because 'the common Celtic background, contacts across the Channel, and the remoteness of Italy caused Gaul and Britain to develop their own linguistic features, embracing phonetic interference from Celtic and the adoption of Celtic loanwords'.

As far as 'the common Celtic background' is concerned, the extent to which Brittonic should be grouped together genetically with Gaulish as *Gallo-Brittonic*, as opposed to with Irish as *Insular Celtic*, is an interesting question for Celticists; but Schrijver makes chronological sense of the issue. He writes (1995: 465) that 'a number of highly specific sound developments in which Irish did not take part, is shared by British and Gaulish'. He then suggests that 'the period of Insular Celtic unity ... dates to before the Roman conquest of Britain, while Gallo-Brittonic developments belong to the early centuries AD, when both Britain and Gaul were dominated by Rome'. So not only were there Romance linguistic links across the Channel at the relevant period, there were Celtic links as well.

As far as this Celtic interference in Latin as mentioned by Adams is concerned, I would like to suppose that there is no reason for this interference not to have extended to the grammatical level as well: as far as copulas are concerned, we noted earlier that Vennemann (2010) claims that Old French had a Proto-Celtic-type two-copula, habitual vs. non-habitual system. According to him, the two Old French copulas were *estre* from Latin ESSE 'to be', via *essere* > *essre* > *estre*; and *ester*, from Latin STARE 'to stand' via *estare* > *estar* > *ester*. The grammatico-semantic distinction between them was not dissimilar to that still to be found in the modern Iberian languages. The present tense paradigms for *estre* (habitual) and *ester* (non-habitual) were (Bonnard & Régnier 1997: 105–6):

estre	*ester*
suis	estois
ies	estas
est	esta
somes	estons
estes	estez
sont	estont

We could therefore readily suppose that the precursor of Old French – Northwestern Romance – also had two copulas. And if this was the case, then there is no reason to suppose that this was any less true of the Northwestern Romance that was spoken in Lowland England than of that spoken in Gaul. Vennemann's claim, it is true, does not seem to receive support from the standard Old French grammars, where *ester* is generally cited as meaning 'stay'. But it does have some plausibility. We know that STARE did become increasingly grammaticalised, with semantic bleaching leading to loss of any connection with 'standing' as such: as Wandruszka (1965: 438) has it, we see that '*stare* von der vollen

Bedeutung "aufrecht stehen" weitgehend entlastet wurde'.[8] The grammaticalisation process was already underway in Vulgar Latin: Väänänen (1967: 97), in a section on *Changement de sens*, cites the development '*être debout* > *être immobile* > *être*', and gives examples such as *in dubio stare* 'to be in doubt'.

And the process clearly did take place to different degrees in the different western Romance languages. For Gascon, for example, Väänänen (1967: 138) says that '*esse* est en partie éliminé . . . en gascon par *stare*'. The results of the process can also be seen beyond Northwestern Romance in that even modern Italian *stare* is not infrequently translatable into English as 'be'; there is also some evidence of copula-like status in Sicilian (Vennemann 2010); and Sardinian *istare* also shows some grammaticalisation in that it can be used to form the progressive (Jones 1993). Pountain, too, says (1982: 158) that 'it is clear that the histories of *ESSER and STARE should be thought of as a Romance, rather than simply an Ibero-Romance phenomenon'; and he talks of 'a general drift towards the proliferation of copular verbs' (1982: 159). So it is perfectly reasonable to suppose that STARE might very well have acquired copula or copula-like status in Northwestern Romance.

Perhaps the strongest argument in favour of Vennemann's claim that STARE became sufficiently grammaticalised in Old French for it to be interpretable as a genuine copula, however, is the ultimate fate that befell *ester*. What happened was that there was increasing confusion in Northwestern Romance/Old French between ESSE and STARE, with *ester* eventually being merged – swallowed up, almost – by *estre*, modern *être*, and effectively disappearing (with the function of the full lexical verb meaning 'to stay' being taken over by *rester*[9]).

It is widely thought that this distinction between the two verbs in Old French gradually came to be lost as a result of phonological changes. Wandruszka (1965: 438) says: 'Im Französischen erklärt man das meist mit der lautlichen Verschmelzung der beiden Verben, so wie das spanische und portugiesische *ser* sein Partizip *sido* der Veschmelzung mit *sedere* verdankt'.[10] There certainly was a phonological component to this loss of *ester*: 'im Französischen wurde *stare* zu *ester*: die französische Lautentwicklung machte verschiedene Formen dieses Verbums denen von *esse* > *estre* > *être* "sein" so ähnlich, daß es schließlich in *estre* aufging'[11] (1965: 425).

But phonological change cannot be the whole story. Wandruszka says that from his examples 'man sieht, wie nahe *stare* und *esse* sich in den romanischen Sprachen

---

[8] *Stare* has been largely relieved of the full meaning 'stand upright'.

[9] As kindly pointed out to me by Mike Jones.

[10] In French, this is most often explained in terms of the phonological merger of the two verbs, just as Spanish and Portuguese *ser* owes its participle *sido* to the merger with *sedere*.

[11] 'in French, *stare* became *ester*: this French sound-change made the different forms of the verb so similar to those of *esse* > *estre* > *être* "to be" that in the end it was absorbed by *estre*'.

gekommen sind'.[12] But 'im Italienischen und Katalanischen hat auch ohne eine solche Verschmelzung *stare* sein Partizip an *esse* weitergegeben'[13] (Wandruszka, 1965: 438); and, as Wandruszka says, English has two phonologically identical verbs *to lie*, but they show no signs of merging!

The loss of the distinction between Old French *estre* and *ester* must surely imply something much more than just phonetic similarity. There must have been some close grammatically functional similarity between the two forms in order, for example, for *stare* to pass on its participle *statum* to *esse* (Wandruszka, 1965: 438). Otherwise it is hard to see how the past and present participles of *ester* could have ended up replacing the participles of *estre*: the past participle of *ester* survives in modern French, after transfer to *estre*, in the form of *été* 'been', and the present participle as *étant* 'being'. Indeed, the whole imperfect indicative of Old French *estre* eventually also had its origins in *ester*: the forms *estoie, estoies, estoit, estions, estiez, estoient* are said by Elcock (1960: 136) to have originated when the old imperfect from ESSE, ERAM, gave way to the *estoie* derived from STABAM (from STARE), after the infinitives *estre* and *ester* became confused. This could hardly have happened without some kind of parallelism. There was indeed a 'lautliche Verschmelzung'; but there was a grammatico-semantic one as well. Spalinger also uses the term *Verschmelzung* 'fusion, merger', but, as she sees it, this undoubtedly also involved a 'semantische Annäherung' – a semantic convergence (Spalinger 1955: 129). This analysis of what happened sits well with the supposition that it was eventually only the habitual/non-habitual copula function which separated the two sets of forms semantically – and then even that disappeared.

Of course, if there was a two-copula system in Northwestern Romance, it is not clear how confidently we could ascribe the presence of this system to Celtic (and thus perhaps to Vasconic) influence; but the case would be strong. And the system certainly would represent a good example of complexification vis-à-vis earlier forms of Latin: the addition of a grammatical category, habitual vs. non-habitual, that was not present at earlier stages of Classical Latin.

Brittonic Celtic and Old English

The next major episode of language contact in Britain was that which occurred, initially in the eastern part of the island, as a result of the arrival of the West Germanic tribes who had crossed the North Sea from mainland coastal regions of what are now Belgium, the Netherlands, northwestern Germany and Danish Jutland. As we saw before, this process started in the fourth century AD, but

---

[12] 'one can see how close *stare* and *esse* have come to each other in the Romance languages'.
[13] 'in Italian and Catalan, *stare* has donated its participle to *esse* even without such a merger'.

major permanent West Germanic settlements in England did not begin appearing in any significant way until the middle of the fifth century.

Celtic and Latin, as we noted, experienced considerable contact in mainland northwestern Europe before they did so in England. But Celtic and Germanic speakers, too, had also come into contact with each other earlier on the mainland, as a result of the southward migrations of Germanic peoples out of southern Scandinavia into what is now Germany some time before the first millennium BC. Following Hutterer (1975 [2008]), Hawkins (1990) suggests, as I interpret his map (1990: 60), that by 1000 BC Germanic was spoken all along the coastline of what is now Germany from the mouth of the Ems eastwards to the mouth of the Oder in the region of Stettin/Szczeczin; and then inland as far perhaps as the regions of Hanover/Hannover and Berlin. By 500 BC, further geographical expansion meant that Germanic speakers were now to be found from the North Sea coast, starting well to the south of the Rhine Delta – so, in modern Belgium – to as far east as the river Vistula/Wisła/Weichsel, which runs through today's Warsaw/Warszawa/Warschau; and stretching as far south perhaps as Amiens in the west and Cracow/Kraków/Krakau in the east. In all of those areas there would have been contact with Celtic speakers. Schumacher (2009: 247), who provides an in-depth consideration of the possible linguistic consequences, locates the main area of Germano-Celtic contact at this time as being situated 'upstream along the Rhine from its mouth, then across the middle of Germany, through the Czech Republic, and into the western part of Slovakia'. Now, however, contact began to occur in England itself, between the West Germanic of the westward-migrating Jutes, Angles, Saxons and Frisians, and the specially British form of Celtic, Brittonic.

The possible relevance of Vennemann's Vasconic hypothesis for the linguistic history of English now comes from his insight about the *transitivity of language contact* (Vennemann 2002): if there are several historical layers of language contact, then a substratum language can itself have a substratum. One much-mentioned example of a possible linguistic contact phenomenon resulting from this meeting of Brittonic and West Germanic is the distinction between the two paradigms of the copula – the functional differentiation of two forms of *be* mentioned above as perhaps resulting in Celtic from contact with Vasconic, and also in connection with Northwestern Romance. If Vasconic had an influence on Celtic in mainland Europe, and if Celtic had an influence on continental West Germanic and/or on pre–Old English in Britain – as we just supposed it might have had on Northwestern Romance – then it could indeed be said that Old English was influenced by Vasconic.

The Old English distinction, unique in Germanic, between the two different copulas *wesan* and *beon* has long been known. Wischer (2011) points out that Bethge (1900) and Dieter (1900) had both noticed that copula forms derived from an Indo-European **b*-root were not found in North Germanic or East

Germanic and, more importantly, that only Old English of the West Germanic languages had two complete paradigms. The two paradigms are as follows (from Wischer 2011):

	Indicative		Subjunctive		Imperative	
1.	*ēom*	*bēo*	*sīe*	*bēo*	*sīe/wes*	*bēo*
2.	*eart*	*bist*	*sīe*	*bēo*		
3.	*is*	*biþ*	*sīe*	*bēo*		
pl.	*āron*	*bēoþ*	*sīen*	*bēon*	*wesaþ*	*bēoþ*

Following on from the work of Tolkien (1963, 1983), whose arguments in favour of Celtic influence on Old English have been highly influential, Lutz (2010) points out that not only did Old English have these two different present tense declensions for the copula, but that this was actually also a functional distinction as in Celtic.

The importance of this for our current story is persuasively made by the distinguished Celtic linguistic scholar Anders Ahlqvist (2010), who points out, again following Tolkien, that the functional distinction lay in the fact that the Old English *eom* declension of *wesan* was used only for non-habitual meanings, while the *b-* declension of *beon* was employed for the expression of the habitual. According to Ahlqvist, this system is not only peculiar to Old English amongst the Germanic languages; the distinction is also precisely the one which is found in Welsh — Ahlqvist writes of 'a curious parallelism'. And not only that — there is also the remarkable phonological similarity between the actual forms of Old Welsh and Old English: the 'true present' in both languages has forms without *b-*, while the habitual has forms with *b-*. More particularly, the Welsh form corresponding to the Old English third-person singular habitual *b*-form *biþ* is *bydd*, which goes back to earlier **bið*. Ahlqvist stresses that this resemblance — or indeed identity — is even more remarkable because of the short vowel in Old English *biþ*.

Wischer (2011) agrees and shows that her detailed and extensive corpus-based analyses of the two parallel sets of forms — and a comparison with the Celtic languages — supports the thesis that the emergence of the double paradigm in Old English 'can only be assigned to Insular Celtic influence'.

It is true that Laker (2002) points out that the present-tense paradigms of the verb *be* actually have two different stems in the other West Germanic languages as well. Old Saxon had the present-tense singular 1, 2, 3 forms *bium, bist, is*, for example — compare the simpler North Germanic system: Old Norse *em, ert, er*. This suggests, Laker argues, that there were originally two functionally distinct paradigms of *be* in continental West Germanic as well as in Old English — with the functionality of the distinction having been lost by the time we get to the historical record. This same situation is now found in modern English, of course: we have the two separate stems, as in *am, be* etc., but they are no longer used distinctively.

Latin and Brittonic

While this complexification was taking place in the English Lowlands, a rather different type of development was occurring in the Highlands of England. Schrijver (2009) has presented us with a language-contact–based insight in which he not only suggests that language contact in England had remarkable linguistic consequences for Brittonic, but also presents a specific scenario for how this might have happened.

Jackson (1953) says that nearly all of the many sound changes which converted Brittonic/Brythonic into its descendant languages, Welsh, Cornish and Breton, took place between the middle of the fifth and the end of the sixth century, and – in a remarkable claim – that the evolution was so rapid 'we can be fairly sure that Vortigern around 450 could not have understood Aneirin around 600' (1953: 690). More importantly, it is also well known that considerable grammatical simplification occurred in Brittonic between approximately 450 and 600: Jackson refers to the 'break-up of the case system' (1953: 691) as having been completed by about 600. The linguistic changes which occurred in British overall were to 'alter its whole appearance' and 'to modify fundamentally its syntax' (1953: 691).

From a sociolinguistic-typological point of view, we can suggest that it is not a coincidence that the massive changes in Brittonic occurred precisely when they did. After the first Anglo-Saxon uprising in eastern England, much of fifth-century Celtic Britain was a socially very unstable place indeed. There were battles, murder, destruction, flight, migration, emigration, enslavement, land-taking – in other words very considerable upheaval. This is certainly Jackson's interpretation of the relationship between the social and linguistic events: he says (1953: 690) that 'periods of unusually marked linguistic corruption [sic] are sometimes associated with great social upheavals, or with invasion and conquest'. Schrijver, however, has a more detailed suggestion about this. He argues, specifically, that it was large-scale language shift involving the adult second-language learning of Brittonic which led to the simplification. But who was it, at that period of history, who was learning Brittonic as a second language? Schrijver says that it was the very large numbers of upper-class British refugees who were fleeing from Lowland England to the Highland zone, to escape the same Anglo-Saxon revolt which also led to the flight to Brittany. These refugees were Romanised Celts who were by now native speakers of Latin/British Northwestern Romance and who, on arriving in the still Brittonic-speaking Highland north and west, were obliged to learn their ancestral but forgotten language as best they could. They were so numerous that the effects of the simplifications they introduced into the inflectional systems of Late British were in subsequent generations passed on even to the children of native speakers.

In the Highland zone, then, there was language shift from British Latin to Brittonic, just as there had earlier been a shift in the Lowland zone from Brittonic to Latin. But the two-copula system survived this episode of contact-induced linguistic change (as we shall see), which is not surprising given that there was very probably a similar two-copula system in the Northwestern Romance spoken by the upper-class refugee Celts, meaning that they were not faced with any enormous difficulties when it came to acquiring this system.

Welsh, Nordic and English

There is, then, evidence that Celtic survived for some considerable time after the beginnings of the Anglo-Saxon takeover of England. There is similar evidence for Latin: as we have seen, Schrijver believes that Latin survived into the seventh century (2009: 195). We can therefore suppose that there was a period of a number of generations, perhaps during the sixth and seventh centuries, when there were three languages spoken in England which all had the two-copula system: Brittonic/ Late British, British Latin/Northwestern Romance, and Old English. However, the fate of the two-copula system when it came to the second millennium was a less happy one: by the medieval period it had been greatly weakened.

If Northwestern Romance had survived in England, we can suppose that it would have undergone the same development as happened in Old French. We saw that Old French may well have had a functional, habitual/non-habitual distinction between the two paradigms of *estre* and *ester*, but that *ester* was swallowed up by *estre* in the medieval period. It is true that *ester* survived in the sense that it has replaced a number of the original forms of *estre*, including the original past participle *étu* with its own *été*, but the crucial point for our purposes is that any functional semantico-grammatical distinction that might have existed between habitual/non-habitual was completely lost.

The distinction fared no better in English. Wischer tells us that 'towards the end of the Old English period this distinction blurred, and a new mixed paradigm emerged in Middle English' (2011: 230). And Lass (1992: 140), referring to the work of Mossé (1952), talks of the 'dismemberment' of the system in Early Middle English – so presumably by about 1200 – with 'various portions spread over the dialects' (see also Laing 2011). The widespread survival in some modern dialects of variants such as *I be*, alongside the *I am* of other dialects, testifies to the endurance of different forms from the two Old English paradigms; but nowhere has the actual grammatical distinction been maintained.

Could this loss too be accounted for as having been the result of language contact? This seems perfectly possible. We have already noted that the presence of the copula distinction in Northwestern Romance may have played a role in its preservation in Late British, in spite of the simplification that was otherwise taking place. We can then suppose that its presence in Late British similarly helped its survival in Old English, even under adult language contact. But contact with Old Norse would have been a different matter. As mentioned earlier, Dieter (1900) noticed that copula forms derived from an Indo-European *b-root were not found at all in North Germanic or East Germanic. North Germanic, which had not been in contact with Celtic, had never acquired the two-copula system; and it would therefore have been absent from Old Norse as it arrived in Britain. Lutz states that 'the distinction is abandoned in early Middle English, earlier in Northern than in Southern and Southwestern texts' (Lutz 2009: 233), a geographical indication of the probability of North Germanic influence.

However, the situation in Brittonic was a rather happier one as far as the survival of the two-copula system was concerned. This emerges from Simon Evans's (1964) *Grammar of Middle Welsh* (i.e., Welsh as written between approximately 1150 and 1400 – a period when Brittonic was also still being spoken in Cornwall and, at least at the beginning of the period, in Cumbria and Strathclyde). The survival of the two-copula system is made very clear by Evans's reference to the fact that Middle Welsh had both simple or non-habitual and consuetudinal or habitual forms of the copula (with the habitual also being used to express the future). He cites (1964: 136) the following present-tense paradigms of the two forms of *to be* (somewhat simplified here):

1sg	wyf	bydaf	
2sg	wyt	bydy	
3sg	yw	byd	
1pl	ym	bydwn	
2pl	ywch	bydwch	
3pl	ynt	bydant	

Indeed, something very like this system has survived right into Modern Welsh, with the *byd* paradigm (modern *bydd*) still being used for habituality. In Evans's analysis of Middle Welsh, he has it that the habitual paradigm can also be used to express futurity. King (2003: 168) puts it the other way round for Modern Welsh – future forms are also used to express 'a repeated or habitual action' – but this of course amounts to the same thing. The modern habitual paradigm is (King 2003: 145, 157):

sg.	pl.
bydda	byddwn
byddi	byddwch
bydd	byddan

This also extends (King 1993: 172) to the use of the *bydd* paradigm in periphrastic verbs forms: the 'periphrastic tense is also used as a habitual present'. King gives the example of *Bydda i'n mynd yno bob wythnos* 'I go there every week':

bydda i'n mynd yno bob wythnos
am I+PROG go there every week

There are indications, however, that the system is currently being lost: as reported by David Willis (personal communication, 2011), younger speakers are now tending to use the simple present to express habituality. This report is supported by the observation made by Jones (2010: 74), who says that the simple present is now the preferred choice for expressing habituality 'for some speakers'.

It would be easy to ascribe this development to contact with English, and indeed it may well be right to do so: it is certainly the case that the younger speakers in question will all be bilingual in Welsh and English. And if it is right to do so, then we can conclude that the phenomenon of language contact which led to the introduction, perhaps 4,000 years ago, of the two-copula system into Southern Britain, and then to its very long-term maintenance, is now, very many generations indeed later, also leading to its gradual demise.

4 The First Three Thousand Years: Contact in Prehistoric and Early Historic English

There are many factors which have contributed to the linguistic character of modern English, but one of them is undoubtedly contact.[1] In this chapter, I will be concerned to approach the notion of language contact, and its role in the history of English, from what I hope will be a nuanced, sociolinguistic-typological perspective. By this I mean that sociolinguistics shows us that, as we have seen in earlier chapters, language contact is not a unitary phenomenon, as it sometimes seems from the literature: the linguistic consequences of language contact can vary enormously depending on the particular sociolinguistic conditions in which it takes place (Trudgill, 2011).[2]

Contact can often, for example, lead to simplification, as we have already noted. This is the kind of development which occurs as a result of short-term adult and therefore imperfect language learning – seen at its most extreme in the case of pidgins. But contact can also lead to complexification, as a result of long-term contact – typically co-territorial, and involving child-language bilingualism. In these situations, additional grammatical categories can be transferred to a language from neighbouring languages, as typically seen in *Sprachbund*-type situations, with resulting added complexity.

In its examination of contact from a sociolinguistically informed point of view, this chapter deals specifically with those language-contact events involving English which have had structural consequences for mother-tongue English as a whole (Kastovsky & Mettinger 2001; Vennemann 2011; Miller 2012). There have been many other relatively recent, less major contact events which have influenced only specific varieties of the language: I have argued, for example (Trudgill 2010), that the absence of third-person singular present-tense -*s* in the dialects of East Anglia is due to the fact that, in 1600, one third of the population of the English city of Norwich were Dutch- and French-speaking people. And colonial varieties of English have experienced particular contact events in their individual situations – though linguistic influences on mother-tongue colonial English varieties, other than at the lexical level, have mainly been from other European languages, such

---

[1] This chapter does not deal with English-based creoles, nor second-language varieties such as West African English, nor shift varieties of English with a clear substrate, such as Highland Scottish English.

[2] For the, rather extensive, role played by dialect contact, see Trudgill (2012).

as Afrikaans in South Africa and German/Yiddish in the USA, rather than from the indigenous languages (Trudgill 2004).

But the history of the English language generally is a story which has been intimately connected with language contact from the very beginning. If we are looking for contact-based explanations as to why English as a whole is like it is, then we have to go back a very long way.

The Prehistory

The Proto-Germanic language that English descends from was linguistically rather unusual within the Indo-European language family. It had many idiosyncratic features in its lexis, grammar and pronunciation; and many of these idiosyncrasies – aspects of which are still to be found to this day in modern English – are often thought of as being the result of language contact (Hawkins 1990; Polomé 1990).

The First Germanic Sound Shift, which gives us innovative /f/ in English *foot* as opposed to the original Indo-European /p/ in French *pied*, Greek πόδι, Lithuanian *péda,* has been argued by Wiik (2003), if controversially, to be the result of a Finnic substrate, Finnic being the parent language of modern Finnish, Estonian and Sami (Lappish). The hypothesis would be that on their journey westwards from the borderlands of Europe and Asia – if that is where the Indo-European homeland was located, as seems likely – Indo-European speakers came into contact with Finnic speakers. Some of these Finnic speakers went through a process of language shift, with resulting substratum effects.

It has also been hypothesised that language contact and language shift occurred in the southern Scandinavian homeland of Proto-Germanic itself, after the Indo-European dialect in question had arrived there. Schrijver (2003) provides a detailed phonological discussion of the possibility of a connection between Indo-European /Germanic and Sami, perhaps through some shared, now lost substrate. And Vennemann (2003a, 2003b, 2010a, 2010b) has put forth an adventurous but important hypothesis about what happened. As we saw in Chapter 3, he argues – controversially (see Sheynin 2004) but with support (e.g., Mailhammer 2011) – that the people who were already in residence when Indo-European speakers first arrived in southern Scandinavia were speakers of a language which was a member of the language family he calls Vasconic. This is the family which is today represented by Basque as the only modern survivor.

It could perhaps be this episode of contact which would account for the several simplifications which occurred in the transition from Indo-European to Germanic, arguably as a result of pidginisation brought about by adult-language learning.[3] Braunmüller (2008) cites a number of examples of simplification which he ascribes

---

[3] This term in no way implies that any kind of pidgin language was involved.

to contact, all of which remain visible in modern English. Proto-Germanic, for example, had only two inflected tenses (present and past), and it had lost the Indo-European subjunctive (the form called subjunctive in Germanic continues the Indo-European optative). In addition, the Indo-European sigmatic aorist tense had gone.

Another possible example of contact-induced simplification is the development in Germanic of predictable word stress. In Indo-European, the location of the main stress in a word was unpredictable; but in Germanic this had changed so that all words had their stress on the first syllable (Lehmann 1961). This is something that we can still see in modern English, where all original Germanic words have this stress pattern unless the first syllable is some form of prefix.

A final candidate for the label of simplification is the growth in Germanic of weak dental preterites (Prokosch 1939: 194), giving English *want-wanted* as opposed to the Indo-European-type strong verbs of the type *sing-sang-sung*. One possible mechanism leading to this development was the grammaticalisation of the weak verb *dō* 'do' (e.g., Braunmüller 2008; Kiparksy 2009). But in any case, the consequence was that part of the verb system was entirely regular and would have been more readily learnable by non-native adult learners.

But Vennemann's hypothesis does not stop there. Contact with Vasconic, he argues, cannot explain all the peculiarities of Germanic. One of these peculiarities is the fact that Proto-Germanic had a vocabulary which was as much as one third non-Indo-European in origin, as a number of linguists have suggested (Feist 1932). Hawkins (1990) reports that the Germanic words which are not of Indo-European origin belong to the core of the basic vocabulary; they include common words, such as those to do with maritime travel like *sea*, *ship*, *boat*, *sail*, as well as words for *sword*, *shield*, *eel*, *calf*, *lamb*, *king* and very many others.

Hawkins has no suggestion as to which language these words might have been borrowed from, but Vennemann (2000, 2001) does have a proposal which is not without support from others (see Coates 2009). He claims that the vocabulary is not Vasconic. Rather, the lexical items in question originate in a language he calls 'Semitidic', which was a member of the Afro-Asiatic (formerly 'Hamito-Semitic') family. Vennemann's view is that sea-faring Semitidic-speaking people travelled north as colonisers from the western Mediterranean along the Atlantic coastline of Europe, to the islands and along the major rivers, reaching southern Sweden in about 2500 BC. In this Germanic homeland they formed a minority ruling class, and eventually went through a process of language shift – but not without first bequeathing a large amount of vocabulary to the Indo-European dialect which became Germanic (see also Mailhammer 2011).

So we can speculate – and it is speculation – that the ancestor of modern English, Proto-Germanic, was a dialect of the Indo-European language which came originally from the borderlands of Asia and Europe and which was influenced in its phonology by contact with Finnic; in its grammar and phonology by contact with the ancestor of modern Basque; and in its lexis by contact with Afro-Asiatic. The

development of Proto-Germanic occurred during and/or after the westward movement of Indo-European speakers across northern Europe into southern
Scandinavia, and it seems possible or even probable that language contact played
an important role in determining the actual linguistic nature of Germanic
(Mailhammer 2012).

West Germanic–Continental Celtic Contact

The next important series of contact-induced linguistic events which ultimately
influenced the nature of English took place as a result of further migrations. Some
time before the first millennium BC, groups of speakers of Germanic moved southwards out of their southern Scandinavian homeland into what is now Germany
(Hawkins 1990). There they came into contact with speakers of another Indo-
European language which was already in place: Celtic (Roberge 2010).

As already noted in Chapter 3, Hawkins' map (1990: 60), following Hutterer
(1975 [2008]), suggests that, by 1000 BC, Germanic was spoken all along the
coastline of Germany, from the mouth of the Ems eastwards to the mouth of the
Oder in the region of Stettin; and then inland as far as the regions of Hanover and
Berlin. Five centuries later, by about 500 BC, considerable further geographical
expansion had taken place. Germanic speakers were now to be found in an area
stretching from the North Sea coast, starting well to the south of the Rhine Delta –
so in modern Belgium – to as far east as the river Vistula, which runs through
today's Warsaw; and then as far south perhaps as Amiens in the west and Cracow in
the east.

In all of those areas there was contact with Celtic speakers. As we saw in the
previous chapter, Schumacher (2009) argues that there was a contact zone which
ran from the Rhine delta through Germany and on into Slovakia. One much-
mentioned example of a possible linguistic contact phenomenon resulting from
this meeting of Celtic and Germanic has to do with the West Germanic copula
(Keller 1925, Schumacher 2009), as discussed in Chapter 3. Old English, as we saw
there, had a distinction between two different copulas, *wesan* and *beon*.

English–Insular Celtic Contact: the Early Period

As is well known, West Germanic tribes eventually crossed the North Sea to Britain
from coastal regions of what are now Belgium, the Netherlands, northwestern
Germany, and western Danish Jutland. This process started in the fourth
century AD, but permanent West Germanic settlements in England did not begin
appearing in any significant way until the middle of the fifth century.

As a result of this migration, Celtic and Germanic continued or resumed contact in England itself, where the contact was between the West Germanic of the westward-migrating Jutes, Angles, Saxons, and Frisians, and the specifically British form of Celtic, Brittonic. Once again, this contact had some rather major linguistic consequences, something which has not always been acknowledged in the literature but has now become widely accepted (see, for instance, volume 13 of *English Language and Linguistics* 2009). The importance of this form of contact for the English language is underlined by the fact that there is further evidence, in addition to the presence of the two-copula system, suggesting that contact between Late British and Old English was initially of the complexification type, involving additive borrowing. A number of writers, including Ahlqvist (2010), Filppula (2003), Laker (2008), Lutz (2010) and Vennemann (2000) have discussed the acquisition by Old English of other morphological categories from Late British. One example concerns the grammaticalisation of the progressive aspect (Mittendorf & Poppe 2000; White 2002; Filppula 2003; Lutz 2010): the progressive is generally considered not to be a typical feature of the Germanic languages, and therefore to be a good candidate in English for influence from Brittonic, where it was and is an established feature (see also Keller 1925). Ahlqvist gives a reasoned and highly persuasive account – and one informed by a profound knowledge of Celtic linguistics and of the relative chronologies involved – showing that the argument that the English progressive results from influence from a Celtic source is a sound one.

The non-linguistic importance of this observation is that sociolinguistic typology indicates that, if there was language contact leading to the adoption of Late British features into Old English of this grammatical type, this must have occurred at a time when Old English speakers were relatively few in number, and the relationship between the two ethnic groups was one that was developing, for a period, on a basis of relative equality (Trudgill 2010, 2011).

In this particular case, contact of this type must have taken place in the earlier decades of Anglo-Saxon settlement in the Lowland zone. Morris (1973) describes a situation which gives a clear impression of the historical and social background against which this might have happened. He paints a picture in which, after the withdrawal of Roman imperial government and administration from the island in 410, an independent Romano-Celtic Britain continued to maintain Roman civilisation for a number of decades. Then threats from outside, perhaps raids by the Picts from northern Scotland, led to invitations from the British to small groups of Anglo-Saxons to assist in the defence of the nation, particularly the east coast, probably in the late 420s. By about 442, however, many more Anglo-Saxons had arrived, and they had become numerous enough to revolt against their British hosts. As we saw above, it was at some point after this that some thousands of Brittonic speakers emigrated across the Channel to Brittany.

But the British fought back and, by about 495, they had subdued the Anglo-Saxons, who then remained for the most part confined, as a majority population, to

Norfolk, Kent and Sussex. There were plenty of ethnic English elsewhere, but they were in a minority: according to McMahon (2011: 257) 'the genetic evidence indicates that there was a significant movement of continental populations (males at least) into the east and south of Britain around the 5th century, but for most of the country the incomers represented a relative minority'. Morris (1973: 136) says that the 'small size [of English communities] made them harmless, necessarily subject allies of the British'. For example, in Driffield, Yorkshire, the 'British and English lived side by side and the government may have been British'. Moreover, 'throughout Britain the English lived in very small communities' and all of them 'were surrounded by stronger British neighbours; some of them were doubtless ruled by British kings' (Morris 1973: 282). Conflicts between different groups of Anglo-Saxons also led them to military alliances with the British.

A second Anglo-Saxon revolt against the British then began in the 570s, and was eventually to lead to Anglo-Saxon control of most of England and the domination by the Germanic population of the Celtic: the last British military victory over the English was in 655, perhaps in Wiltshire.

So it was during the period from approximately 420 to 600 that Old English speakers were dominated in most parts of Britain by Brittonic speakers, a situation which led to competent bilingualism on the part of the Germanic speakers, and thus to the borrowing of Celtic grammatical categories into English – a form of complexification typical of long-term co-territorial contact situations involving child bilingualism (see Trudgill 2011b).

English–Insular Celtic Contact: the Later Period

Contact with Brittonic was responsible, as we have just seen, for additive complexification in Old English. But it was also responsible for simplification. This is in no way paradoxical. The differential linguistic consequences have to do with changes in the sociolinguistic context over the centuries of contact: there was an early period of Celtic dominance in which complexification occurred, up until about 600, and then a later period of Germanic dominance during which simplification took place.

Old English was a highly synthetic fusional inflecting language, as discussed earlier. Though nothing like as complex as Ancient Greek, it had three numbers; five cases; inflectional case-marking on nouns, adjectives, demonstratives and pronouns; strong versus weak nominal declensions; inflectional person-marking on verbs; and large numbers of irregular 'strong' verbs, which also made a distinction between the root vowels of singular and plural preterite forms. There were also large numbers of conjugations and declensions.

Middle English, on the other hand, was much less inflecting and fusional, showing a clear move towards a much more isolating type of morphology. It had two numbers rather than three; three cases rather than five; and many fewer inflections, conjugations and declensions. There was also a reduction in case-marking and in subjunctive verb forms; and the distinction between the root vowels of the singular and plural preterite forms of strong verbs also disappeared, as did the strong/weak nominal declensions.

It is uncontroversial to suggest that this simplification in Old English was due at least in part to language contact. Many authors have argued for this explanation. James Milroy, whose memory this volume is dedicated to, says of the simplification which occurred that 'it seems clear that such a sweeping change is at least to some extent associated with language contact' (1992: 203). His case is a strong one, because simplification is very well known to be associated with language contact, and this thesis would therefore seem to be relatively uncontroversial.

It is, however, more controversial to argue a case in favour of the role of Celtic in this contact, many scholars accepting that it was in fact contact with Old Norse that was responsible (as we shall see). To argue persuasively for the role of Brittonic, it has been necessary for writers who favour this hypothesis to counter two wide-spread beliefs.

The first is that Celtic could not have been influential because it died out too early, the Brittonic-speaking population having fled, or been killed off or assimilated. However, there is now a lot of evidence to suggest that this was not the case – Celtic actually survived even in the Lowlands of England for many centuries. Consider the following from Morris (1973):

spoken Welsh was common in the 7th century . . . British monks probably preached in Norfolk, and also in Hertfordshire, about the 590s; their activity implies a considerable population who understood their language. (p. 314)

near Peterborough Guthlac was troubled about 705 by the still independent British of the Fenland who were to retain their speech and untamed hostility into the 11th century. (p. 314)

the population of the English kingdoms in the seventh century consisted of an uneven mixture of men of mixed Germanic origins and of descendants of the Roman British, called Welshman, who are likely to have constituted the larger number in many regions. (p. 316)

But Brittonic, as we have already seen, would have survived much more strongly and for much longer in the Highlands of Britain – and especially in the remotest Highland fringes: Strathclyde (southwestern Scotland), Cumbria (northwestern England) and Devon (southwestern England), as well as, obviously, Wales and Cornwall. Tristram (2004: 113) suggests that in some areas of the Midlands and Northern zone, speakers of the post-conquest Anglian and Mercian dialects ruled the native population of the Britons as their slaves. These continued to speak Brittonic, their native language, for perhaps as many as six or seven generations, before they shifted to Old English. Gelling (1993: 55) allows for more than four hundred years for the shift from Brittonic to Old English to have been completed, and suggests that the process was only complete around 900 AD.

The second anti-Celtic argument is that the chronology does not work, in that the simplification which occurred in Old English did not happen until centuries after the Celtic Brittonic language had died out in England (and the Old English-speaking areas of Scotland). Against this point, Tristram (2004) has argued for the relevance of the persistence of a written-language/spoken-language diglossia in Anglo-Saxon England, with an insight stemming from Wagner (1959: 151):

Daß sich das Germanische im angelsächsischen England einige Jahrhunderte ziemlich gut erhalten konnte, hängt mit dem Vorhandensein einer ags. Aristokratie und einer ags. Schrift- und Dichtersprache zusammen. Mit der normannischen Eroberung wird dieser germanischen Herrenschicht die Spitze gebrochen und der Entwicklung einer britischen Sprache freier Lauf gewährt.[4]

This insight was further developed by Vennemann (2001: 364):

Substratal influence originates in the lower strata of a society and usually takes centuries to reach the written language, and regularly only after a period of social upheaval. That this applies to Irish was argued by Pokorny (1927–30), and that it applies to English is a fact well known to every Anglicist: Middle English is the period during which the language of the old ruling class dies out because the new ruling class speaks French; and when this French-speaking ruling class switches to English, that English is the Celticized English of the lower strata.

Tristram's specific suggestion is that simplification occurred in Old English very much earlier than has hitherto been thought, at a time when contact with Celtic would have provided a very reasonable explanation. But these fundamental changes occurred in the spoken language without making their way into the written language – which provides the only data that we now have. The written evidence that has survived came from the pens of a small upper-class elite who preserved a knowledge of how Old English was supposed to be written, long after the original morphological complexity had disappeared from everyday speech. According to Tristram (2004), 'the theocratic elite of late Anglo-Saxon England deliberately enforced the standardization of Old English as a means of political control' (p. 113); and 'only the language of the elite, the high variety of Old English narrowly monitored and standardised, seems to have been codified in writing, and it was this version of the language which remained remarkably constant over many centuries' (p. 202).

---

[4] 'The fact that for some centuries Germanic survived rather well in Anglo-Saxon England is linked to the existence of an Anglo-Saxon aristocracy and a written Anglo-Saxon literary language. After the Norman Conquest, the leadership of this Germanic ruling class was broken and the development of a British language given a free rein.'

Evidence of simplification then appears in the written record only after the social breakdown brought about by the Norman Conquest had led to the disappearance of this diglossia, producing the first evidence available to us of changes which had occurred several centuries earlier:

Unfortunately, we know nothing about spoken Old English to the extent that it differed from the language as it was committed to writing, which was an instrument of power enforcement in the hands of a very few monastics belonging to the elite. In Old English literature we seldom hear about non-aristocratic people; they were given no voice. The spoken language only became visible (literally) after the Norman Conquest, after William the Conqueror effectively replaced the Anglo-Saxon aristocracy by Norman-French-speaking barons, clerics and their followers. Spoken Old English therefore only started to be admitted to the realm of writing at the beginning of the twelfth century. (Tristram 2006: 203)

We can compare this situation to the way in which, in places such as France, the knowledge of how Latin was supposed to be written survived even though massive linguistic changes had produced a situation in which the population as a whole were now not speaking Latin as such at all but the precursor to Old French. As Clackson and Horrocks (2007: 262) say, nonstandard spoken Latin of the later Empire 'is hidden behind the façade of the uniform written idiom which we find in most texts'.

It makes sense, then, to argue that simplification in Old English was the result of adult language contact, after 600 AD and mainly in the Highland zone of England, between Old English and a substratum variety spoken by subjugated Late British speakers, with eventual shift to Old English. Crucially, in those Highland areas where Brittonic survived the West Germanic takeover, its speakers were in a very different type of contact situation with Old English speakers than had been the case before 600 AD. Brittonic or Late British was now in a substratal, not adstratal relationship with Old English; and something like a caste system was probably in operation. The Britons were often slaves, a point made by Lutz (2010), amongst others: Lutz devotes extensive discussion to the important work on Anglo-Saxon slavery by Pelteret (1995). And according to Whitelock (1952: 111) 'the unfree class consisted of persons of different origins. Some were the descendants of the British population, as the word for "Briton" to mean simply "slave" testifies. And the menial tasks described in some Anglo-Saxon riddles are performed by "Britons"'.

A number of other writers (see Woolf 2007) have actually described the social situation as being one of 'apartheid': Thomas et al. (2008: 2419) write that the genetic evidence suggests that 'an apartheid-like social structure remains the most plausible model to explain the high degree of northwest continental European male-line ancestry in England', and that 'people of indigenous ethnicity were at an economic and legal disadvantage compared with those having Anglo-Saxon ethnicity – leading to differential reproductive success – and that the two groups were, to an extent, reproductively isolated'. Also 'from the textual evidence we have, the social barriers between the free and land-holding elite of Anglo-Saxon society and their dependents were perhaps fairly stable until the advent of the Normans' (Tristram 2004: 202). And Morris (1973: 314) asserts that 'a class of persons of inferior Welsh status existed in some numbers in much of England from the English conquest until after the Norman conquest and later'. So the two linguistic groups were hardly 'on good social terms', in Mithun's phrase (see Chapter 3).

Residential patterns would also have been significant: as Coates (2007: 190) says, separate villages where 'homogeneous slave communities might be retained' could 'lead to "slave coloured" varieties of English'. There is considerable evidence for this residential separation from place names. Ekwall (1960) lists about fifty different places in England containing the Old English element *walh, wealh* 'Briton, serf', including Walbrook, Walburn, Walcott, Walden, Walford, Wallington, Walmer, Walshford, Walworth and Walton – there are as many as twenty Waltons with this origin.

Demography would also have been very important for these developments – there were relatively few native-speakers of Old English around to act as linguistic models. 'The current discourse [of historians and archaeologists] advocates the theory of an elite take-over of the c. two-million Romano-British population by Anglo-Saxon "fringe barbarians"' (Härke 2002: 167). Morris (1973: 304) too believes that 'in Northumbria, a very few English ruled a large British population' – and the English 'were too few to colonise the west'. As far as the actual linguistic processes are concerned, Tristram (2004: 202) says that if we assume that the native Britons in the South West, the Midlands and the North slowly shifted to Old English in the course of two to four centuries (fifth to ninth), the type of linguistic contact and of language acquisition would have had to be that of the adult-learner type. She suggests that for Britons acquiring Old English, especially in the Highland zone, the first step would have been one of unstructured adult acquisition of the Old English target dialects as L2.

This pidginised form of Old English would have been increasingly passed on to subsequent generations: 'children would have learned the imperfectly acquired L2 from their parents as their L1 and subsequently passed on their linguistic knowledge of the modified target language to their own children' (Tristram 2004: 202); and the simplified version of the language eventually became the dominant variety, not least because of the relatively small size of the Anglo-Saxon elite, as just mentioned.

Importantly, Schrijver has also argued that contact between Insular Celtic and Old English had far-reaching consequences at the phonological level, as Celtic speakers shifted to English. He writes (2009: 201) of 'the probability that the development of Anglo-Saxon phonology and phonetics was fuelled by language shift' and says that:

the phonology of the language of the Germanic speaking settlers who spread across southern and eastern Britain was changed drastically between c. 400 and 700. In all dialects of Old English, from northern Northumbrian to Kentish and West Saxon, almost the same phonemic-phonetic system arose . . . The simplest explanation of this state of affairs is that phonetic-phonological developments were fuelled by a language shift of a pre-settlement population which stretched all the way from the Tweed to Wiltshire and which in its original language had that same phonemic-phonetic system. The shifting population introduced its traditional phonetics and phonology into the language of the Anglo-Saxon settlers, where those features survived and were perpetuated.

One example cited by Schrijver is 'breaking', the development of front-to-back diphthongs out of monophthongs in back contexts in Old English, such that for example the front vowels *i, e, æ* became the opening (falling) diphthongs *io, eo, ea*, as in *feh > feoh* 'money, property, cattle'.

Recall too that Schrijver also believes that, during the course of the Roman occupation, the Lowland zone of England ceased to be monolingual-Brittonic speaking and that a British form of Vulgar Latin had developed which was extremely widely used by the Celts. Crucially, as indicated by the subtitle of his 2002 paper 'The rise and fall of British Latin: evidence from English and Brittonic', Schrijver argues that Old English phonology was the product of contact with a Celtic-influenced British Latin as well as with Brittonic itself – we once again see Vennemann's *transitivity of contact* in operation. This was because, while

city folk and the rural elite fled to the Highland Zone . . . the rural poor, small farmers and agricultural labourers may have stayed on, hoping to strike a deal with the new powers, and in so far as they succeeded, they would have imported into Old English a comparatively lower-class Latin accent, phonetically similar to the original Celtic. (Schrijver, 2009: 209)

English–Old Norse Contact

It seems, then, that it was limited contact between a minority of Old English speakers and a majority of socially inferior adult Brittonic speakers in Highland England which set the process of simplification in later Old English going, as the Britons shifted to (their form of) English, and Brittonic was eventually lost. Since it was especially in the Highland zone that this pidginised form of Old English came to dominate, it is not surprising that it is in the north of England that we see the earliest and greatest degree of linguistic simplification in the historical record.

However, this northern locus has more usually been cited as evidence in favour of the argument that simplification in Old English was the result of contact with Old Norse. The Old Norse-speaking population was, after all, also geographically concentrated in the north of England. This view concerning the role of Old Norse is inherited from Bradley (1904: 32), who said that 'we know for a fact that those districts in which the Danes had settled are precisely those in which English grammar became simplified most rapidly'. Poussa has it that contact with Old Scandinavian was responsible for 'the fundamental changes which took place between standard literary Old English and Chancery Standard English, such as the loss of grammatical gender and the extreme simplification of inflexions' (Poussa 1982: 84). Kroch et al. (1995) make the same point. Further extensive and detailed discussions of the nature, extent and consequences of Old Norse–Old English contact are found in Townend (2002), and in Thomason and Kaufman (1988: 275–304).

However, a sociolinguistic-typological perspective on linguistic change suggests that contact with Old Norse is most unlikely to be the explanation for the simplification. Large-scale Viking settlements took place mainly during the ninth and tenth centuries, and led to many areas of eastern and, especially, northern England containing a heavily Scandinavian or Scandinavianised population, as famously witnessed by the hundreds of Norse place-names. The numbers of Scandinavians who actually arrived and settled in Britain is, however, unknown and the subject of much controversy (Härke 2002; Holman 2007).

What we know of the relevant sociolinguistic conditions suggests, however, that contact between Old English and Old Norse speakers in northern England very quickly turned into one of long-term co-territorial co-habitation and intermarriage – very unlike the relationship which existed during the second stage of contact between Anglo-Saxons and subjugated and enslaved Britons. Townend sees the significance of 'Anglo-Scandinavian integration and the continued practice of mixed marriage' (2002: 204). And Laing and Laing (1979: 185) speak of 'the cultural fusion of Angle and Dane in the north'.

Moreover, not only did large numbers of words make their way from Old Norse into English (unlike Brittonic words) but, as a very persuasive piece of actual linguistic evidence for the intensity of the long-term contact, the English third-person plural pronominal forms *they*, *them*, *their*, *theirs* also have their origins in Old Norse, as is well known. The borrowing of pronouns from one language to another is a rather rare type of development which one never sees in short-term adult contact situations, but only in long-term co-territorial contact of the type which typifies the growth of linguistic areas or *Sprachbünde*. According to Nichols and Peterson (1996: 242), the 'borrowing of pronouns points to *unusually close contact*' [my italics].

The fact that the contact was 'unusually close', and sufficiently intimate and long term that pronouns could be borrowed, would seem to render much less tenable the popular thesis that it was contact with Old Norse which led to simplification in Late Old English. Old Norse and Old English 'were roughly adstratal in Viking Age England' (Townend 2002: 204). Contact between Old

Norse and Old English was not of the sociolinguistic type that makes for simplification, which typically results from short-term adult second-language learning from limited exposure (Trudgill 2011b). Rather, the North Germanic people would have had every opportunity to learn this closely related language in a non-pidginised form: this was co-territorial, long-term contact involving child bilingualism and therefore perfect acquisition.

This point of view is strongly supported by work of Emonds and Faarlund (2014), who cite the Norse character of a number of Middle English syntactic constructions as compared to Old English. For example, van Riemsdijk (1978) makes the strong claim that the only languages in the world which permit fully developed preposition stranding are members of the North Germanic language family – plus English, as in *Reven ble skutt på* 'The fox was shot at' (Holmberg & Rijkhoff 1998).

According to Emonds and Faarlund (2014), most languages disallow it completely, and West Germanic Dutch allows it only under very restrictive conditions – which was also the situation in Old English. According to Hoekstra (1994), it is also disallowed in Frisian. (However, for a discussion of the work of scholars who have suggested possible Brittonic influence on the development of English preposition stranding, see Roma 2007.)

A second example is provided by the fact that in North Germanic and English, the original Germanic genitive *-s* ending has become a phrasal clitic which can be postposed to phrases as well as to head nouns, as seen in these Norwegian and English examples: *Sjåførens feil* 'The driver's fault'; and *Sjåføren av lastebilens feil* 'The driver of the lorry's fault'. In continental West Germanic, *-s* continues to be simply a genitive case inflection on head nouns only. Emonds and Faarlund mention only Dutch and German, but this is equally true of North Frisian (Löfstedt 1968; Hoekstra 2010) and West Frisian (Hoekstra 2006).

A third point is that there was a switch between Old English and Middle English from verbal prefixes to post-verbal particles. In modern German and Dutch, directional and aspectual particles still have to precede non-finite and clause-final finite verbs, as in example *Sie will den Brief herausnehmen* 'She wants the letter out-take'. This was also the situation in Old English. But these grammatical prefixes disappeared in Middle English, and instead English developed a system of post-verbal particles which took over the role of the prefixes. Modern English *She wants to take the letter out* exactly reflects the Scandinavian structure, as in Danish *Hun vil tage brevet ud* 'She wants take letter-the out'.

Fourth, the infinitival marker *to* always occurred immediately adjacent to the verb in Old English, as it still does in Dutch and German. In Scandinavian, on the other hand, the marker is a free morpheme which can be separated from the verb by adverbs and negatives. The English infinitival *to* operates in exactly the same way, as in *Det er viktig å alltid komma i tide* 'It is important to always come on time'.

It seems rather clear from Emonds and Faarlund's work, then, that the character of Modern English has indeed been influenced by Old Norse to some degree in syntax, as well as in lexis.

English–French Contact

It is equally clear, too, that contact with Norman – and other forms of – French has also had a very considerable impact on the nature of English. As is mentioned in all histories of the English language, this is especially true of English lexis, with 40 per cent of modern English vocabulary often being cited as the proportion of French-based words in the modern language (Rothwell 1998).

Is it possible, however, that there was also some grammatical influence from French? Dalton-Puffer (1996) has provided us with an extensive and detailed account of the role of French in the development of modern English derivational morphology. But this was initially a direct consequence of the transfer of massive amounts French vocabulary to English – as was also, to an extent, the phonemicisation of /v/ and /z/.

But otherwise, any role for French in the shaping of English grammar would seem, on the face of it, to be unlikely. After all, how would this have happened? The number of native Norman French[5] speakers in England was never very high – Carpenter (2004) gives a figure of 8,000 for the year 1086, out of a total population of perhaps 3 million (Hatcher & Bailey 2001). These figures are extremely approximate but, even so, we can be fairly sure that more than 99 per cent of the population of England in 1100 were English (or Norse or Brittonic) speaking. The proportion of French speakers, whatever it was, would have been even lower in Scotland and, especially, Wales; and very many of them were elite aristocratic members of a ruling class who had very little contact with the bulk of the Germanic-speaking population.

Bailey and Maroldt (1977), however, suggest that the influence of French on English was very considerable. Indeed, they go further than this and argue that Middle English was actually a 'creole' which developed as a result of contact and interaction between English and Norman French. This is clearly a misuse of the term 'creole', as has been powerfully and carefully demonstrated by Görlach (1986) and others; and Bailey and Maroldt's arguments have not been widely accepted (e.g., Danchev 1997 – though see Dalton-Puffer 1995 and Rothwell 1998). But their putative examples of French grammatical influence should nevertheless be considered.

The examples of influence Bailey and Maroldt cite include:

---

[5] More accurately, Anglo-Norman, which demonstrated a certain amount of dialect mixture of Norman with Picard and other varieties (Trotter 2000).

1. The analytic gradation of polysyllabic adjectives, as with Modern English *more/most beautiful*. West Germanic languages, including Old English, use the bound morphemes *-er* and *-est* regardless of the length of the adjective, as in German *Sie ist interessanter als ihr Mann* 'She is interesting-er than her husband'. Middle and Modern English do not do this, and here Bailey and Maroldt see the influence of French, cf. Modern French *(la) plus intéressante*.

   Interestingly, however, their thesis is undermined here by Emonds and Faarlund, who argue that analytic comparative and superlative forms of English adjectives are actually due to Old Norse rather than Old French influence. They point to the fact that North Germanic also uses free words meaning 'more' and 'most' for the gradation of longer adjectives, as in Norwegian *Det var det mest underlege* . . . 'That was the most remarkable . . . '

   The chronological and demographic case for the influence of Old Norse is also more powerful than that for French. In particular, the Scandinavian proportion of the population – although, as we have just noted, not known with any certainty – was much higher, especially in the North of England.

2. Bailey and Maroldt also cite as being the result of Norman French influence the use of oblique forms of personal pronouns in all functions in English except for non-conjoined subjects, as in *Well done him! John and me left* and *Who did that? Them!*.[6] They compare this to the similar usage in Modern French of the oblique forms *lui, moi, toi, eux*.

   Here too, however, Emonds and Faarlund claim Scandinavian influence. They argue that the modern English pattern is reflected in modern Danish, where we have: *Mig og Ole gik i bio* 'Me and Ole went to the cinema'; *Ole er bedre kvalificeret end dem* 'Ole is better qualified than them'; *Hvem vil have en øl til? Os to/ Ikke mig/ Hende derovre* 'Who wants another beer? Us two. Not me. Her over there.'

   Other examples given by Bailey and Maroldt, however, perhaps deserve a more sympathetic consideration: they suggest, for instance, that the development of English *wh*-interrogative pronouns into relative pronouns took place under French influence. In the modern languages, the pronouns *who* and *qui* both operate as relatives as well as interrogatives, something which is not generally true in North Germanic.

Conclusion

English is the result, in part, of millennia of language contact. At some points, contact has led to the transfer of additional grammatical categories and has thus added complexity to the structure of English. This was the case, it has been argued,

[6] My examples.

with the borrowing of the progressive aspect from Brittonic Celtic. At other points, contact has led to simplification as with, it has been argued, the loss of Old English morphology due to adult language learning by native speakers of Brittonic in a substratum situation in Highland England. And at yet other points it has simply led to replacive borrowing, as with the replacement of verbal prefixes by post-verbal particles under Old Norse influence.

In spite of all these different episodes of contact, however, English is still by general agreement an Indo-European Germanic language. But we can see, in its modern structures, the results of contact between the Germanic languages Old English and Old Norse, as well as contact with other Indo-European languages: Celtic Brittonic, and Italic Latin and Anglo-Norman. Less certainly, it may also show traces of contact with Continental Celtic and, even less certainly, with Finnic, Afro-Asiatic and Vasconic.

5   Verner's Law, Germanic Dialects and the English Dialect 'Default Singulars'

Adger and Smith (2005: 155) write that 'one of the most common features of vernacular dialects [of English] world wide' is the occurrence of plural *was* as in *we was, you was, they was*. This, occurring as it does alongside singular *was* as in *I was, she was*, obviously represents a regularisation in comparison with Standard English. Indeed, there is a widespread perception in the international English-linguistics community in general that this phenomenon is so widespread as to be the norm in varieties of English other than Standard English, to the extent that it may be a 'vernacular universal' (Chambers 2001; Walker 2007; Filppula, Klemola & Paulasto 2008) or a 'vernacular primitive' (Chambers 1995: 242). As Tagliamonte (2008) states, 'according to Chambers' theory of "vernacular roots," certain variables appear to be primitives of vernacular dialects in the sense that they recur ubiquitously all over the world'. Others have correctly remarked, however, that since forms equivalent to 'plural *was*' are not 'common to spoken vernaculars [of other languages] in general' (Lauttamus et al. 2008), then it may be better described specifically as an 'angloversal' (Kortmann & Szmrecsanyi 2004: 1150).

One suggestion very current in the variationist literature is that this predominance of generalised *was* in English is predictable in the sense that *was*-generalisation represents a case of the 'default singular'. It is agreed in linguistic typology that singular number is unmarked, as opposed to plural and other possible numbers, in all the languages of the world that have a number distinction, with plural forms being, in general, longer than and derived from the singular (although Haspelmath [2006: 31] has pointed out that this can be overridden by frequency effects, such that, for example, Welsh *pluen* 'feather' has the plural *plu*).

This can be interpreted as giving rise to the principle of the *default singular*, which is illustrated in a number of grammatical facts such as the use in English of singular verb forms with interrogatives such as *who*? (as in 'who is coming?') even if more than one person is expected. It has also been suggested by variationists that it is the principle of the default singular that is operative in English constructions of the type *there's lots of people/ there was lots of people*, which too is often labelled 'vernacular' or 'nonstandard' despite the fact that it is used by most native speakers of English, including Standard English in speech even if not in writing. Both singular *was* and plural *there's/there was* are thus regarded as instances of the same phenomenon, and as Tagliamonte (2008) writes, 'default singulars are perhaps the proto-typical exemplar of these [vernacular] roots since they are mentioned in virtually every discussion (Chambers 2000, 2001, 2003, 2004)'.[1]

In this chapter, I argue that while the principle of the default singular of the *who is coming type?* is a sound one, it is not appropriate as a description of or an explanation for *was*-generalisation in varieties of English. I leave aside such inelegant assertions as Pittman's (2004: 125) claim that *The boys was interested* 'shows singular agreement with a plural subject'. It does no such thing, of course: it shows rather that *was* is the plural as well as the singular verb form in this particular dialect.[2] I shall argue that what is involved here is very much not a question of singular versus plural, with *was* representing a case of the 'default singular'. My suggestion is that it is a matter of r-forms of the past tense of the verb BE versus s-forms, with forms such as *were, war, wor* representing the r-variant and forms such as *was, wiz, wus* representing the s-variant. This s/r-alternation, as is well known, is a Germanic alternation of very considerable antiquity but one which has been analogically levelled out in most Germanic dialects over the past millennium.

Crucially, examination of these different Germanic dialects shows that in very many cases, it is the r-forms which have survived, suggesting that the success of s-forms, where they have been victorious, is very much *not* due to the fact that they are singular. If some general principle were at work here, then we would expect s-forms to predominate in all the dialects. In fact, the history of the dialects of the Germanic languages as a whole shows that we are dealing here with a process of analogical levelling that does not favour *either* the s-forms *or* the r-forms. The term 'default singular' thus has absolutely no explanatory value whatsoever in this case and is in fact quite wrong. It has only come to be used in connection with *was/were* by certain linguists because they have erroneously ignored a very large number of the English dialects of England as well as nearly all the other Germanic languages. Not only is it most definitely not a 'vernacular universal'; there is no way it can even be said to be an 'angloversal' either.

History

The Standard English alternation between singular *was* and plural *were* is the result of a very ancient linguistic change.[3] Germanic past-tense forms of BE descend from

---

[1] As far as I know, the 'default singular' argument has not been used in any attempt to account for those English dialects that have present-tense forms such as *we goes, they walks*, probably because there are perhaps even more dialects that have *he go, she walk*.

[2] I acknowledge that it may well represent the outcome of a diachronic change of some centuries' standing such that the originally singular form was generalised to the plural.

[3] I shall use this convenient shorthand in spite of the fact that in modern Standard English, *you* is singular as well as plural.

an Indo-European root meaning 'dwell, remain', as in Sanskrit *vasati* 'he dwells', which came down into Germanic as *wesan* (Lass 1992: 139). The stem-final consonant reconstructed for Proto-Indo-European, then, was /s/. Then Verner's Law came into operation, which is the label given to the Germanic sound change which occurred sometime between 2000 BC and 500 BC and which led to the voicing of voiceless fricatives in voiced environments after unstressed syllables – in Proto-Germanic, stress in preterite plural forms was on the second syllable – and hence to the alternation /s/ ~ /z/ (Hock & Joseph 1996: 121). A later, specifically North and West Germanic change /z/ > /r/ then led to the /s/ ~ /r/ alternation that we still see in modern Standard English.[4] For example, in Proto-Scandinavian, **was/*wa:zun* 'was/were' had become **was/*wa:run* by 550 AD. East Germanic Gothic *wisan* 'to remain', on the other hand, retained *s* throughout the paradigm: *was, wast, was, wesum, wesuð, wesun*.

Maintenance of the S/R-Alternation

Unlike Proto-Scandinavian, Old English – at least as we mainly know it, that is, from late West Saxon – retained the ancient alternation (Lass 1992: 140):

	Indicative		Subjunctive	
	sg.	pl.	sg.	pl.
1st	wæs	wæron	wære	wæren
2nd	wære	wæron	wære	wæren
3rd	wæs	wæron	wære	wæren

Note that the r-forms were very much in the majority in this paradigm, occurring in the second-person singular, and in the subjunctive singular for all persons (although, of course, this would not necessarily have translated into total dominance of r-forms in terms of tokens). Crucially, from the very beginning, there was no total coincidence between s-forms and the grammatical category 'singular'.

The alternation was retained into Middle English, with the Southeast Midland dialects around 1400 having the following forms (Lass 1992: 141):

	Indicative		Subjunctive	
	sg.	pl.	sg.	pl.
1st	was	weren	were	weren
2nd	were	weren	were	weren
3rd	was	weren	were	weren

Here the s/r-alternation persists but r-forms still predominate.

---

[4] In modern English, of course, West Germanic /s/ appears as /z/ in the relevant forms, while in non-rhotic dialects, /r/ is most often Ø.

The dominance of the r-forms was subsequently weakened, however. The gradual loss of the subjunctive reduced the incidence of r-forms, as did the development of new analogical forms of the second-person singular such as *wast, werst* (prior to the loss of the second-person singular altogether). The s/r-alternation did survive, as it does to this day in Standard English, with the r-forms still predominating:

	Indicative	
	sg.	pl.
1st	was	were
2nd	were	were
3rd	was	were

Insofar as the subjunctive still survives, it is, of course, also characterised by r-forms: *If I were you.*

This same s/r-alternation also survives in Dutch.[5] In Middle Dutch, the paradigm was the following (Van Loey 1973: 93):

	Indicative		Subjunctive	
	sg.	pl.	sg.	pl.
1st	was	waren	ware	waren
2nd	waers	waert	waers	waert
3rd	was	waren	ware	waren

In Modern Standard Dutch, it is

	sg.	pl.
1st	was	waren
2nd	was	waren
3rd	was	waren

In nonstandard Dutch/Flemish dialects, on the other hand, the situation appears to be more complex. This is partly because we now have so much information about these dialects from the Morphological Atlas of the Dutch Dialects (MAND) project. It is also, however, because a number of partial generalisation processes have taken place which have led to mixed paradigms, as well as because of the introduction of forms with -n, -d and zero. A typical mixed paradigm is found in the West Flemish dialect of Bruges:

	sg.	pl.
1st	waren	waren
2nd	waar	waart
3rd	was	waren

---

[5] My information on Dutch comes from Wim Vandenbussche, Jacques Van Keymeulen and Martijn Wieling.

In the West Flemish of Ieper, there is a different mixed paradigm:

	sg.	pl.
1st	waren	waren
2nd	was	was
3rd	was	waren

And a majority of Dutch dialects have in some way preserved the s/r alternation.

The alternation survives, too, in the mainland dialects of North Frisian,[6] in Schleswig-Holstein. In the Bökingharde dialect, the forms are the following (Walker 1980):

	sg.	pl.
1st	wus	wjarn
2nd	wjarst	wjarn
3rd	wus	wjarn

And the alternation is also found in Sater Frisian (the last vestige of East Frisian):

	sg.	pl.
1st	waas	wieren
2nd	wierst	wieren
3rd	waas	wieren

However, it is important to note that this survival of the ancient alternation is relatively unusual in Germanic. In *all* Germanic varieties other than English and those Dutch and Frisian dialects just mentioned, analogical generalisation or levelling out of the alternation has taken place, and in some cases took place very many centuries ago. Crucially for my argument, *the generalisation can go either way*, with s-forms replacing r-forms or vice versa.

S-Generalisation

We have already noted that very many dialects of English have the s-generalisation (Britain 2002): *I was, you was, she was, we was, they was*. This is the dominant form in the colonial nonstandard Englishes of Ireland (and Liverpool), North America and the Southern Hemisphere (cf. Eisikovits 1991). It is also usual in Scots, as well as in the southeast and far north of England.

Certain other varieties of modern Germanic also have s-generalisation. Afrikaans has total s-generalisation (Donaldson 1994):

	sg.	pl.
1st	was	was
2nd	was	was
3rd	was	was

---

[6] My information on Frisian, here and below, comes from Alastair Walker. See also Munske (2001).

And some Westphalian dialects of Plattdeutsch have s-generalisation as well (Durrell 1989), although a singular/plural distinction is formally maintained[7]:

	sg.	pl.
1st	was	wassen
2nd	wast	wassen
3rd	was	wassen

S-generalisation is also found in the Low German dialects of East Frisia and of parts of Eastphalia (Matras & Reershemius 2003):

	sg.	pl.
1st	was	wasn
2nd	wast	wasn
3rd	was	wasn

S-generalisation also occurs in a number of dialects of Dutch.

R-Generalisation

It does not seem, however, that in the Germanic languages generally it is s-generalisation that predominates. In fact, a much more common pattern would appear to be the generalisation of r-forms, which in some cases goes back many centuries. In Old Norse, for example, a regularised r-based paradigm had 'become general by about 1100' (Gordon 1957: 308), or perhaps more likely, by 1200 (Noreen 1923):

	sg.	pl.
1st	var	va:rum
2nd	vart	va:ruð
3rd	var	va:ru

Here we would not want to say that the older Scandinavian languages were operating a 'default plural' mechanism, because obviously the singular/plural distinction was still preserved. We simply say that the alternation between r and s was regularised, with the r-stems being generalised to the whole paradigm. Subsequently, the modern Continental Scandinavian languages have lost all person and number distinctions, with *var* being the invariant form throughout:

	sg.	pl.
1st	var	var
2nd	var	var
3rd	var	var

---

[7] Thanks to Martin Durrell and Alastair Walker for information on Low German.

However, modern Icelandic and Faroese have maintained person and number marking to this day – for example, Faroese,

	sg.	pl.
1st	var	vóru
2nd	vart	vóru
3rd	var	vóru

with, once again, the r-variants being found throughout.

In Standard German, r-generalisation has also taken place[8]:

	Indicative		Subjunctive	
	sg.	pl.	sg.	pl.
1st	war	waren	wäre	wären
2nd	warst	wart	wärest	wäret
3rd	war	waren	wäre	wären

This is also true of all the other German dialects that have retained a preterite form of BE.[9]

Luxembourgish, too, has r-generalisation[10]:

	sg.	pl.
1st	war	waren
2nd	waars	waart
3rd	war	waren

Other Germanic varieties which have r-generalisation include most varieties of Low German, as well as the island dialects of North Frisian. The following is a typical Low German paradigm:

	sg.	pl.
1st	weer	weern
2nd	weerst	weern
3rd	weer	weern

And the following is the paradigm in the dialect of the island of Sylt, which exemplifies the island dialects of North Frisian (Föhr, Amrum, Sylt, Heligoland):

	sg.	pl.
1st	wiar	wiar
2nd	wiarst	wiar
3rd	wiar	wiar

---

[8] Note, however, the past participle *gewesen*.

[9] Many of them have lost the preterite; Swiss German, for example, typically uses the verb forms of the perfect tense instead. This is also true of Yiddish.

[10] Data kindly supplied by Kristine Horner.

A number of Flemish dialects also have r-generalisation. According the MAND data, there is one sizable area in West Flanders where this is true, two areas in East Flanders, and a large area of Belgian Limburg.[11]

A Pan-Germanic Perspective

Two things are clear from this pan-Germanic perspective. First, Standard English has lagged behind most of the other Germanic dialects, with alternation between *r* and *s* representing a conservative holdout against the regularising trend. This places it together with a few other conservative dialects: Standard Dutch, a number of Dutch dialects, mainland North Frisian and the few remaining speakers of East Frisian.

Secondly, very many Germanic varieties, indeed a majority, do *not* have s-generalisation but r-generalisation: Icelandic, Faroese, Norwegian, Swedish, Danish, German, most Low German, island North Frisian and some Flemish dialects. Apart from English, s-generalisation is found only in Afrikaans, some Dutch dialects and a minority of Low German dialects.

Looking at the Germanic languages as a whole, then, it really would be rather surprising if r-generalisation were not found in some English dialects also. And the fact is, of course, that it very much is.

R-Generalisation in English Dialects

Chambers (2004: 131) points out that his term 'default singulars' highlights only one form of regularisation, and that certain nonstandard dialects do have *were* in all persons and both numbers: *I were, you were, it were, we were, they were.*[12] Indeed, importantly, the picture in England is very different from elsewhere in the English-speaking world. Britain (2002: 19) writes that 'extensive levelling to *were* in positive polarity clauses also exists', but he goes on to note that 'the literature provides little detail of its present socio-geographical distribution'. However, the picture has now become much clearer, as a result of Britain's paper and of Klemola's (2006) county-by-county analysis of the Survey of English Dialects tape recordings. Klemola helpfully shows that r-generalisation is very much the nonstandard norm in a very large and well-defined geographical area starting in Lancashire and Yorkshire in the north of England and extending through the central Midlands as far south as Bedfordshire. The other counties included in the area are Derbyshire, Staffordshire, Nottinghamshire,

---

[11] The MAND material was kindly made available to me by Martijn Wieling.

[12] Other dialects have *was* in all persons and both numbers in the affirmative but *were* in all persons and both numbers in the negative: *I was, you was, I weren't, you weren't* (Britain 2002; Trudgill 2003; Chambers 2004).

Leicestershire, Rutland, Northamptonshire, Cambridgeshire and Huntingdonshire. *Were*-levelling is also very common in a second contiguous area in the southwest of England which covers Somerset, Wiltshire and Dorset – so we are talking about millions of speakers.

Many other writers confirm this picture. Beal (2004: 122) states that vernaculars in large areas of the north of England have regularised in favour of *were* rather than *was*. Shorrocks (1999), too, tells us that *were* is the norm in Bolton, Lancashire – and Moore (2003) agrees. Petyt (1985) cites it as the norm in the West Riding of Yorkshire, and other similar evidence is provided by Anderwald (2001, 2002), Pietsch (2005) and Britain (2007: 91). Anyone needing any further evidence can also watch the British television soap opera *Coronation Street*, set in Salford, Greater Manchester, where the scriptwriters give all the local-dialect-speaking characters generalised *were* forms.

It also seems likely that r-generalisation was formerly more widespread in England even than it is now. For example, the local dialects of Norfolk now have generalised *s* in positive verb forms (Trudgill 2003). But Norfolk adjoins Cambridgeshire, which comes into Klemola's r-zone, as confirmed by Ojanen (1982); and Forby ([1830] 1969: 141) writes with respect to the early nineteenth-century Norfolk dialect of 'our constant use of *war* for *was*' (where it is clear that *war* is /waː(r)/). Britain (2002) suggests that *war* was the older form in the Fens also.

A reasonable supposition would therefore be that s-generalisation in England was initially particularly associated with the Home Counties – the counties around London – and other areas of southeastern England. From there it was transported to, and became the majority variant in, most of the colonial Englishes. In England, it has subsequently spread outward from the southeast, like so many other features, to take over some formerly r-generalisation areas – a view also argued for by Britain (2002) and strongly supported by the map he provides. However, s-generalisation in Scotland and the far north of England – Cumbria, Durham and Northumberland – must be a separate development.

The preponderance of s-forms in world English, then, is recent, and a coincidence. Germanic varieties in general seem to have plumped for both *r* and *s* more or less at random with, for example, most Low German dialects settling for *r* but some going for *s* instead. Indeed, it seems that up until the eighteenth century at least, r-generalisation predominated in the English-speaking world, until the influence of the English southeast began to make itself felt.

Conclusion

The levelling that we have been looking at here is all, of course, part of a much wider Germanic pattern concerning the analogical elimination of the effects of Verner's Law. Levelling to *was* or *were* is part of a broader picture of the loss of the s/r-alternation: German has *verlieren, verlor*, but English has *lose, lost*; Standard Dutch has *kiezen, gekozen* and English *choose, chosen*, but German has *küren, gekürt* (cf. the Old English preterite plural form *curon*).

We cannot say why some varieties generalised *s* and others *r*, and I suggest that we should not even try because the outcomes are genuinely random. The facts strongly suggest that analogical levelling can select either one of the available routes, and that it would be an error to attempt to locate explanations in terms of more natural, marked or frequent categories winning out. Attempts to account for outcomes of analogical levelling in terms of markedness and/or frequency – and the literature contains many such attempts (e.g., Smith 2001) – are not likely to succeed, as indeed they do not in this case. As Durrell (1999) points out, Low German strong verb preterites have been levelled in favour of the past subjunctive forms – forms which were *neither* the least marked *nor* the most frequent. The application of analogy is notoriously 'capricious',[13] and it is this very capriciousness that has led to the *kiezen/choose/küren* alternation just mentioned: 'the occurrence of analogy is generally quite unpredictable' (Trask 1996: 109). In particular, 'the direction of levelling is unpredictable, at least across different languages and dialects' (Hock & Joseph 1996: 156). Many other linguists support this view. Ritt (1992: 100), for instance, speaks of 'the unpredictable working of analogical levelling'; and Dresher (2000: 67) writes that, when it comes to the direction of analogical levelling, 'the choice may be random'.

The fact that s-generalisation dominates in *was* versus *were* in current world English is due, to a great extent, to the spread of forms from the heavily populated English southeast, where *was* just happened to be the norm, to neighbouring areas of England and to the anglophone colonies. It is not due to the typological status of singulars as unmarked and the concomitant status of *was* as 'default singular'. From a purely linguistic perspective, the generalisation of English *was/were* could have gone either way, and if we look at the Germanic languages as a whole, instead of just at English, it certainly has.

---

[13] I owe this adjective to Brian Joseph.

6 Deep into the Pacific: the Austronesian Migrations and the Linguistic Consequences of Isolation

As is well-known, the Austronesian language family includes more than 1,200 members (Pawley & Ross 1993: 429); it is found over a bigger area of the globe than any other family, stretching from Madagascar, in the western Indian Ocean, to Easter Island, in the eastern Pacific; and it covers 70 degrees of latitude, from Hawai'i in the north to New Zealand in the south.

Of particular relevance to this chapter are the migrations which led to this enormous spread, especially the remarkable settlement of the islands of the remote Pacific Ocean by the Polynesians. Current thinking (Blust 1999; Pawley 1999) suggests that the pedigree of the Polynesian languages is as follows. Proto-Austronesian split into several first-order subgroups (Blust 1999, thinks as many as ten). All but one of these groups are located in Taiwan. The exception is Malayo-Polynesian, which thus contains all the Austronesian languages spoken outside Taiwan. Malayo-Polynesian then split into a number of groups, including Central–Eastern Malayo-Polynesian. Next, Central and Eastern Malayo-Polynesian split from one another, and subsequently Eastern Malayo-Polynesian subdivided into a number of groups, one of them being Oceanic. The Oceanic languages include all the languages that were formerly labelled as Micronesian, Melanesian and Polynesian.

One of the sub-branches of Proto-Oceanic is Central Pacific (Geraghty 1983, 1986; Pawley 1996a, 1996b, 1999). Central Pacific formed an extensive dialect chain: Polynesian is thought to have diverged from the eastern end of this chain (Geraghty 1983), and Rotuman from the northwestern end (Pawley 1996a). The approximate chronology of these developments appears to be as follows (Pawley & Ross 1993; Pawley 1996a, 1999; Kirch & Green 2001):

Proto-Austronesian: 4000–2500 BC
Proto-Malayo-Polynesian
Proto-Central-Eastern Malayo-Polynesian
Proto-Eastern Malayo-Polynesian
Proto-Oceanic: 1500–1300 BC
Proto-Central Pacific: 1000–800 BC
Proto-Polynesian: 500 BC–200 AD

Possible homelands for these proto-languages are as follows (Pawley & Ross 1992; Kirch and Green 2001):

Austronesian	Taiwan
Malayo-Polynesian	Philippines
Eastern M-P	Moluccas (Maluku)
Central Eastern M-P	Cenderawasih Bay, Irian Jaya
Oceanic	Bismarck Archipelago, Papua New Guinea
Central Pacific	Fiji
Polynesian	Tonga-Samoa-Uvea-Futuna

The well known, although not entirely accepted (see Marck 1999, 2000), outline of the structure of the Polynesian family can be portrayed, in a somewhat simplified form, as follows. Proto-Polynesian split initially into Tongic and Nuclear Polynesian. Nuclear Polynesian then subdivided into Samoic-Outlier and Eastern Polynesian. The main Samoic languages are Samoan, Uvean, Futunan, Tokelauan, Pukapuka (Cook islands) and Tuvaluan. The Outliers are languages which are the result of, as it were, backwards migration of Polynesian speakers into Micronesia, Vanuatu, the Loyalty islands and the Solomons (as we shall discuss). The Eastern group divided into Central Eastern and Rapanui (Easter Island). The main Central Eastern Polynesian languages are Marquesan, Mangarevan and Tahitian (French Polynesia), Rarotongan and Penrhyn (Cook Islands), Hawai'ian and New Zealand Maori. Tahitian, Penrhyn, Rarotongan and Maori form the Tahitic sub-branch; Marquesan, Mangarevan and Hawai'ian the Marquesic subbranch. (More recently, Fischer [2001] has argued that Mangarevan and Eastern Tuamotuan are part of a separate Southeastern branch, parallel to Central Eastern, but that both these languages received some input from Southeast Marquesan.)

It is probable that the split into Tongic and Nuclear Polynesian occurred 100 BC–200 AD, with a probable homeland for Nuclear Polynesian being Samoa. The migration eastwards that led to the establishment of eastern Polynesian, perhaps in the Tahiti area, could have been around 500 AD (Kirch & Green, 2001). The chronological end point of the major colonisation of the Pacific by Austronesians lies with the settlement of the North Island of New Zealand, perhaps around 1000 AD, probably from Rarotonga, by the ancestors of the Maori, and the subsequent settlement of parts of the South Island.

The final, minor acts of Polynesian expansion probably involved migration from Mangareva to Rapa in the southern Australs, around 1300 (Fischer 2001); and from New Zealand to the Chatham Islands, probably around 1400. The Moriori language of the Chathams is now extinct.

The chronology for the development of New Zealand Maori might thus be something like this:

Proto-Polynesian: 500 BC
Nuclear Polynesian: 200 BC
Eastern Polynesian: 0–500 AD
Central Eastern Polynesian: c. 500 AD
Tahitic: 500–1000 AD
Maori: 1000 AD

All of the Central Eastern languages retained a good degree of mutual intelligibility at least until the beginning of the nineteenth century.

I have suggested in earlier chapters that there is a challenging issue for linguistic typology which involves the relationships which might exist between societal type and aspects of linguistic structure. Linguistic-typological studies have provided us with insights into the range of structures available in human languages, into what the constraints on these structures might be, and into relationships between different typological characteristics. But we do not yet have explanations for why, of all the possible structures available to human languages, particular languages select particular structures and not others. A legitimate sociolinguistic viewpoint would be that some such explanations may be available, and that some of these might be social in nature; that is, the distribution of linguistic features over languages may not be totally random when viewed from a social perspective.

It will be recalled that the sociolinguistic factors I have suggested as possibly being relevant revolve around language contact versus isolation; and community size and network structure. They include:

1. Small, isolated, low-contact communities with tight social network structures are more likely to be able to maintain linguistic norms and ensure the transmission of linguistic complexity from one generation to another. Such communities are thus likely to be more linguistically conservative (i.e., to show a slower rate of linguistic change); and more likely to demonstrate complexities and irregularities. Though changes are less likely to occur in such communities, these changes may also tend to be of a more marked type, because of the ability of tightly networked societies to, as it were, force such changes through; and the languages of such communities may therefore be more likely to have more marked forms and structures. Thus, Faroese is a language which is more conservative and more morphologically complex than the closely related Norwegian, and one which has experienced more marked phonological changes.

2. Small, isolated, low-contact communities with tight social network structures will have large amounts of shared information in common and will therefore be able to tolerate lower degrees of linguistic redundancy of certain types. It is possible, for example, that such communities may therefore show a higher incidence of fast speech phenomena, and higher

proportions of phonological changes due to the institutionalisation of such fast speech phenomena.

3. On the other hand, communities involved in large amounts of language contact, to the extent that this is contact between adolescents and adults who are beyond the critical threshold for language acquisition, are likely to demonstrate linguistic pidginisation, including simplification, as a result of imperfect language learning. Thus, the languages of such communities are likely to show greater degrees of regularisation. The most extreme forms of such languages are, of course, creoles.

Phoneme Inventories

The dispersal over a period of more than 5,000 years of the Austronesian language family into the Pacific, culminating in the settlement of New Zealand, was accompanied by a remarkable series of phonological developments involving phoneme inventories. Two of the Polynesian languages at the extreme geographical end points of this dispersal, Hawai'ian in the far north and Rurutu in the far southern Australs, are remarkable in that they have very small phoneme inventories indeed. In particular, both of them have only eight consonants. South Island Maori (now extinct), which also lay at the extreme end point of a migration route, is also sometimes claimed to have had eight consonants (Biggs 1978: 708–9), but nine seems more probable (Harlow 1987). Importantly, moreover, these unusually small inventories are simply the phonological end point of a millennia-long reduction in the number of consonants as languages spread further and further into the Pacific:

Language	Consonants
Proto-Austronesian	23
Proto-Malayo-Polynesian	20
Proto-Oceanic	23
Proto-Central Pacific	21
Proto-Polynesian	13
Nuclear Polynesian	11
Central Eastern Polynesian	10
Hawai'ian	8

The reduction was effected as follows: Proto-Austronesian (see Tryon 1993), which was spoken, as we have seen, around 4000 BC, had a phoneme inventory including twenty-three consonants:

```
m   n       ŋ
p   t       k   q   ʔ
b   d   ɟ   g
ts
dz
s       ʃ           h
z
    l   ļ
    r           ʁ
```

Ross (1992) posits a reduction to twenty consonants for Proto Malayo-Polynesian. Proto Oceanic (Lynch et al. 2002: 63) had a slightly larger system, although a number of the additions had low functional load:

```
mw m   n   ɲ   ŋ
pw p   t   c   k   q
bw b   d   ɟ   g
       s
       r           R
       dr
       l
w          j
```

Proto Central Pacific is believed to have had about twenty-one consonants (Pawley, personal communication). Proto-Polynesian, whose separate identity has to post-date the settlement of the Tonga and Samoa, demonstrates a rather dramatic loss of consonants, with a system considerably reduced as compared to that of Proto-Austronesian and Proto-Oceanic. It had (see Clark 1976; Krupa 1982) a consonant inventory of only thirteen consonants:

```
m   n   ŋ
p   t   k   ʔ
f   s       h
v
l
r
```

This was somewhat reduced in Nuclear Polynesian (the ancestor of all modern Polynesian language groups except Tongic) by the loss of /h/, and the merger of /r/ with /l/, giving a system of eleven consonants.

In Central Eastern Polynesian, which postdates the eastward expansion of the Polynesian peoples into the more remote areas of the Pacific, this was further reduced to ten consonants as a result of the loss of /ʔ/. This is already a very minimal consonant system, especially bearing in mind that there were only five vowels. Then, however, and remarkably, Hawai'ian, whose separation from the other eastern Polynesian languages obviously postdates the settlement of Hawai'i from the Marquesas (see Sutton 1994), reduced the consonant system even further to eight, as mentioned above, by merging /f/ and /s/ as /h/, and merging /ŋ/ with /n/. In addition to this, /k/ became /ʔ/ and /t/ changed to /k/:

```
m n
p   k   ʔ
        h
v
  l
```

The Rurutu language of the Austral Islands (Tubuai), situated on the extreme southern fringes of French Polynesia, also developed an extremely attenuated consonant system in which the glottal stop had three different historical sources:

```
m n
p t     ʔ
f
v
r
```

And, while New Zealand North Island Maori has ten consonants, the same number as in Central Eastern Polynesian:

```
m   n
p   t   k
wh          h
w
r
```

in South Island Maori (Harlow 1987), now extinct, this was also reduced, as we mentioned above, to nine, as /ŋ/ merged with /k/ (/r/ also became /l/):

```
m   n
p   t   k
f           h
w
l
```

There is also a claim (Biggs 1978) that /f/ merged with /h/, giving an eight-consonant system:

```
m   n
p   t   k
w
l
h
```

Similar reductions of consonant inventories can be found in some of the Polynesian Outlier languages spoken on small isolated atolls on the fringes of Micronesia and

Melanesia: Kapingamarangi, for example, has nine consonants. Nine-consonant systems are also found in Mangarevan, spoken in the Gambier Islands about 1,600 kms
southeast of Tahiti, and some forms of Marquesan (Clark 1976: 20; Krupa 1982: 26).

Possible Sociolinguistic Explanations

The question I now want to pose is this: is there any connection between this
geographical penetration, deeper and deeper into the formerly uninhabited
Pacific, and the loss of consonants? Andy Pawley (personal communication)
paints a very nice picture of Polynesians setting off in their canoes, throwing
consonants overboard as they go. But is there anything which linguists can
actually say about this? Is it just a coincidence that the gradual centuries-long
but dramatic and pioneering dispersal of the ancestors of the modern Polynesians
from mainland Asia into more and more remote areas of the hitherto uninhabited
Pacific Ocean was accompanied by an equally gradual but no less dramatic
reduction in the size of the phonological inventories of the languages spoken
by these people? In particular, is an explanation available that might link this
aspect of linguistic structure to aspects of societal structure? One encouraging
pointer that such an explanation for the loss of consonants in Austronesian might
be at hand is that we can suppose that the two factors of isolation and small
community size would have become increasingly relevant as Polynesian groups
advanced further and further into the remote Pacific.

Contact and Isolation

The issue of the relationship between societal type and size of phonological
inventories (see Trudgill 1998) has been addressed by Haudricourt (1961), who
cites the Caucasian language Ubykh, which had a very large phoneme inventory
including seventy-eight consonants. He points out that this large-inventory (and
now dead) language was spoken by a smaller population in a smaller geographical
area than the other, related Caucasian languages which had smaller inventories. He
also points to North America, where East Coast Amerindian languages have fewer
than twenty consonants (e.g., Oneida has ten), while the further west one goes, the
bigger the inventories get and the more languages there are, or at least were, per
square mile. Is this, he asks, just a coincidence?

   Given that languages generally both lose and develop new phonemes over time,
how do we explain this relationship between geographical language density and
phoneme inventories? Nichols has one answer. She writes (1992: 193): 'It can be
concluded that contact among languages fosters complexity, or, put differently,

diversity among neighbouring languages fosters complexity in each of the languages.' (I would point out that such contact will, of course, have to be of a very particular type, namely long-term contact situations involving childhood – and therefore proficient – bilingualism. As indicated, adult language contact tends to lead, on the contrary, to simplification.) Large inventories will be favoured by stable contact situations because the long-term presence of many neighbouring languages means that segments can readily be borrowed from one language to another, thus leading to increased inventories, such as the well-known borrowing of velaric-ingressive stops by some Bantu languages from the Khoisan languages of southern Africa. This process can also be seen in the case of certain Polynesian languages. Some Polynesian Outlier languages which came into contact with phonologically more complex languages, as in parts of Melanesia, have added consonants. For example, Rennellese has thirteen consonants, Emae fifteen, Mele-Fila sixteen and West Uvean twenty-six (Clark 1994). Large phonological inventories, then, may be the result of borrowing.

But what of small inventories? Why do some varieties have very small numbers of vowels and consonants? An obvious suggestion is that this may result from relatively mechanical factors associated with language contact of the type involving adult language contact and acquisition. The point is that simplification, both in language contact and in dialect contact situations (see Chambers 1995: 160), is brought about by the imperfect language learning of adults and post-adolescents (McWhorter 1997). Simplification may very well lead to loss of phonological contrasts: the smaller the inventory, the easier it is to learn, which is why the most extreme products of pidginisation, pidgin languages themselves, tend to have small phoneme inventories. Labov has also maintained (1994) that, in dialect contact situations, mergers tend to spread at the expense of contrasts. Isolated dialects are thus those which are likely to avoid mergers most strongly (and thus have larger phonological inventories). Obviously, other things being equal, mergers also lead to smaller inventories. So, long-term contact involving child bilingualism may produce large inventories through borrowing; and adult language contact may produce smaller inventories through imperfect learning, pidginisation and simplification.

Unfortunately, however, this latter cannot be the only explanation for small inventories. The Polynesian languages which we have been focussing on in particular, namely those which have only eight consonants, can be supposed to have been relatively isolated, low-contact languages. Haudricourt (1961) attempts an explanation for this. Small inventories, he says, are the result of the impoverishment which occurs in situations characterised by monolingualism and isolation (the opposite of the situation obtaining in the Caucasus) – and/or by non-egalitarian bilingualism. Haudricourt (1961: 9) suggests that in certain situations the superiority of a dominant group in a diglossic bilingual environment may be so obvious they no longer have any need to articulate well to be understood – they may confuse two different phonemes or no longer pronounce one – no one will dare to mock them. This is why we find fewer consonants in the language of the Iroquois who terrorised their neighbours, or in the languages of the people of Tahiti and Hawai'i who combine island isolation with significant demographic development as compared to other less favoured archipelagos. [my translation]

Community Size and Network Structure

This is not an especially happy thesis, but it does perhaps contain the germs of an explanation. Maddieson (1984) argues that there is no actual evidence that languages such as Hawai'ian show signs that they suffer from problems due to lack of contrastive possibilities. Let us suppose, however, that a small number of available syllables, and therefore a relatively small amount of redundancy may, other things being equal, lead to greater communicative difficulty. If this is so, then we should probably turn away in this case from high contact versus low contact as an explanatory factor. We should turn instead to the other major factor mentioned above, community size and network structure, as being the most important.

My argument here is as follows: initial small community size (the number of people who could arrive on a relatively small number of relatively small boats) would have led to tight social networks, which would have implied large amounts of shared background information – a situation in which communication with a relatively low level of phonological redundancy would have been relatively tolerable. There is, however, a problem here. One group of languages which, like the Caucasian languages, is known to have very large phoneme inventories are the San languages of southern Africa: on one analysis, !Xũ has ninety-five consonants (Maddieson 1984), for example. It seems unlikely that we can explain this, in Nichols' terms, as being due to a high degree of contact, especially since very many of the consonants are clicks which, although they have been borrowed from San into a few southern African Bantu languages, are otherwise unknown in the area outside the Khoisan grouping. Why then do we find this extreme contrast between two different sets of languages traditionally spoken in small, isolated communities, the San and (some of the) Polynesians?

Contact Again

I suggest that the answer lies in psycholinguistic issues to do with memory. One of the biggest difficulties encountered by adult non-native learners in contact situations has to do with learning and remembering – which is one reason why irregularities tend to disappear in such situations, most dramatically in the case of pidgin languages. At the phonological level, learning and remembering are probably less likely to cause particular difficulties than at other linguistic levels, but they will nevertheless be relevant in one of three ways.

1. First, Khoisan-type consonant systems are unlikely to be present in high-contact language situations because of the inherent difficulty for adults and adolescents of remembering and mastering such a rich series of articulations.
2. On the other hand, languages such as South Island Maori and Hawa'ian will cause problems of memory load of a very different type. According to Maddieson (1984), Hawa'ian has only 162 possible syllables. This inevitably leads to a situation no doubt even more extreme than that in North Island Maori, of which Harlow (2001) says a very high proportion of all possible words consisting of two morae actually occur. This is of course what leads to the lack of contrastive possibilities previously mentioned. I suggest that while this lack of contrastive possibilities is entirely unproblematical for native speakers, it does cause problems for non-natives. The problem lies in the relative lack of distinctiveness between one vocabulary item and another, due to the necessarily high level of usage of all possible syllables. The problem is one of *confusability of constituents*.

Consider the case of Maori, which also has, as we have seen, a small phoneme inventory. I submit that learning and remembering, as an adult, which of the following twenty-three words is which, is no easy task:

pakake	minke whale
paakaakaa	brown
pakeke	hard
paakeekee	grate
pakikau	wing
paakiki	inquisitive
pakoke	random
pakoki	distort
pakoko	dried up
paakoko	childless
paakoukou	shoulder blade
piikaokao	cockerel
pookaakaa	stormy
pookeka	chant
pookeekee	gloomy
poukoki	stilts
puukaakaa	burning fiercely
puukaki	source of river
puukeekee	armpit
puukeko	swamp hen
puukiki	stunted
pukoko	lichen
pukukai	greedy

It is no easy task because, according to Lively et al. (1994: 274), there are *neighbourhood effects* (also called *lexical similarity effects*) having to do with what other words a given word has to be differentiated from (Luce & Pisoni 1998). 'Neighbours' are words which differ from a given target word by only one phoneme (see also, Luce 1986; Goldinger et al. 1989). Lively et al. show that words of equal frequency are identified less accurately if they come from 'dense neighbourhoods' than if they are from 'sparse neighbourhoods' (1994: 275). A word that has neighbours which are higher in frequency tends to have its recognition speed and accuracy depressed.

Therefore, if we can generalise from recognition to memory, my point is made – and it seems clear that we can generalise in this way, since recognition obviously depends on memory.

3. There is also the issue of word length. Nettle (1995, 1999) has shown that there is a connection between inventory size and word length. It is rather obvious that this should be so on purely mathematical grounds (although it has been disputed by Maddieson 1984): the smaller the phoneme inventory, the longer words, on average, have to be. The length of lexical items, moreover, in terms of syllables and segments, will have an effect on memory load. The less there is to remember, the easier language acquisition is (on the length effect, see Garman 1990: 251–3). The longer a word is, in terms of syllables and/or segments, the more difficult it will be, other things being equal, to remember.

Conclusion

In summary, it seems that we have reached the following conclusions concerning contact, isolation, community size and phoneme inventories:

1. In cases where there is long-term language contact involving child-language acquisition, high degrees of language contact may lead to **larger** phoneme inventories, as a result of borrowing, as suggested by Nichols.
2. Situations involving adult-language contact, on the other hand, are likely to favour **medium-sized** phoneme inventories (i.e., inventories which are not so large as to be difficult for adolescents and adults to remember and acquire, but not so small as to cause confusability of constituents and high word length).
3. Low degrees of language contact may lead to languages with **small** inventories, because the memory load difficulties caused by confusability and word length will not be relevant, since post-critical threshold learning is not involved. They may also just as well lead, however, to **large** inventories, because, equally, the memory load difficulties caused by the acquisition of large numbers of phonemes will not be relevant either.

4. Large community size will favour **medium-sized** phoneme inventories (i.e., inventories which are not so small as to cause communicative difficulties as a result of a low degree of redundancy).

5. Languages spoken in small communities can develop **very small** inventories since lower degrees of redundancy can be tolerated because of the large amounts of shared information present. Small communities can also, equally, develop **very large** inventories because of the ability of such communities to encourage continued adherence to norms from one generation to another, however complex they may be.

In the case of the Polynesian languages with very small inventories, we can point to a process whereby increasing isolation and diminution in community size, as migrations carried settlers to ever more remote parts of the Pacific, was accompanied by ever smaller phoneme inventories, as per points 3 and 5. As points 3 and 5 show, however, the correct generalisation is not that such languages will necessarily have very small inventories, but that they will be more likely to have *either* very small inventories *or* very large ones. Non-isolated languages spoken in larger communities will, on the other hand, tend to have medium-sized inventories.

The factors of isolation and small community size can quite simply lead to the development of unusual phonological systems, as has also been suggested by Nettle (1999: 147): these systems may be either unusually small, as in the case of South Island Maori and Hawaiian; or unusually large, as in the case of !Xuˉ.

7 The Hellenistic Koiné 320 BC to 550 AD and Its Medieval and Early Modern Congeners

During the period of colonial expansion from the fifteenth century onwards, a number of Western European languages were transplanted to other continents. This produced new varieties of these languages which were different from those of the metropolitan homeland. Well-known examples include the English of the USA, the French of Canada, the Portuguese of Brazil and the Spanish of Argentina.

Two Fallacies

There are two major fallacies in the literature concerning these colonial varieties. The first is the **Monogenesis Fallacy**. Examples of this include Wagner's (1920) assertion that Latin American Spanish was originally just a variety of European Andalusian Spanish. Rivard (1914) similarly argued that Canadian French was nothing but transplanted European French from Normandy. Hammarström (1980) equally suggested that Australian English was simply transplanted Cockney (London English), and the same argument was also made for New Zealand English by Wall (1938). The failure here to acknowledge any role for dialect contact and dialect mixture is perplexing.

The second is the **Identity Fallacy**. Many scholars who, quite rightly, do not accept the monogenetic fallacy, nevertheless do subscribe to the fallacy that these new overseas varieties, which they agree are polygenetic, develop in colonies as a result of the role of identity. Moore (1999) writes that 'with language one of the most significant markers of national identity, it's not surprising that post-colonial societies like Australia, the United States, Canada, New Zealand, *should want to* distinguish their language from that of the mother tongue' [my italics]. Macaulay (2002: 239) also says that 'I fully expect new dialects to develop in places where a sense of local identity becomes strong enough to create deep-seated loyalty.' And Tuten (2003: 29) asserts that 'speakers accommodate to the speech of their interlocutors *in order to* promote a sense of common identity' [my italics]. The belief that speakers develop new varieties knowingly and deliberately is particularly disturbing here.

The First Koiné

The Monogenetic Fallacy and the Identity Fallacy can both be investigated with
benefit from the perspective of the first polygenetic colonial variety known to us,
namely the colonial Greek of the Hellenistic Koiné – Η Ελληνιστική Κοινή. As is
well known, this was the Greek spoken and written between approximately 320 BC
and 550 AD in Greece, with some regional diversity (Horrocks 1997: 60–4), and in
those areas of North Africa, the Middle East and Central Asia which were under the
control or influence of Greeks or Hellenised rulers, following the fourth-century BC
conquests of Alexander the Great.

From the point of view of the Monogenesis Fallacy, it is important to note that the
Hellenistic Koiné was very much not just transplanted Attic Greek. The Koiné was
based mainly on the Attic and Ionic dialects of Greece, but there was considerable
admixture due to dialect levelling with other dialects, notably Aeolic and Doric
(Browning 1969; Mackridge 1985; Horrocks 1997). Similarly, colonial European
varieties did not arrive fully formed in the new colonial locations in Africa and
Asia. They came about as the result of the coming together of different dialects from
different homeland locations; and of the dialect mixture which this led to.

It is also significant that there was clear second-language influence. Greek became
the standard language of commerce and government across the imperial territories,
and was, for several centuries, spoken alongside many indigenous languages. The
Koiné became the lingua franca of much of the Mediterranean area and the Middle
East, and was adopted as a second language by the native people of these regions. This
helped produce significant changes in vocabulary, pronunciation and grammar. There
was particular influence on the Koiné from contact with Egyptian/Coptic and Aramaic.
The Koiné was also 'submitted to a process of morphological simplification' (Adrados
2005) – morphological categories of the dual and the optative were both lost, for
instance. There was also considerable phonological simplification: most analyses
suppose that Attic Greek as spoken during the 400s BC had no fewer than twenty-
two distinctive vowels (Allen 1987), while the Koiné had only six (Horrocks 1997: 104).
Many of the European colonial varieties similarly show influence from other languages
encountered during the colonisation process, as well as simplification, with the
colonial Dutch of South Africa, Afrikaans, being a particularly striking example.

From the point of view of the Identity Fallacy, there is no evidence that the
Hellenistic Koiné came into being because Greek speakers wanted to symbolise
some new 'Middle-Eastern Greek' or 'Egyptian-Greek' or 'Central-Asian-Greek'
identity. Similarly, Australian English and Canadian French did not come into
being because their speakers wanted to establish and signal new colonial
identities. The point is that 'identity' is not necessary as an explanatory factor,
because the formation of new mixed dialects is what always happens. There is
no known case of new mixed colonial dialects not developing. Whenever large

numbers of people speaking different varieties of the same language come into close contact for a sufficient period of time in a new colonial situation, a new mixed-variety language emerges. Dialect contact of this type *always* leads to dialect mixture, and the formation of new mixed dialects (Trudgill 1986, 2004).

To illustrate this point, I now put forward a series of examples of colonial koinéisation, in chronological order, which taken together paint a powerful picture of the inevitability of colonial koiné formation.

Colonial Arabic

From the 600s AD onwards, Islamic expansion out of the Arabian peninsula led to the coming together of Arabic dialects from different parts of Arabia. A koiné developed in the garrison towns of Mesopotamia, where pre-Islamic Arabic dialects combined to form a new mixed dialect.

This koiné spread into the Middle East and North Africa during the eighth century, and formed the basis of most modern Arabic dialects (Ferguson 1959). Language contact also occurred. As with the Hellenistic Koiné, the Arabic Koiné came to be widely used as a second-language lingua franca by speakers of Aramaic, Coptic, Berber, Greek and many others

Colonial Norse: Icelandic

Iceland was settled from mainland Scandinavia, mainly between 874 AD and 930 AD. There were around 20,000 to 30,000 settlers, approximately 85 per cent of whom came from Norway, with around 4 per cent from Sweden and some 11 per cent Norwegians from the Hebrides. Of the settlers from Norway, 80 per cent were from western Norway, 10 per cent from the east and 10 per cent from the north. The Icelandic language which eventually developed was clearly a result of dialect mixture: 'Icelandic is a colonial dialect and a study of the development of Icelandic sheds much light on the mechanism of the development of mixed colonial dialects' (Chapman 1962: 23). According to Thrainsson (1994: 142) 'dialect levelling took place, since it does not appear that settlers speaking the same dialect formed any kind of dialectal colonies within Iceland'.

Colonial German: the Ostkolonisation

Up until about 900 AD, the border between the Germanic and the Slavic-speaking areas of central Europe ran along a line from the southern shore of the Baltic Sea by Kiel in Germany (Polish Kilonia), up the river Elbe (Polish Łaba) as far south as Magdedurg, and then along its southwestern tributary, the Saale (Polish Sołaẉ̨a), as far as Hof. It then travelled south along the Danube from Regensburg (modern Czech Řezno) through Passau (Czech Pasov) and then east. Between about 900 and 1350, however, the germano-phone area expanded considerably as a result of large-scale eastwards expansion of German-speaking peoples into the relatively less populated Slavic- and Baltic-speaking areas beyond that line. This eastwards colonial movement of Germanic speakers, which is known as the 'Ostkolonisation', saw the boundary gradually move eastwards into what is now eastern Germany, and then beyond into what is now Poland and Lithuania, though a Slavic-speaking population remained in the majority in many areas until the 1200s (Trudgill 2008).

The first stage of this northern 'East Colonisation' – *Ostkolonisation* or *Ostsiedlung* – took place across the river Saale and as far as the middle Elbe. This occurred by means of three main colonisation routes (Frings 1932). The first was from the Netherlands and northern Germany, via Magdeburg and Leipzig (Slavic Lipsk). The second was from central Germany via Erfurt and Leipzig. And the third was from southern Germany via Bamberg and Chemnitz (Slavic Kamjenica). The crucial point is that settlers arriving along the first route brought with them Northern dialects – Low Franconian and Low German; the second stream brought Central German dialects such as Hessian and Thuringian; and the third group brought Southern dialects, Bavarian and Alemannic. These three routes, and so the three sets of dialects, converged in what is now Saxony, the main focus of this convergence being on the town of Meissen (Slavic Misni), which had become a German-speaking city by 929. Meissen then formed the main jumping-off point for German-speaking onward colonisation further east to Dresden (Slavic Drezdany), which was a German city by 1206, and then on into Silesia and beyond.

The linguistic consequences in the Meissen area of this contact between different dialects – which all had their origins further west – were of great interest to Frings (1932). According to him, in the area of Meissen during the twelfth and thirteenth centuries, a new colonial dialect of German developed (see Bergmann 1990) which was due to this mixture of settlers from the different areas. It was a 'kolonial Ausgleichssprache' ('colonial levelled language') – in other words, a koiné – which Frings described as resulting from a mixture of Low Franconian, Low German, Central German and Upper German dialect forms (Ebert et al. 1936). This fourteenth-century mixed, levelled *Ausgleichssprache* was carried east across the Rivers Oder and Neisse as far east as places such as Königsberg (Kaliningrad, Russia), Memel (Klaipda, Lithuania) and Krakau/Cracow (Kraków, Poland). The new mixed dialect once again developed in conjunction with language contact, in this case with speakers of the original Baltic (Old Prussian – now extinct – and

Lithuanian) and Slavic languages of the area (Pomeranian (extinct), Cashubian and Polish).

Colonial English I: Ireland

English first arrived in Ireland in 1169 in connection with the Anglo-Norman invasion. Once there, it experienced language contact with Irish Gaelic; and indeed by the sixteenth century English had almost disappeared, with the Anglo-Normans assimilating to Irish Gaelic language and culture. But the English which did remain still showed signs of the original settlement by English speakers from different dialect areas of England: Anglo-Irish texts from the 1300s/1400s are written in an English which is a mixture of features of the dialects of Herefordshire, Gloucestershire, Somerset, Devon, Shropshire, and to a lesser extent Cheshire and Lancashire (Samuels 1972).

The Iberian Reconquest

There is currently a linguistic continuum along the northern edge of the Iberian peninsula, from the Atlantic Ocean via the southern edge of the Pyrenees as far as the Mediterranean, which consists of Ibero-Romance dialect areas which differ significantly from one another and which are rather small geographically. From west to east these are Galician, Asturian, Old Castilian, Aragonese and Catalan. In the south, on the other hand, in the coastal areas of the Algarve (Portugal), and Andalusia and Murcia (Spain), the degree of dialect differentiation is much reduced, and the dialect areas become bigger and fewer in number. This pattern is the result of dialect mixture processes – very like those that took place in East-Central Germany – which occurred during the reconquest of the peninsula by Ibero-Romance-speaking Christians as they gradually wrested control of the area from the Moslem Moors.

The expansion of Arabic-speaking Muslims out of the Arabian peninsula, as described, had reached the shores of southern Europe via North Africa in 711 AD, when Islamic forces crossed the Straits of Gibraltar and started taking control of southern Iberia. These forces brought their Arabic language with them, but along with them also came speakers of the indigenous Berber languages of North Africa from areas which are now Libya, Tunisia, Algeria and Morocco. During the reconquest, the southward-expanding Iberian Romance dialects thus came into contact with dialects of Arabic and Berber, but also with Mozarabic (Wright 1982; Harris 1988), the dialects descended from popular Latin which were spoken in the Middle Ages (often bilingually with Arabic) in Islamic Spain, or in areas recently reconquered from Islamic Spain. These varieties were spoken not only by Mozarabs (Christians living under Moorish rule), but also by Muslims and Jews living in the same territories at the same time (Penny 1998: 327), and some written records survive in the Arabic and Hebrew scripts.

Mozarabic had considerable regional variation (Galmés de Fuentes 1983), and indeed there was a west-to-east dialect continuum in the south of the peninsula, similar to the one in the north, which Penny refers to as the 'Mozarabic bridge' (2000: 83). Penny also says that these Mozarabic dialects were 'probably mutually comprehensible with the varieties of Portuguese, Castilian and Catalan with which they came into contact after the Reconquest of each area where Mozarabic was spoken' (1998: 327), and we can therefore be reasonably confident that this was genuinely dialect contact rather than language contact. Penny adds that some scholars have argued that, as Mozarabic was being absorbed by the northern languages, it exercised influence on them, 'but the only clear evidence of such influence belongs to the field of vocabulary' (2000: 83).

There were three different linguistic strands to the Iberian koinéisation process: the southwards expansion of Galician/Portuguese into the Algarve; the southwards movement of Castilian, finally ending up in Andalusia; and the southwards spread of Catalan into Valencia.

A Reconquista: Galician/Portuguese

Lisbon was taken from the Moors in 1147, and Faro on the Mediterranean coast in the Algarve fell in 1249. The southwards movement of Romance dialects from Galicia down through Portugal to the Algarve led to the development of a new koinéised variety, with the new mixed Southern Portuguese dialect emerging from contact between Galician-Portuguese, Asturian, Castilian, Aragonese and Mozarabic (Fernandes 2011). According to Fernandes, modern southern Portuguese diminutives can be accounted for, not so much in terms of the evolution of Mozarabic, but as a result of changes produced by contact between Galician-Portuguese, Asturian, Castilian, Aragonese, Catalan, Mozarabic and even, she suggests, French.

La Reconquista: Spanish

The linguistic consequences of the southwards expansion for Spanish have been described by Penny (1991, 2000) and Tuten (2003): the dialect mixture that resulted from the expansion explains a number of important developments in the language, and accounts for some of the characteristics of the modern language. There were three principal stages, Penny argues, in the development of Spanish during which dialect contact produced *Ausgleichsprachen*, via koineisation and rekoinéisation. The first phase of the expansion (Tuten, 2003) lasted from the ninth to the eleventh centuries, and focussed on Burgos, in north central Spain, where Ibero-Romance speakers from Asturias, Navarre, Leon and northern Castile came into contact as part of the southwards expansion. The second phase of koineisation took place between the eleventh and thirteenth centuries and focussed on the central city of Toledo, where again large-scale dialect mixture occurred as in-migrants gathered from different areas further north. Finally, the third phase occurred between the thirteenth and fourteenth centuries, and was concentrated on Seville, in Andalusia. Once again, dialect mixture occurred as populations with different dialects moved in from the north.

Tuten (2003) argues that one of the linguistic consequences of this series of mixtures was the disappearance from Castilian of contracted forms of preposition-plus-definite-article which are found in many Romance languages, such as Italian *nei* 'in the'. This is one of the most dramatic changes in the history of Spanish, and according to Tuten, it has never been explained. His explanation is that in the Burgos dialect mixture, there were a number of different contracted variants of forms like *en+los* 'in the-plural' (e.g., Galician *nos*, Leonese *enos*, Aragonese *ennos*, Riojan/northern Castilian *enos*). Post-koineisation Burgos Castilian simplified this situation by creating more analytical interdialect (Trudgill 1986) forms such as *en los*. Tuten suggests that during koinéisation, speakers developed interdialect forms which were more transparent in that their 'component parts also appeared regularly in other contexts' (2003: 119).

La Reconquesta: Catalan

Also at about the same time, a very similar kind of process was happening on the eastern edge of Iberia. Catalan was spreading south from its original homeland in the northeast of the peninsula into the province of Valencia (Baldinger 1958; Ferrando 1989) as a result of the Christian reconquest. The annexation was led by the Aragonese-Catalan king, James I, from his Aragonese capital in Saragossa, but the Catalans were also heavily involved (Bishko 1975). The campaign lasted from 1232 until 1245, when James had gained control of the east coast down as far as Murcia which, it had been agreed, should go to Castile. Once again, dialect contact occurred as the new territory was settled by northern colonists – although the section of the northern Iberian dialect continuum from which the incomers came was much shorter geographically than in the case of Castilian, as also in the case of Galician-Portuguese. The major dialects that came into contact were, from west to east: Aragonese; Western Catalan, from the Lleida area; and Eastern Catalan, from the Barcelona area. According to Alarcos (1983: 57–78), the outcome of this contact was a mixture of these three major dialects.

When the new Valencian variety emerged it actually resembled Western Catalan, but this did not mean that Western Catalan had dominated in the process. The similarity to Western Catalan was a kind of coincidence. Alarcos (1983: 75) tells us that many of the features of the Valencian vowel system are 'fàcilment explicable com un fenomen d'anivellament entre diversos estrats lingüístics'. Changes which had affected the Western Vulgar Latin vowel system, with different changes happening in different regions, led to Old Eastern Catalan having a three-way distinction between the stressed vowels of *entre* 'between', *herba* 'grass' and *terra* 'land' as /ə/, /e/ and /ɛ/: /əntrə/ ~ /erbə/ ~ /tɛrə/'land'. This corresponded to a two-way distinction in Aragonese between /e/ and /ie/: /entre/ BUT /ierba/ and /tiera/; and to a different two-way distinction in Western Catalan, between /e/ and /ɛ/: /entre/, /erba/ BUT /tɛra/. Then, 'en el necessari procés d'igualació entre uns parlants i altres, devien abandonar-se aquelles articulacions que només fes servir un dels grups' (Alarcos 1983: 75). The forms which were abandoned were therefore /ie/ and /ə/, which produced the Valencian two-way distinction, /entre/ – /erba/ BUT /tɛra/, which is coincidentally the same as Western Catalan.

Colonial Russian

Russian dialectologists usually classify Russian dialects into three geographical groups: North, Central and South. They also, however, classify dialects chronologically. The distinction here is between the Primary Dialects, meaning those which were formed before 1550; and the Secondary Dialects. The Secondary Dialects are those that were formed as a result of Russian colonial expansion after 1550, northwards towards the Arctic Ocean and eastwards towards Siberia and the Far East: the Russian language had reached the Pacific Ocean by 1650 (Cubberley 2002).

The secondary dialects of the new Russian-speaking territories were koinés based on dialects originally spoken further west or south. For example, Northern Kazakhstan Russian dialects are a mixture of Northern and Southern Primary Dialects. There is also considerable dialectal intermixture in the Central Ural mountains area, as well as in the Kuznetsk Basin (the coal-mining area between Novosibirsk and Mongolia). The Maritime Province of Siberia in the area around Vladivostok also has mixed koinéised dialects (Matthews 1953; Karabulatova 2013).

Colonial Spanish: Latin America

A fourth stage in the koinéisation of Spanish occurred in the Americas. During the sixteenth century, Spain took control of large areas of North, Central and South America, and the Caribbean. As many as 2 million Spanish speakers crossed the

Atlantic. Spanish came into contact with many different Amerindian languages; while new koinés developed as a result of dialect contact between different European Spanish dialects and subsequent dialect mixture: 'a linguistic alchemy acted on the kaleidoscopic jumble of Peninsula languages and dialects to yield Latin American Spanish' (Lipski 1994: 46). In the words of Penny (2000: 137), 'the distribution of features in American Spanish can often be reasonably sought in the processes of immigration from Spain and the patterns of *dialect mixing* which sprang from these processes' [my italics].

Colonial Portuguese: Brazil

A further stage in the koinéisation of Portuguese also took place in the Americas, in Brazil. During the sixteenth century, Portugal took control of large areas of South America, and 2 million Portuguese speakers eventually crossed the Atlantic from Portugal, Madeira and the Azores. Like Spanish, Portuguese came into contact with many different Amerindian languages, as well as African languages through slavery. A new Brazilian Portuguese koiné arose as 'immigrants from both the north and south of Portugal, in approximately equal numbers, carried their respective dialects to Brazil; the coming together of such diverse dialects in a single overseas center must have set up conditions leading to a sort of *linguistic compromise*, a new kind of dialect' [my italics] (Maioso Camara 1972: 20).

Colonial Dutch: Afrikaans

The settlement by Dutch of the Cape in South Africa began in 1652; and the variety of Colonial Dutch which eventually emerged is now known as Afrikaans. This language is the result of the mixing of 'Germanic dialects in close contact' (Combrink 1978: 72) – with a majority of speakers coming from North Holland, South Holland and Utrecht – but also of considerable contact with the indigenous Khoisan and other languages, and thus simplification and admixture.

Colonial French I: Canada

French settlement began in Quebec in 1608. Colonial Quebequois French was clearly a mixed dialect. Canadian French was from very early on a dialect not exactly like any European French dialect (Morin 1994). Mougeon and Beniak (1994: 26) say that the particular conditions associated with emigration to New France [Canada] and with life in the new colony on the St Lawrence led to 'a unique mixture ["brassage"] of central

French, varieties of regional French and perhaps even of certain patois . . . From this mixture there developed a new form of the French language . . . a unified, coherent, distinctive Quebec variety' [my translation]. They also speak of a 'fusion dialectale'. Poirier (1994: 256) reports that 'philological studies have proved the existence, in the middle of the 17th century, of a koiné along the St Lawrence which was strongly influenced by the dialects of different French provinces' [my translation].

Colonial English II: North America

The establishment of English speakers beyond the British Isles began in the Americas with the 1607 Jamestown settlement in Virginia, now in the USA; the settlement, beginning in 1609, of the uninhabited island of Bermuda; the 1610 settlement in Newfoundland, now part of Canada; and the New England settlement of the 'Pilgrim Fathers' in Massachusetts (USA) in 1620. By 1690 there were anglophone colonies all along the east coast of North America from Maine, New Hampshire, Rhode Island, Connecticut, New York, New Jersey, Pennsylvania, Virginia, Delaware, Maryland and North Carolina down to South Carolina, a distance of around 1,500 kilometres/ 900 miles. The new dialects which emerged were again koinés. They were each of them, according to Kurath (1949), a unique blend of British types of speech. Modern regional variation along the east coast of the USA thus came about because the initial mixtures were different in each location (Algeo 2001).

The anglophone colonists were also in contact not only with speakers of Amerindian languages, but also in certain cases with Dutch, French and Spanish speakers.

Colonial English III: Australia

The British penal colony of New South Wales was established in 1788, when a thousand mostly anglophone convicts from the British Isles together with prison guards and their families arrived. There is agreement that Australian English results from a mixing together of different British Isles dialects: 'The ingredients of the mixing bowl were very much the same, and at different times and in different places the same process was carried out and the same end point achieved' (Bernard 1981: 104).

Colonial English IV: South Africa

The second major anglophone settlement in the Southern Hemisphere took place in South Africa. This first occurred on the Cape, from 1820, followed by anglophone colonisation of Natal from 1824. Again the picture is one of koinéisation. According to a leading authority, South African English derives from a mixture of 'at least twenty regional (geographical) dialects: out of these dialects there grew up, in a remarkably short space of time, a form of English which was not identical with any one of them, but presented a unique set of dialectal features deriving from several British dialects' (Lanham 1967: 20).

Colonial English V: New Zealand

The third major anglophone Southern Hemisphere settlement was in New Zealand, which had started to receive visits from English speakers from the end of the 1700s. However, major arrivals of large groups of immigrants did not begin until the 1840s. Data from the Origins of New Zealand English project (Gordon et al. 2004) show that the speech of the first generation of New Zealand-born anglophones had a wide range of features from many British dialects, and it is clear that the outcome, from around 1900, was a new mixed dialect (Trudgill 2004).

Colonial French II: New Caledonia

A new French koiné also emerged in the South Pacific in the nineteenth century, as a result of European immigration. New Caledonia was originally entirely Austronesian speaking, but it has been controlled by France since 1854. The population today is around 250,000, with about 25 per cent of those being native French speakers of European origin. The distinctive new colonial French of New Caledonia has resulted from a mixture of dialects from metropolitan France – mainly forms from southern France, but together with forms from the area around Paris (Hollyman 1979; Darot et al. 1993).

Colonial Japanese

The northern Japanese island of Hokkaido was originally inhabited by speakers of Orok, a Tungusic language, and Ainu and Nivkh, both isolates. There was a small Japanese settlement during the 1300s, but extensive Japanese colonisation began in the 1860s. Since then, distinctive colonial Hokkaido varieties of Japanese have developed on the island. These new varieties clearly result from a mixture of dialects from different more southerly parts of Japan, notably Tokyo and northern Honshu (see Shibata 1999).

Transplanted Polish

After 1945, the national boundaries of Poland were changed very drastically. Over 40 per cent of the land area of eastern pre-war Poland, inhabited by more than 4 million native Polish speakers, was transferred to the Soviet Union. These areas are now parts of Lithuania, Belarus and Ukraine. On the other hand, large areas of Germany which had lain to the north and west of pre-war Poland were now transferred to Poland. German speakers were moved back to the west of the Rivers Oder and Neisse, thus reversing the population movements of the medieval *Ostkolonisation* described above, and were replaced by Polish speakers. Polish speakers in the new western territories came from many different areas, mostly in the east, and contact between their different regional dialects led to the development of what Polish dialectologists call *Nowe dialekty mieszane* 'new mixed dialects'. The mixtures differed from place to place, and so the new dialects also vary. In the rural northwest of the new Poland, for example, the mixture is of Polish dialects from Ukraine plus dialects from Greater Poland (Urbańczyk 1976).

The Hellenistic Koiné

The Koiné is, of course, very special historically in that it is the very first example of large scale koinéisation known to linguists and philologists. Importantly, both Ancient Greek and Koiné Greek were also, as is well known, vehicles of important writings which have provided us with a permanent record of the linguistic changes which occurred as between the former and the latter. But all of the examples of colonial new-dialect formation just listed above show that there was nothing unusual linguistically about the Hellenistic Koiné.

The Hellenistic Koiné, it turns out, was very typical. Colonial dialects are always mixed dialects: when speakers from different areas of some linguistic homeland mix together in a new colonial location, their dialects also mix together, and the outcome is a new mixed dialect. The evidence from the nineteen different colonial scenarios presented above paint a very clear picture: colonial dialect mixture necessarily, and inevitably, leads to the establishment of new dialects. The monogenesis-of-colonial-dialects thesis is quite wrong.

But why does this happen? Why does colonial dialect mixture necessarily, and inevitably, lead to the establishment of new dialects? The answer does not lie in 'identity': the identity thesis is also quite wrong. Any process of new-identity formation that may occur is much less inevitable than new-dialect formation and, when it does occur, typically *post-dates* new-dialect formation. Did any kind of new colonial identity result from the gradual movement east of German dialects?

Probably not. Why would the movement south of Christian Romance-speakers in Iberia have led to a new and different 'deep-seated loyalty'? It surely did not. There is no reason either to suppose that speakers of the new mixed dialects of western Poland have ever subscribed to anything other than an already-existing identity as Polish.

The fact that colonial dialect mixture universally leads to new-dialect formation, as illustrated with these numerous examples, indicates rather strongly that some universal of human linguistic and social behaviour must be involved. According to Keller (1994: 96) this universal is that human beings, as speakers, operate according to the powerful maxim: 'Talk like the others talk'. This is impossible to disagree with. If this were not true, there would be no local dialects. The fact that everyone who grows up in the same community speaks in the same way is not generally regarded by linguists as needing any kind of linguistic discussion or explanation. This is what always happens, and must result from some universal of human behaviour.

Behavioural Coordination

I suggest in fact that Keller's maxim is just one aspect of a broader general principle of behavioural coordination. Behavioural coordination is found in humans and in other primates and is due to 'innate biological basis of interactional synchrony' – mutual adaptation is 'pervasive in face to-face interaction, and is the essential characteristic of every interpersonal interaction' (Pelech 2002: 10). Linguistic accommodation between speakers occurs because it is an aspect of 'the automatic behaviors manifested during social interaction' (Capella 1997: 80).

Koiné-formation is inevitable because it derives from accommodation in face-to-face interaction. Koiné-formation takes place principally in the speech of children; and the particular phonological and grammatical variants from the dialect mix which end up in the new koiné is not haphazard (Trudgill 2004). As Samuels (1972) has it, 'the numerically superior forms are selected irrespective of their original area of provenance'. We can assume that this was how the Hellenistic Koiné was formed; and that this is how all new mixed colonial dialects are formed.

8 Indo-European Feminines: Contact, Diffusion and Gender Loss around the North Sea

As we noted in Chapter 2, the very earliest known form of Proto-Indo-European had only two grammatical genders: Fortson (2010: 114) tells us that 'the oldest preserved branch of Indo-European, Anatolian, had only a two-way distinction between animate or common gender and inanimate or neuter'. According to Ringe (2006: 24), however, all the extant modern Indo-European varieties descend from the non-Anatolian branch of Proto-Indo-European, which he calls North Indo-European, which represents a more complex and innovative stage of Proto-Indo-European in which, at some point after 4200 BC, 'a three-way contrast in grammatical gender between masculine, feminine, and neuter' (Fortson 2010: 114) had developed. It is widely agreed that the innovation which gave rise to the new tripartite system was precisely the development of the new feminine gender.

This chapter is devoted to a study of how, some six millennia later, this 'new' gender began to be lost again, in parts of northwestern Europe. How exactly the feminine initially developed is the subject of much discussion – as Corbett says, the origins of the Indo-European gender system 'lie so far back' in time that much work on them 'has been largely speculative' (1991: 168) – though Luraghi (2009) does provide a very helpful summary. But it should be a rather easier task to work out how and why this development came to be undone again after some 6,000 years in the area around the North Sea.

Many modern Indo-European languages such as Czech and German still preserve the three genders, complete with the 'new' feminine: they have a grammatical gender system which shows the faithful preservation, over a period of at least 6,000 years, of all three North Proto-Indo-European grammatical genders. Though nothing like as pervasive as in some other modern Indo-European languages such as Polish or Greek, the gender system of Standard Norwegian Nynorsk also distinguishes between masculine, feminine and neuter in a number of important nominal categories to the extent that gender-markers occur frequently in all utterances of any length. Crucially, although the third-person singular pronouns *han* 'he' and *hon* 'she' are generally used to pronominalise human and other animates according to their natural gender (i.e., sex), the system as a whole still operates on an entirely grammatical-gender basis, as in older Indo-European as well as in modern languages such as German:

the wall ... it	*vegg-en ... han*	'wall-the ... he'
the book ... it	*bok-a ... hon*	'book-the ... she'
the child ... it	*barn-et ... det*	'child-the ... it'

However, there are a number of other modern Indo-European varieties, including Norwegian varieties, which have only two genders. These include all of the western Romance languages, where the reduction from three to two genders was achieved through the loss of the Latin neuter, not the feminine. Similarly, in the two-gender dialect of Slovenian of the bilingual area of Sele Fara in southern Austria (Priestly 1983), it is the neuter gender which has disappeared and been replaced by the masculine. And this is also true of Albanian, Latvian, Lithuanian, Welsh, Gaelic, Hindi and Pashto.

In this chapter, however, I want to focus more specifically on the reduction of three genders to two through the loss of the feminine, not least because this is more perplexing than the loss of the neuter. Grammatical gender systems of the Indo-European type are based on 'small systems of noun classes as in French or German' (Dixon 2002: 452) where the class assignment of inanimates is arbitrary but the categories are derived from the natural gender of animates (i.e., they are semantically derived, sex-based gender categories). It is therefore very odd, as Hickey (2000) points out, that varieties such as modern Standard Danish and Standard Swedish have actually lost the fundamental distinction in inanimates between masculines and feminines which the whole sex-based grammatical gender system is founded on.

My goal here is to explore this phenomenon of feminine gender-loss and maintenance in West Germanic varieties such as Dutch, and in North Germanic varieties such as Norwegian. Within the Germanic language family there are very many varieties which, like Nynorsk, still preserve the original three genders – Icelandic, for instance. On the other hand, there are Germanic varieties, like English – which have lost grammatical gender altogether.[1] And there are yet others, like Bergen Norwegian and Standard Danish, which have lost the feminine and thus have only two genders.

Bergen

The Norwegian of the city of Bergen holds a special place in the study of Norwegian dialectology (e.g., Skjekkeland 1997), being generally considered to be aberrant in a number of respects in the context of regional varieties of Norwegian. One respect in which it is highly unusual has to do with the unique

---

[1] Other non-Germanic Indo-European languages which have lost gender include Cappadocian Greek (Janse 2009), Armenian, Farsi and Bengali.

position which the grammatical-gender system of the Bergen dialect has amongst Norwegian dialects. Bergen has acquired a system with only two genders, common and neuter, through the loss of the newest of the three Indo-European genders, the feminine, which became merged with the masculine in a new 'common gender'. Thus, in Bergen, the distinct feminine definite and indefinite articles have disappeared and the markers of the common gender are all original masculines, for example, *bok-en* cf. Nynorsk *bok-a* 'the book', *en bok* cf. Nynorsk *ei bok* 'a book'.

This is more than just a formal matter, since the originally feminine nouns are now also pronominalised using the original masculine pronoun *han* 'he'. The feminine third-person singular pronoun *hon* 'she' does survive, but is used only for natural gender (i.e., to pronominalise feminine nouns referring to females). Thus, in the basilectal Bergen dialect (Nesse 2005), we have:

vegg-en . . . han	wall-the . . . 'he' cf.	Nynorsk *vegg-en . . . han*	
bok-en . . . han	book-the . . . 'he' cf.	Nynorsk *bok-a . . . hon*	
kvinn-en . . . hon	woman-the . . . 'she' cf.	Nynorsk *kvinn-a . . . hon.*	

My exploration of gender loss will be from the perspective of sociolinguistic typology (Trudgill 2011). I will be asking whether it is possible to provide sociolinguistically based explanations for why different Germanic varieties vary to the extent of having respectively one, two or three genders[2] – where I am using the term 'explanation' in what McMahon refers to as a 'lower-key' kind of way to refer to 'relief from puzzlement about some phenomenon' (1994: 45). Can we give a sensible sociolinguistic account of why most Norwegian dialects have preserved the feminine gender while certain other Germanic varieties have not? What different social factors might be involved, separately or in combination?

I Contact

The reduction of three genders to two in Bergen is a clear example of simplification; and a number of writers have ascribed this simplification to language contact. Ernst Håkon Jahr has developed a specific contact-based explanation for this loss of the feminine in Bergen (Jahr 1995, 1998, 2001) in which he argues that this development in the town was the result of the 'heavy influence of language contact between Norwegian and Low German' (2001: 100) during the Hanse period (Mørck 2018: 348–51). Nesse (2002) makes the same kind of point in more detail. Jahr's explanation hinges on the fact that 'voksne som lærer nye språk,

---

[2] To write of varieties with 'one gender' is obviously anomalous, but I notice that I have done it anyway.

kjennetegnes ved å være "imperfect adult learners" i forhold til hva barn er'.[3] Jahr's explanation, that is, is couched in terms of the simplification which is well-known to be associated with the imperfect language learning abilities of adults in contact situations (Trudgill 2011).

Other writers have discussed whether this should be considered to be *dialect contact* rather than language contact (Trudgill 2000; and see also Chapter 2, and below), supposing that Low German might have been rather mutually intelligible with Norwegian at the time in question, and noting that the gender reduction was partial, from three to two, rather than the total loss of gender altogether.

Jahr (1995, 1998, 2001) points out that it is very significant that the only other area of Norway apart from Bergen where this distinction has been lost is in the area of strong Sami-Norwegian contact in the Norwegian North. This contact explanation, however, turns out to be controversial. Perridon (2003) strongly disputes these language-contact-based arguments (see also, Heide 2003): 'the hypothesis that language contact with Low German was (co-)responsible for a number of changes in the grammar of the dialect of Bergen does not explain anything' (Perridon 2003: 254). The traditional explanation for this development, which he favours, is simply phonological. In Bergen, 'after the quantity shift, there were no longer long segments in unstressed or lightly stressed syllables, the opposition between long and short *n*'s in the definite forms of nouns was hence lost: *hestinn* "horse DEF-SG-M" became *hesten*, with the same ending as *bokin* "book DEF-SG-F" → *boken*'. In other dialects, though, 'short final -*n* fell, often after having nasalised the preceding vowel [i], [æ] or [e], which later turned into [a], e.g. *solin* → *solĩ* → *sola* "sun-DEF", or *soli* in non-nasalising dialects' (2003: 254), and so the gender distinction was preserved. So Perridon would seem to be correct at least to the extent that the merger of the masculine and feminine articles was linked to phonological change. Kusmenko (2000), however, argues that to say that the latter brought about the former is actually to confuse cause and effect.

Kusmenko (1996, 2000) also suggests that gender simplification may be due to large-scale confusion on the part of speakers in contact situations about masculine/feminine/neuter grammatical gender membership (which is after all arbitrary). For example, confusion resulting from contact between and bilingualism in Dutch and West Frisian (as we shall see) might be due to Dutch/Frisian gender mismatches: it is certainly the case that 'there are a good many Frisian nouns whose gender differs from that of their Dutch cognates' (Visser 2011: 32). Kusmenko also makes a similar point about simplification in Jutish Danish, North Frisian and Schleswig Low German, where nouns also belonged to different genders in the different languages. Haugen (1976) similarly suggests that the entry of new loanwords from Low German into the Nordic big-city dialects might have caused problems of gender assignment which contributed to the merger of masculine and feminine.

---

[3] 'adults who learn new languages are characterised as being imperfect adult learners in comparison to children'.

In Perridon's disagreement with Jahr we can see a conflict between two opposing types of attitude towards explanations for linguistic changes. On the one hand, we see sociolinguists looking to language contact and other social factors as explanations for the simplification involved in gender loss and reduction. On the other hand, we see other scholars who are part of a tradition of linguists who see no need for any explanation other than the internal-linguistic (see Delsing 2002). Some of these go as far as to overtly question the role of sociolinguistic factors at all – Perridon is only one of a number of non-sociolinguists who are contact-sceptics who feel no need for a sociolinguistic explanation for something which seems to them to be just a straight-forward consequence of internally generated linguistic change. In this case, Perridon argues that it was phonological change that was the key; but a number of linguists have also argued for the role of morphology (e.g., Enger 2010).

My own goal in this paper – to attempt to account for why gender has been reduced in some varieties but not others – leads me to take the side of Jahr in this dispute. While Perridon's account of the sound changes involved is undoubtedly correct, what he does not attempt to do is to explain why the process of phonological change which he describes led to the two different grammatical outcomes in the two different types of variety: why did sound change lead to the loss of the feminine gender in precisely the Bergen variety; and to the preservation of the feminine elsewhere?

Perhaps Perridon's point of view would be that that there is nothing specific about Bergen that is relevant here at all – that there is a random element in linguistic change which means that it is impossible to account for why a particular linguistic change happened when and where it did, rather than at some other time and in some other place – I did, after all, myself point to the random nature of the operation of analogy in Chapter 5. But the instinct of the sociolinguist is at least to try to move towards a further reduction in puzzlement.

It is, therefore, very fortunate for the sociolinguist that there is indeed something very obviously sociolinguistic-typological to be said about the Scandinavian loss of the feminine. Haugen (1976: 288) explains that the three grammatical genders are preserved 'in the overwhelming majority of Scandinavian dialects down to the present' but that certain varieties have reduced the number of genders to two. These latter varieties are the Norwegian of Bergen already mentioned, together with Standard Danish and Swedish, plus a number of Danish (Arboe 2008) and Swedish dialects. The feminine gender is most weakly preserved in contemporary Swedish in those varieties which are spoken in the vicinity of Stockholm, as well as in Skåne/Scania, the area nearest to Copenhagen (Andersson 2011). Note Perridon's (2003: 241) own description:

Masculine and feminine gender have coalesced into a common gender ... in Copenhagen, and hence in Standard Danish; in Central Sweden (the area around Stockholm; Uppland) and hence in Standard Swedish; and in Bergen.

The denial of the role of contact means that for Perridon it has to be a *total coincidence* that three of the areas in which feminine-gender loss has occurred just happened to be, at the relevant period in history: the largest city in Denmark; *and* the largest city in Sweden; *and* the largest city in Norway.

From the point of view of sociolinguistic typology, moreover, this is actually *most unlikely* to be just a coincidence. Kusmenko (2000) makes the point that it cannot be coincidental that at the time of the supremacy of the Low German of the Hanseatic League these three cities, with their large populations of foreigners, lost the feminine, while the immediately surrounding rural areas without the foreigners did not. Eventually this loss did also spread to the environs of Stockholm, and of Copenhagen – the dialects of Sealand outside Copenhagen merged masculine and feminine only at the beginning of the twentieth century – but in the case of Bergen it has still not happened.

Copenhagen

Pedersen (1999) writes that in Copenhagen the masculine-feminine distinction was totally lost during the period 1450–1600, during which time Copenhagen was experiencing a five-fold increase in the number of its inhabitants. Koinéisation, as discussed in the previous chapter, is a very common occurrence in large urban areas (Trudgill 1986) as a result of the dialect contact which accompanies in-migration and dialect-mixture during urbanisation. Pedersen has just such an explanation for feminine-loss in Copenhagen – and hence in Standard Danish. The gender merger, she argues, was due to contact between the dialects of Zealand and the dialects of (the now Swedish) Scania, as well as Low German dialects which would at that time perhaps have been somewhat mutually intelligible with Scandinavian, as we have discussed.

From a mechanical linguistic perspective, it is relatively simple to see how gender-loss could result from dialect levelling. For example, in the three varieties involved in the dialect contact, eight different forms would have been found for the first person singular possessive pronoun. All eight forms were phonologically very similar, but the masculine/feminine distinction was effected in different ways in the different varieties, and the situation was further complicated by the three different case forms in Low German. The eventual new Copenhagen dialect outcome represented a kind of simplified common-denominator compromise between the eight forms, in which the masculine-feminine distinction had gone missing:

Dialect-mixture input:

	Masc.	*fem.*
Zealand	min	me:n
Scania	mi:n	mi:n

Low Germ.	nom.	mi:n	mi:ne
	acc.	mi:nen	mi:ne
	dat.	mi:nem	mi:ner

Koine output: mi:n 'my'

We can suppose that similar processes may have been at work in Stockholm and Bergen.

Afrikaans/Dutch/Flemish

In his anti-contact argument, Perridon refers in particular to the fact that Jahr says that the large-scale presence of Low German-speaking Hanseatic traders in Bergen leads us to expect to find more language contact effects, such as simplification, in Bergen than in Oslo or Tønsberg. Perridon (2003: 254) counters with the observation that it cannot have been like that because 'in Belgium there was an intensive language contact between French and Dutch, but just in this area the three gender system is still very much alive', and therefore a contact-based explanation for why gender-loss occurred in Bergen does not make sense.

It is particularly odd, however, that Perridon has chosen Dutch as an example to make his anti-contact case here, because there is one variety of Dutch which is universally accepted (Duke 2010) as having undergone simplification, including gender loss, precisely as a result of language contact. As we saw in Chapter 2, the Southern African language Afrikaans is derived historically from Dutch; and is explained by Roberge (1995) as having undergone much simplification relative to its source language because of its history of contact with indigenous and other languages. Typologically, Afrikaans is best described as a creoloid (Trudgill 1983) because, although simplification has occurred, there has been a continuous native-speaker tradition throughout its history, and the Dutch/Afrikaans language has been transmitted from one generation to another since the arrival of Dutch speakers in the 1600s.

Dialect contact was also important, as is often the case in colonial situations (Trudgill 2004a), and as it undoubtedly also was in Copenhagen. Combrink (1978) sees a large role for dialect contact in the simplification, as we saw in Chapter 7, and ascribes this in part to 'interdialectal noise deletion'.

Some modern Afrikaans native speakers are thus the direct genetic as well as cultural descendants of earlier generations of Dutch speakers. But according to Combrink (1978), the population of Cape Town in 1795 was about 1,500, and approximately 1,000 of these were 'slaves that had come from Guinea, Mozambique, and the far East' and 'people of Khoin extraction, most of whom had given up their mother tongue and could speak only the Cape Dutch' (1978: 77). Dutch was acquired by very large numbers of non-native speakers, initially speakers of the indigenous Khoi and San languages, and then by speakers of Bantu languages, and immigrant speakers of German, French, Portuguese, Malagasy, Malay, Indonesian languages and others. There was much mixing and intermarriage, as the current 'Coloured' population of South Africa shows. Women in particular were quite likely to be native speakers of some language other than Dutch. This led to a situation where the nature of transmission became crucial: so many people initially acquired and used Dutch as an L2 that, in later generations, children were born who became, as it were, native speakers of non-native Dutch. A non-native variety became nativised and, in time, the dominant, and subsequently only, variety.

The role of contact in the formation of Afrikaans was clearly so massive that it would be foolish to ascribe the loss of gender to any other cause. And in adult language contact situations, grammatical gender is very much a prime candidate for loss. Dahl points out that many linguistic phenomena are *cross-linguistically dispensable* (i.e., there are languages which manage very well without them); and gender is clearly one such. As Hickey (2000) says: 'grammatical gender . . . is largely semantically redundant'. Also, gender systems are 'mature phenomena' which take a very long time to develop diachronically and which tend to be 'most recalcitrant in second language learning' (Dahl 2004: 286). It is therefore not surprising that loss of gender 'appears to be highly correlated with the degree of external contacts' (Dahl 2004: 200).

To be fair to Perridon, we should also consider in more detail his specific point about the consequences of contact between Dutch and French in Europe. From the point of view of sociolinguistic-typology, however, the Germanic/Romance border does not provide a good comparison with Bergen at all. What Perridon says about contact in Belgium is of course quite true; but there is a failure of sociolinguistic sensitivity and imagination here. When he attempts to shine light on the situation in Bergen by pointing out that 'in Belgium there was an intensive language contact between French and Dutch, but just in this area the three gender system is still very much alive', Perridon is not comparing like with like. He is using the term 'contact' in an unsubtle and undifferentiated way, and one which turns out to be somewhat naïve from a sociolinguistic point of view. The fact is that we need to analyse the concept 'contact' in more detail.

In our search for explanatory factors, we need to distinguish sociolinguistically between two major types of language contact which have two very different linguistic outcomes. As I have argued in Trudgill (2011), simplification in language contact, such as loss of gender, does not result from contact *as such*. It results from post-critical threshold learning (Lenneberg 1967) which, as the previous quotation from Jahr makes clear, is what he is talking about. Simplification will occur only to the extent that *adult* second-language learning dominates in short term-contact situations.

The contact between French and Dutch that Perridon refers to is precisely the sort of contact where we would *not* expect to observe any simplification (see Trudgill 2010a).

The situation on the language frontier in what is now Belgium is very different from the situation in medieval Bergen, where contact involved Low German-speaking adults who were mostly short-term migrants. In Belgium, the contact was and continues to be a stable, very many centuries-old contact environment involving whole communities, including children, rather than the 'imperfect adult learners' that Jahr refers to. Ryckeboer (2002) speaks, for instance, of 'generations and generations of bilinguals' in the French/Flemish border contact zone. And Willemyns (2002) writes of the 'mutual influence due to the extremely long duration of language contact' and of fluent bilingual speakers who practise code-switching.

In French-Flanders, the degree of intensity of the Romance-Germanic contact and the length of its duration can be judged from the extent to which grammatical influence has been mutually exercised by the local varieties of West Flemish and Picard on each another. In the Flemish varieties of France we find conjunctions such as *puisque dat, parce que, soit*; and prepositions such as *à force van, grâce van* (Ryckeboer 2002).

The Flemish dialect in France also shows syntactic characteristics that reflect . . . the age-old influence of French [including the] extra-position of some adverbial complements and even inherent complements, [which are] very common in French Flemish [while] another syntactic feature of the French Flemish dialect is the almost complete absence of inversion (for 97%) after topicalisation of a non-subject constituent. (Ryckeboer 2002: 37)

Similarly, according to Callebout and Ryckeboer (1997), the local Picard dialects demonstrate Germanic features such as preposed adjectives: *du frais café*; and the postposition of prepositions and adverbs as in *crier après, venir avec, faire sans*. Compounding can also occur in the Germanic manner, as in *piedsente* cf. French *sentier pedestre* and Dutch *voetpad*.

Perridon then continues his argument by making a contrast between Belgium and the northern part of the Dutch-speaking area. He writes that 'in Holland, on the other hand, there was little or no contact between Dutch and French (or other languages), yet the dialects in this area lost the distinction between feminine and masculine gender for reference to non-persons'. It is, of course, quite true that the metropolitan varieties in the north of the Netherlandic-speaking area, including Standard Dutch, have merged feminine and masculine, while dialects of the Flemish south (and neighbouring areas) have retained the three original genders (De Vogelaer 2009). As we saw in Chapter 2, Standard Dutch has the definite article forms *de* (common gender – masc./fem.) and *het* (neut.), while the southern dialects have *den* (masc.) *de* (fem.), and *'t* (neut.), with corresponding differences of adjectival agreement (Taeldeman 2005: 62):

Flemish:	*den dunnen Boer* vs.	*de dunne boerin*
Standard Dutch:	*de dunne Boer* vs.	*de dunne boerin*
	'the thin farmer'	'the thin farmer's wife'
cf. Afrikaans	*die maer Boer* vs.	*die maer boervrou*

Importantly, the effects of this merger can also be seen in grammatical (as opposed to natural) gender:

Flemish:	*De tafel – ze* (= 'she')
Standard Dutch:	*De tafel – hij* (= 'he')
	'The table – it'
cf. Afrikaans	*Die tafel – dit* (= 'it')

The noun *tafel* was originally feminine in all varieties of Dutch, and is therefore pronominalised by 'she' in varieties which preserve the feminine. In Standard Dutch, where the feminine has been lost, all common gender nouns regardless of historical gender status are now pronominalised by 'he' – except for animate feminines such as *vrouw* 'woman' – very much as in Bergen Norwegian (De Vogelaer & De Sutter 2011).

But this ties in very nicely with what we have said about urbanisation, dialect contact, koineisation and simplification. Gender-simplification in Dutch occurred in the highly urbanised north of the area; but has not occurred in the much less urbanised areas of the Dutch-speaking south, where there was less in-migration, much less dialect contact and therefore much less simplification. The northern gender reduction was due to the considerable amount of in-migration from other Dutch-speaking dialect areas that occurred, as we saw in Chapter 2, during the period of rapid population expansion in the now highly urbanised north of the Netherlands after the surrender of Antwerp to the Spanish in 1585, when all Protestants were forced to leave, and to further in-migration during the Dutch Golden Age of the seventeenth century (Geerts 1966; Trudgill 2013).

High German

Perridon is not the only scholar to object to the contact-and-simplification thesis. Campbell and Poser (2008: 362) take a similar line to Perridon's by citing the case of High German. They discuss the approach taken to contact and simplification in, for example, Trudgill (2002), and pose a question which is similar to the one posed by Perridon for Bergen. They ask: if Trudgill is right about simplification being a consequence of language contact, then why has German, a language which has a long history of being learned as an L2 and being used as a lingua franca, not been simplified like the mainland Scandinavian languages that Trudgill points to?

It is certainly true that Standard German has retained the three Indo-European genders, and this applies too to the nonstandard dialects of central and southern Germany, Switzerland and Austria. It is also true that Campbell and Poser's question needs answering. In my view, though, it is not the right question. The question should not so much be why the acquisition of German by non-native speakers has not led to simplification. After all, in a situation where a continuous native-speaker tradition is maintained (Thomason & Kaufmann 1988), why would it? When pidgins develop, this is because there is an intergenerational break in transmission, and the result is effectively a new language. But where native speakers transmit their language from one generation to another in the normal way, as with German, the fact that there may also be non-natives around who are speaking simplified versions of the language will normally have no effect on this transmission whatsoever. No language is currently used more by non-native speakers than English, but the mainstream native varieties of English are currently showing no serious signs of large-scale, ongoing, new simplification.

The real question is the reverse of Campbell and Poser's question. Consider Bergen once again. It has been argued, as we have seen, that simplification occurred in Bergen as a result of contact with Low German speakers. But how did this work? How are we to unpack the phrase 'as a result of'? It would be no surprise if the Norwegian spoken by native speakers of Low German was simplified, as undoubtedly it was: Wessén (1970: 169) writes 'mit der Zeit gingen die Deutschen zwar dazu über, Nordisch zu sprechen, aber sie vermochten nie, den richtigen Gebrauch der nordischen Beugungsformen zu lernen'.[4] But the big question is: why should this simplification have spread to the speech of native Norwegians, and thus to subsequent generations?

Again, the focus has to be refined onto *type* of contact – it is not adequate to refer to 'contact' as an undifferentiated concept. And the clue here lies in the case of Afrikaans. The answer to the Bergen question must lie, as with Afrikaans, in two factors central to contact processes: demography and transmission. As far as *demography* is concerned, we have some information about Bergen. According to Rambø (2008), who quotes also from Nesse (2001), the population of Bergen in the 1400s may have been around 7,000. Of these perhaps 2,000 were Germans, with that number rising to perhaps 4,000 (then out of 9,000) in the summer months. There were also other foreigners, including Dutch, English and Scottish. Elsewhere, Blomkvist (1979) says that in the 100 years from 1250 between a third and a half of the population of Kalmar, Sweden, were German. And Dahlbäck (1998) shows that in 1460, Stockholm had a population that was one third German.

Although there was a very long-term presence of these foreign communities in Bergen and other Scandinavian cities, the non-Norwegians did not typically settle as individuals in Bergen or elsewhere for the long-term. They formed large but predominantly male and, unlike in South Africa, transient populations. In short-term contact, which is what this must have been for individual adults, we know that dialect mixture and levelling do occur as a result of contact via accommodation in face-to face interaction (Trudgill 1986). In the Bergen case, if Low German and Norwegian were mutually intelligible (Duke 2010), as they may have been at this

---

[4] 'with time the Germans did switch to speaking Scandinavian, but they never managed to learn the correct usage of Scandinavian inflections'.

time – Nesse (2005) says that a normal communication pattern was one of passive bilingualism – we can count Low German/Norwegian interactions as instances of dialect contact. If they were not intelligible – recall that Wessén (1970) claims that the Hanseatic Germans did start to speak Scandinavian – then we can also suppose that there was dialect contact of a different kind, between native Bergen Norwegian and the non-native Norwegian of Low German speakers. In-migration from rural areas of western Norway, involving what can uncontroversially be labelled dialect contact, will also have been important.

My suggestion is that when the proportion of non-native speakers becomes as close to 50 per cent as this – the proportion of non-native speakers of Norwegian in Bergen was certainly very high (4,000 out of 9,000) – the number of face-to-face dialect-contact-type interactions, and therefore potential instances of accommodation (Trudgill 1986), would have reached a threshold level at which some aspects of the non-native variety could transfer to the native. If the demography is right, natives can and will accommodate, to different extents, to non-natives. And the point about 'different extents' is important: overall simplification in Bergen Norwegian is actually rather slight, especially when compared to Afrikaans.

II Diffusion

Contact, then, must surely be a vital part of the explanation we are looking for. However, it is often a good idea to look at the possibility of multi-causality in linguistic change: there are so many developments which can take place in linguistic change that the fact that some particular change *has* actually taken place suggests that there is likely to have been more than one favourable, predisposing factor at work. I now, therefore, want to show that geography, too, has been crucially involved in the loss of the feminine.

The Bergen Norwegian gender system, it turns out, is not very unusual when viewed in its wider geographical context. Bergen is located on the eastern shores of the northern North Sea; and across this sea from Bergen, on its western shores, lies another area where the original three grammatical genders of Germanic have also not been retained, namely Britain. Bergen is about 300 nautical miles from the Scottish coast at Aberdeen, and we know that contact around and across the North Sea has been of considerable historical and cultural importance over the centuries. Can there be a connection between the loss of gender in the two places?

One's first answer has to be, in fact, that it is not immediately obvious that this is anything other than a pure coincidence. But notice then that, ignoring for a moment the island of Britain, Bergen Norwegian was also not the only continental Germanic variety to experience reduction of genders from three to two. Further south, again on the east coast of the North Sea, and at roughly the same time as in Bergen, the metropolitan Dutch varieties of the north of the Netherlandic-speaking area also merged the feminine with the masculine (Geerts 1966), as we just saw. It is perhaps not quite so easy to shrug this off as simply being a coincidence.

And the claim that it is simply a coincidence becomes perhaps even more difficult to maintain when we recall the following. As we have noted, the Flemish and neighbouring dialects – such as that of North Brabant – of the south of the Netherlandic-speaking area did not undergo this change, and retained the three original genders (De Vogelaer 2009), as they still do to this day. What we have not noted before is that the boundary between the innovating northern two-gender dialects and the southern three-gender Dutch dialects is drawn by Dutch dialectologists as running from west to east across the Netherlands, in a rather straight line from the Rhine delta on the North Sea coast. At the eastern end of this line, it takes a brief turn to the north, passing between Zutphen and Enschede, and then another turn back east to meet the Netherlands-Germany border to the east of Hardenberg (De Vogelaer 2009).

Of course, we conventionally divide the dialects of the West Germanic dialect continuum into 'German' and 'Dutch', but this is a politico-sociolinguistic matter since there is no linguistic reason for the division of the continuum into two to be made at the border between Germany and The Netherlands. Linguistically, the more meaningful distinction (Weijnen 2000) is between the Low Franconian dialects of the central and southern Netherlands and northern Belgium, and the Low Saxon Low German dialects of the northeastern Netherlands which are part of the same dialect subgrouping as the Low Saxon dialects of northwestern Germany. So surely we can suppose that this west-east isogloss will not just stop at the national border?

It is initially discouraging for this supposition to find that, according to the three chapters on Low German published in Russ (1989) – Goltz and Walker (1989), Durrell (1989) and Schönfeld (1989) – Low German has three genders, just like High German. This is also the information presented in the Low German grammar by Lindow et al. (1998).

Crucially, though, these works do show that manifestations of gender are fewer than in High German, there being a much smaller role for case in modern Low German; and with no gender marking in the plural. The masculine/feminine distinction in particular survives only rather tenuously. As described by Durrell, manifestations of the masculine/feminine distinction in Westphalian are few, with the nominative singular of the definite article being *de* for both genders, and only the oblique (the result of an earlier simplifying coalescence of accusative and dative) differing in having *den* for the masculine and *de* for feminine (cf. neuter *dat*). Lindow et al. (1998: 143) concur that it is only in the nominative singular oblique case that the masculine and feminine definite article are regularly distinguished in Low German generally. Adjectives, in some varieties only, may also take an -*n* in the masculine oblique case in the strong declension. And demonstratives, possessives and indefinite articles may distinguish between masculine and feminine but do not necessarily do so at all in many dialects.

That is, in much of Low German all it would take for the total formal merger of masculine and feminine to occur would be for a sound change to happen such that the word-final -*n* of the masculine singular oblique definite article was lost (and for the same change to happen in the case-strong adjectives in those varieties where they are also distinct). Importantly for our purposes, although this is not mentioned in the major reference works, it actually turns out that this loss of -*n* is precisely what *has* in fact occurred in a number of different varieties of Low German, though of course for a total gender merger to take place, loss of -*n* was not all that had to happen (cf. Nesse 2005): we can only be confident that native-speaker awareness of masculine vs. feminine gender membership has been lost when the relevant pronouns and other proforms have ceased to be distinct as well.

And of course it does turn out, on closer examination, that the relevant isogloss does not stop at the Netherlands–Germany border at all: the west-east two-gender/three-gender line extends from the Netherlands across into Germany, into the County of Bentheim in the German province of Lower Saxony (Niedersachsen). So the question then arises as to how much further it extends into the Low German-speaking area of this part of western Germany. My major source in tackling this question has been Wahrig-Burfeind (1989). Her extremely detailed work, together with her maps, gives a very strong indication that all of the Low German (Plattdeutsch/Niederdeutsch) dialects spoken in western Lower Saxony have only the two genders. In the Low German spoken in Emsland, Lower Saxony, the 'Synkretismus von Maskulinum und Femininum dominiert' (1989: 57). And further to the north, the loss of the feminine has also been totally carried through in East Frisia: Wahrig-Burfeind (1989: 82–3) discusses the East Frisian Low German (EFLG) merger using data from Wiesenhann (1977); but the fact of this merger is also confirmed in the book-length study of East Frisian Low German by Matras and Reershemius (2003: 18) who write: 'EFLG, like other Low German varieties, has a two-gender system: common (or non-neuter) and neuter. As in Dutch and the Scandinavian languages, common nouns tend to continue historical masculines and feminines, while neuter nouns generally continue historical neuters.' Wahrig-Burfeind shows too that the Low German of the Oldenburg area also lacks a distinct feminine (1989: 57) – which takes us geographically as far east, more or less, as the banks of the River Weser. I am, therefore, also assuming, though I have not actually had this confirmed, that all the intervening areas of Lower Saxony between East Frisia/Emsland and Oldenburg, including at least Cloppenburg, Ammerland and Wesermarsch, also have the merger; it would be rather remarkable if they did not.

Goltz and Walker (1989) divide the Low Saxon dialects of Low German in Germany into six major sub-divisions: according to my assumption, three of them, Ostfriesisch (East Frisian), Oldenburgish (including the Wesermarsch district) and Emsländisch have the merger. In view of this configuration of the two-gender dialects, it is now no surprise to find that, back west on the other side of the international border, in the Low Saxon-speaking areas of the Netherlands around Groningen and in Overijssel, the local dialects also have the syncretism, as the Dutch dialectologists' west-east isogloss indicates (Wahrig-Burfeind 1989). And then, to complete the geographical jigsaw, it is now also rather predictable that we should find that West Frisian, the language spoken in the area between the northern Low Franconian Dutch-speaking area and the Groningen-area Low Saxon, is no different. The West Frisian language follows northern Dutch and northwestern Low German in having exactly the same masculine-feminine syncretism. Old Frisian did have the original three Germanic genders (Bremmer 2009) – as seen, for example, in the nominative singular definite articles *thi, thiu, thet*. But Modern West Frisian has only two: the two-gender system of Modern West Frisian is due to the loss of the feminine just as in Northern Dutch and in Bergen Norwegian (Tiersma 1985: 47).

The only West Frisian exception is the island dialect of Schiermonnikoog, where the feminine survives (Hoekstra 2001a). Wahrig-Burfeind (1989) finds this exception significant, and has a sociolinguistic explanation for the conservatism in terms of the relative geographical isolation of the island community. In fact, in her extraordinarily detailed study of the distribution of gender reduction in the southern North Sea region, she stresses the importance of contact, isolation and spatial diffusion generally.

So it is the whole of the north of the Netherlands, regardless of which of the three languages is spoken there, that has been affected by this Bergen-style simplification; together with a large neighbouring area of northwestern Germany up to the River Weser. These two-gender West Germanic varieties lie in a single contiguous geographical area which comprises West Frisian, the northern dialects of Dutch and the northwestern dialects of Low German. The fact that a long contiguous stretch of the eastern coastline of the North Sea, and adjoining inland areas, from the Rhine delta in the southern Netherlands to the mouth of the Weser in northern Germany, is occupied by varieties of three different languages which have all lost the masculine–feminine distinction, while southern Dutch and inland Low German (see, for example, Durrell 1989) have not, looks to be a geographical pattern of some significance. Surely this cannot be a coincidence?

Staying now on the eastern shores of the North Sea, it is true that if we travel from the mouth of the River Weser eastwards along the German coast, we come first into more conservative territory: the coastal dialects of Low Saxon Low German spoken from Bremerhaven and up into western Holstein do still retain the three genders.

But then the remarkable thing is that one does not have to travel much further along the coast, as the shoreline swings round into a now northerly direction, before one returns to two-gender territory. This territory stretches from the mouth of the River Eider by Tönning upwards. According to Jørgensen (1954), as reported in Wahrig-Burfeind (1989: 50), the three-gender/two-gender line runs east to west from a point south of the Eckernförde Bay – so just to the north of Kiel – and then via Haby and along the River Eider as far as its mouth on the North Sea at Tönning. Wahrig-Burfeind (1989: 75–6), using data from Bock (1933), shows that north of this line the masculine/feminine merger has been totally carried through in the Low Saxon of Schleswig. Schleswig thus represents the fourth of Goltz and Walker's six Low Saxon divisions to have the merger, leaving only Holsteinisch and Nord-Hannoverisch with three genders.

Then, in the island dialects of North Frisian, the feminine has also been lost, though on the islands of Föhr and Amrum it has been lost through merger not with the masculine but with the neuter (Hoekstra 1996, 2001a), as the definite article forms show[5]:

The definite article in Island North Frisian dialects

	m	f	n	pl
Sylt	di	di	dit	di
Helgoland	de	de	deät	de
Föhr	de	det	det	dö
Amrum	di	det	det	jo

And, if we continue northwards along the coast from North Friesland into Denmark, we come next to the Danish dialects of the Jutland peninsula, which have also all, with the exception of the very far north and the very far east, undergone gender reduction (Arboe 2008).

Do we, then, still want to carry on maintaining that this is all a coincidence? Surely it is significant that, along the West Germanic dialect continuum, it is the dialects of central and upland southern Germany, and the Alpine German varieties of Switzerland and Austria, which have preserved the three genders, while it is dialects of the coastal lowlands of the Netherlands which have lost the feminine gender? The spatial pattern of feminine loss in modern Germanic is not random. There is a large area of Europe stretching from the Rhine delta along the North Sea coast up to and including most of Jutland, with a small break only between Wesermarsch (Lower Saxony) and Schleswig, where the local dialects of five Germanic languages all have the two-gender innovation while other dialects of those same five languages do not.

If we now therefore consider Bergen from a more international perspective, it is a remarkable fact that from around 1600 or so, it has been part of a much larger Germanic-speaking area of coastal western Europe around the North Sea where the original Germanic three-gender system has not been retained. As is illustrated in Map 1, gender loss of various kinds has occurred in a unified geographical area in seven different North Sea Germanic languages: varieties of Dutch, West Frisian, Low German, North Frisian and Danish, plus English and Bergen Norwegian. And,

---

[5] Data very kindly supplied by Alastair Walker.

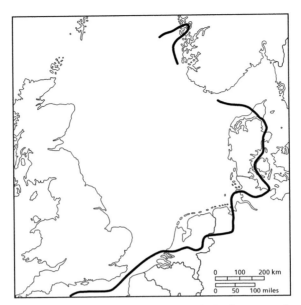

Map 1: The geographical gender-reduction zone c. 1700. To the west and north of the line, Germanic dialects of English, Dutch, West Frisian, Low German, North Frisian, Danish and Bergen Norwegian have all lost the original three-gender system.

again perhaps significantly, this development did not take place in any areas away from the North Sea (except for Stockholm and Copenhagen – as we shall see).

The Linguistics

In considering the question of whether any of this could possibly be a coincidence or not, we now have to concede that, although we are presented with this large contiguous area where the three Germanic genders have been reduced, the actual linguistic outcomes do vary considerably from dialect to dialect.

However, according to Wahrig-Burfeind (1989), there is a regular linguistic change-path or trajectory which Germanic gender loss passes through. It seems that that the different gender-reduction outcomes, albeit not identical, actually simply represent different chronological stages and/or different branchings of the same gender-loss process. The path starts from the baseline of the original Germanic three-gender situation in which pronouns corresponding to 'he', 'she' and 'it' are employed purely on the basis of the grammatical gender of the nominal concerned, as still happens in conservative Germanic varieties such as High German and Norwegian: in the latter, as we already saw, we still find forms such as:

vegg-en . . . han	'wall-the . . . he'	masc.
bok-a . . . ho	'book-the . . . she'	fem.
ku-a . . . ho	'cow-the . . . she'	fem.
jent-a . . . ho	'girl-the . . . she'	fem.

The first development along the path of actual feminine-loss is then one where, as in sixteenth-century Bergen Norwegian, feminine nominals are no longer formally distinct from the masculine, as a result of the loss of the distinction between masculine and feminine articles. But what Nesse in fact shows is that, even after the original merger of the masculine and feminine definite articles, the anaphoric pronouns used for masculine and feminine inanimate nouns did remain distinct – *han* and *hon* – for a period. Awareness of the distinctness of the two genders is signalled in the writings of Mester Absalon[6] (1528–75) in his etymologically correct usage of both the pronouns *hon* and *han* for inanimates (Nesse 2002): *hon* 'she' continued to be used to pronominalise grammatical feminines as well as natural feminines (Nesse 2005). Using the equivalent modern Bergen forms, this would be:

vegg-en . . . han	'wall-the . . . he'
bok-en . . . hon	'book-the . . . she'
ku-en . . . hon	'cow-the . . . she'
jent-en . . . hon	'girl-the . . . she'

It was only later, during the 1600s, that the next and crucial chronological stage for grammatical-gender merger occurred: *hon* 'she' stopped being used to pronominalise original inanimate feminines and was replaced by *han* 'he'. It was of course only when this occurred that the feminine grammatical gender was completely lost:

vegg-en . . . han	'wall-the . . . he'
bok-en . . . han	'book-the . . . he'
ku-en . . . hon	'cow-the . . . she'
jent-en . . . hon	'girl-the . . . she'

The originally feminine nouns were pronominalised with the original masculine pronoun *han* 'he'. And, while the feminine third-person singular pronoun *hon* survived, it was used only for natural gender (i.e., only to pronominalise females). This is also what occurred in northern Dutch. Modern Standard Dutch is like Bergen Norwegian in that it has the definite article forms *de* (common gender or 'uter' – original masculine and feminine) while the southern dialects have *den*

---

[6] Absalon Pederssøn Beyer 'Mester [Master] Absalon' was a Bergen priest, teacher and writer whose diaries 1552–72 provide invaluable historical data (Skard 1972: 32f.).

(masc.), and *de* (fem.), with corresponding differences of adjectival agreement (Taeldeman 2005: 62):

	'the thin farmer'	'the thin farmer's wife'
Flemish:	*den dunnen boer*	*de dunne boerin*
Stand. N. Dutch:	*de dunne boer*	*de dunne boerin*

Importantly, as we saw before, the effects of this merger can be seen in grammatical as well as natural gender:

	'The table . . . it'
Flemish:	*De tafel . . . ze* (= 'she')
Stand. N. Dutch:	*De tafel . . . hij* (= 'he')

The noun *tafel* was originally feminine in all varieties of Dutch and is therefore pronominalised by 'she' in varieties which preserve the feminine. But in northern Standard Dutch, where the feminine has been lost, all common gender nouns regardless of historical gender status are now pronominalised by 'he', except for animate feminines such as *vrouw* 'woman' (De Vogelaer & De Sutter 2011). So this gives us a system as follows, where *boom* 'tree' is an original masculine:

de boom . . . hij	'the tree . . . he'
de tafel . . . hij	'the table . . . he'
de koe . . . zij	'the cow . . . she'
de vrouw . . . zij	'the woman . . . she'

Remarkably, however, Bergen subsequently went one stage further even than this when *han* began to be used even for female non-human animates: in modern Bergen Norwegian, one says *ku-en . . . han* 'cow-the . . . he', whereas Dutch still employs *zij* 'she' for non-human female animates, such as *koe* 'cow'. Thus in the modern basilectal Bergen dialect (Nesse 2005) we have:

vegg-en . . . han	'wall-the . . . he'
bok-en . . . han	'book-the . . . he'
kuen . . . han	'cow-the . . . he'
jent-en . . . hon	'girl-the . . . she'

Hon 'she' in Bergen is entirely restricted to the pronominalisation of nominals signifying women and girls.

There is also another Germanic development which is illustrated in the modern Bergen dialect. Although *han* 'he' is still the pronoun used for all common inanimate nouns (and indeed, as we have just seen, for all animates except humans), it is subject to a grammatical constraint such that *den,* originally 'that', has to be used instead under extraposition or emphasis (Nesse 2005: 224). This is also what has happened in northern Dutch (Shetter 1994: 68), where although *hij* is used for all common gender inanimates, *die,* also originally 'that', has to be used with fronting or stress.

Here we can see the beginnings of another stage of development, as represented in the current systems of Standard Danish and Standard Swedish (Skrzypek 2010), as we have mentioned. In these two-gender Scandinavian varieties, the feminine has merged with the masculine; but there is no longer any pronominalisation of the type *boken . . . han.* Rather, these varieties have developed a newer system in which *han* and *hun/hon* are both reserved for animates, while inanimate common gender nouns (including original feminines) are pronominalised with the new pronoun *den* 'it', derived historically from the masculine distal demonstrative *den* 'that'. In these systems, *han* 'he' has now dropped out of use altogether except for male animates, while *den* 'that' has taken over and is used for all originally masculine and feminine inanimates in all contexts, not just when fronted or stressed. This change is said to have been completed in Standard Swedish during the 1700s (Davidson 1990). In modern Standard Danish, these forms are:

vegg-en . . . den	'wall-the . . . it'
bog-en . . . den	'book-the . . . it'
koen . . . den/hun	'cow-the . . . it/she'
pigen . . . hun	'girl-the . . . she'

The situation in East Frisian Low German is similar. East Frisian Low German, as we saw earlier, also has a two-gender system: common and neuter. As in Dutch and the Scandinavian languages, common nouns derive from historical masculines and feminines. Importantly also, the linguistic details do indicate a truly total gender merger, à la Bergen. According to Matras and Reershemius (2003), in East Frisian Low German, the pronoun *zäi* 'she' is reserved for female animates only, as in Dutch. Wiesenhann (1977), as reported in Wahrig-Burfeind (1989), agrees that East Frisian Low German no longer uses the feminine pronoun for non-animate referents. But, as in Standard Danish and Swedish – and unlike in Bergen and Dutch – inanimate common gender nouns in East Frisian Low German are pronominalised by an originally demonstrative pronoun *däi.* However, *däi* can also used for animates in certain discourse contexts (see Matras & Reershemius 2003: 23, for details), which is not dissimilar to the usage in stressed position of *den* in Bergen and *die* in Dutch. The Low German of Schleswig also has a pronoun system which operates with 'he' and 'she' for animates but has a different common-gender pronoun for non-animates (Bock 1933).

There may then also ensue a yet further step along this path, which can lead to the loss of grammatical gender altogether. According to De Vogelaer and De Sutter (2011), such a process is currently taking place in modern Dutch in that non-animate masculines and feminines are increasingly being treated as neuters, while animates are not, something which Curzan (2003) says also happened in Old English/Middle English, where grammatical gender eventually disappeared altogether to be replaced by a purely natural gender system.

And then the Danish dialects of West Jutland have progressed even further along this path. Above, I simply cited Jutland as an area which was almost entirely two-gender territory. However, there is a very significant difference between the dialects of western Jutland and those of the east of the peninsula. West Jutland has developed an innovative system where gender has been lost and replaced, as in English, by a system which distinguishes between male animates, female animates and inanimates. However, inanimates are further subdivided in West Jutland into two semantically determined classes, namely count vs. mass nominals (Haugen 1976; Arboe 2008; Siemund 2008). The pronominal forms *den* and *det*, as in Standard Danish, have taken over from 'he' and 'she' for inanimates. But the original merged common masculine-plus-feminine gender marked by *den* is used as the nominal class for all inanimate *count* nouns, regardless of historical gender and including original neuters; while all inanimate *mass* nouns behave like original neuters, taking *det*. Haugen (1976: 61) cites the following examples:

Æ ægetræ i vor have, den *er stor* 'The oak-tree in our garden, it's big'
BUT
Ægetræ, det *er best til møble* 'Oak (wood), it's (the) best for furniture'

Some of the neighbouring North Frisian dialects (and some Low German dialects in the same area) have a similar system. Löfstedt (1968: 12) tells us that in modern North Frisian, certain original inanimate masculines and feminines have become neuter, while others have become neuter only when used as mass nouns, and retain their original gender when used as count nouns. Alastair Walker (personal correspondence) kindly supplies a North Frisian example: 'di kafee' (masculine), for example, is a particular cup of coffee, whereas 'dåt kafee' (neuter) is coffee as a substance.

There is, then, some diversity in the linguistic outcomes of gender simplification in the different Germanic languages around the North Sea. But it is possible to see these outcomes as simply representing the same outcome at different stages of development, making the 'coincidence' hypothesis less likely.

The Geography

There is no escaping the picture portrayed in Map 1. Wahrig-Burfeind talks of 'das Phänomen der arealen Gerichtetheit der Genussynkretismus' (1989: 295) – there is a spatial directionality to the spread of the change – and the loss of gender is indeed an innovation which has spread from one area to another even across language boundaries. The geography of the Germanic gender reduction that has occurred around the North Sea makes it look very much as if it is the result of the geographical diffusion of an innovation out of one or a number of centres, in the familiar pattern known to dialectologists and geolinguists with, as is also well-known to students of spatial diffusion, outlying exclaves to which the innovation has jumped such Bergen, Copenhagen and Stockholm (Trudgill 1973; Chambers & Trudgill 1998).

What exactly the route or routes of diffusion were, and what exactly the direction of diffusion was, still remains to be investigated. But Wahrig-Burfeind (1989) points to two geographical areas which seem to have led the way in gender loss: English, where grammatical gender has disappeared altogether; and West Jutish, where it has been replaced by a radically different system.

I would like to argue instead, however, for a modified version of this scenario. The fact that the two different innovating continental masculine–feminine syncret-ism areas – the Jutland Danish/Schleswig Low German/North Frisian area; and the Low Saxon Low German/West Frisian/northern Dutch area – are separated from one another by the small intermediate conservative three-gender Weser-Eider zone involving the Low German dialects of the Bremerhaven and Cuxhaven areas plus Holstein, does indicate the possibility that there were indeed two original kernel areas. But I would suggest that these two areas were rather different from those proposed by Wahrig-Burfeind. The one area was certainly England/Lowland Scotland; but the other, I would argue, must have been the northern Netherlands.

My suggestion is that the southern edge of the intermediate zone, the Weser line, represents the northern limit of diffusion out of some kernel area in the Holland/Friesland area, which is most likely to have been the urban area of the Dutch *Randstad*. We know that gender simplification in Dutch started in the highly urbanised north of the area, focusing on what is now the *Randstad* – the urban conglomeration with a modern population of over 7 million based on the four major cities of Amsterdam, The Hague/Den Haag, Rotterdam and Utrecht; and including also Delft, Dordrecht, Hilversum, Harlem/Haarlem and Leiden. It got under way in this region in the sixteenth century as a result of the considerable amount of in-migration that occurred from other Dutch-speaking dialect areas (Geerts 1966; Trudgill 2013), as we have noted. This zone then formed the heart of the gender-loss zone that was later to extend as far as the Weser and to incorporate dialects of West Frisian and Low German as well as Dutch. The gender merger in Dutch can be seen to have been under way in the 1500s and to have become consolidated by the early 1600s (Geerts 1966). The first available texts showing the spread of the merger to West Frisian then appear in the 1600s (Hoekstra 2001b).

On the other hand, the northern limit of the intermediate zone, the Eider line, can be argued to represent the southern limit of the spatial diffusion of gender-loss out of England – with West Jutland acting as the important focal area, secondary to the primary kernel area on the other side of the North Sea (Perridon 1997). It is clear that England – or Britain – was where Germanic gender loss began. According to Jones (1988), it was a process that began to be evident in English texts from the 900s – and we can also assume a time lag between the appearance of gender loss in English speech and its appearance in the written texts which are all that are left to us.

Chronologically, the next North Sea gender-loss development after English was the one in West Jutland, which occurred well before gender changes anywhere else in Scandinavia or the Rhine-Weser region. Skautrup (1944: 270) says, in connection with the development of the 'helt ny genustype' in West Jutish, that the writer of a section of the Jyske Lov (Jutland Law) written about 1325 certainly had this new West Jutish system because 'han har vanskelighed ved at skelne neutrumsord fra fælleskønsord'.[7]

As is well known, *post hoc* is not necessarily *propter hoc*. But, importantly for our discussion of the possibility of geographical diffusion as an explanatory factor, Perridon (1997: 360) has explored the interesting angle that these two gender-simplification events – in Britain up until the late 1200s, and in West Jutland from at least the early 1300s – are linked, in that the former exported the change to the latter. Russ (1982) has made a similar suggestion; and more recently Dahl (2015) has also given detailed and sympathetic consideration to this possibility.

Perridon writes that, while it is well known that Old Norse had a major impact on English, it has not been usual to suggest that 'the dialect contact in the Danelaw might have had some consequences for the invaders as well'. However, he points out that there are a number of similarities between West Jutlandic and English which might be due to diffusion eastwards across the North Sea; and he specifically mentions the fact that both varieties have lost grammatical gender. What then remains to be explained is why West Jutlandic was more influenced by English than other forms of Danish were, although it is obvious that relative proximity would be relevant.

It is thought that Old Norse as such had probably died out in northern England by the 1200s (Townend 2002). But if English in that part of Britain had started going through gender loss during the 900s at the latest, that gives ample chronological scope for this particular aspect of the anglicisation of any form of Old Norse to be carried back to Jutland.

In discussing how this 'carrying back' might have taken place, Perridon says (1997: 261) that any 'explanation has to start with the fact that West Jutland mainly consists of barren moorlands, which in the past could hardly sustain its population'. This led to a greater proportion of people from this area emigrating to Britain than from anywhere else in Denmark, and 'it is not unreasonable that those who returned to West Jutland after having accumulated some wealth in England' could

---

[7] 'he had difficulty distinguishing between neuter and common-gender words'.

have been, as successful re-migrants, rather influential. Nielsen (2007) points out that contact between English and Jutland Danish may have also been due to the presence of numerous English Christian missionaries in Jutland, particularly during the reign of King Canute from 1016 to 1035.

Nielsen (2007: 102) queries Perridon's thesis on the grounds that the linguistic outcomes were not the same in England and West Jutland. As I have noted above, however, they are not so very different because, in both cases, grammatical gender has been entirely lost and replaced by a noun-class system based on semantics. The difference simply lies in the fact that while the West Jutland classes are, as in English, male, female and neuter, the neuter class in West Jutish is additionally subdivided into mass and count categories. This argument makes particular sense since a not totally dissimilar development has actually also occurred in certain English dialects, as chronicled in a detailed account by Siemund (2008). Traditional dialects in the English southwest, for example, have developed the expression of a pronominal category difference between count and mass nouns (Wagner 2005), such that inanimate count nouns are pronominalised with *he* but mass nouns with *it*:

Pass the loaf – he's over there.
vs.
I likes this bread – it be very tasty.

Nielsen also argues that it could just as well be the case that 'the linguistic parallels between English and the Jutland dialect may have arisen independently ... not least because the two idioms have a shared Germanic heritage which, to some extent, enables them to move in the same direction without being in direct contact' (2007: 102) – a clear reference to 'drift' (Sapir 1921). But we can ask: how likely is it, if we look at the North Sea gender-loss area *as a whole*, that we can explain the remarkably coherent geographical configuration of this phenomenon simply through drift? That drift was operative in all and only this contiguous area would in itself seem to be too much of a coincidence.

On the other hand, a diffusional spread from England to West Jutland, and from there eastwards and southwards to most of the rest of Jutland and down into Schleswig, would account for all of the Danish, Schleswig Low German and North Frisian gender-loss area indicated on Map 1.

It is also quite possible that language shift played a role in the formation of the kernel areas. During the rapid language shift which occurred as speakers of South Jutish abandoned their North Germanic mother tongue and shifted to Low German in the nineteenth century, as a result of political developments and border changes (Kusmenko 1996; Arboe 2008), the two-gender system was simply transferred intact from South Jutish to Low German – a point alluded to in the title of Bock (1933) 'Niederdeutsch auf dänischem Substrat'.

Similarly, the western Low Saxon dialects of Low German – the Groningen and Overijssel variants in the Netherlands; and Ostfriesisch, Oldenburgish and

Emsländisch in Germany – are spoken on or adjacent to territory that is or was Frisian speaking. The Ostfriesisch, Oldenburgish and Emsländisch zones were East Frisian-speaking until the 1400s, and Frisian survived there as a minority language until the 1500s (Matras & Reershemius 2003).

English

We still, however, need to account for the initial loss of gender in English which triggered off the whole process in the first place. Lass, like Perridon with Bergen, sees a role for phonological change, including in this case the weakening and loss of final unstressed syllables, as well as grammatical and semantic developments. But he also attributes the loss of gender mainly to 'a shift towards a system in which sex (or the lack of it) became the primary or sole determinant' as well as 'gradual relaxation of grammatical constraints' (Lass 2000: 106–7) and the resolution of conflicts between natural and grammatical gender in favour of the natural – as in the case of the neuter noun *cild* 'child' referring to a boy being treated as a masculine. Lass's view is in some measure supported by Curzan's (2003) analysis, as we have noted, which showed that masculine and feminine inanimates were increasingly treated as neuters during the relevant period. But this is not really an explanation. It is more of a description of what happened, which does not help us understand why this process took place – nor, crucially, why it took place in English and not in the other early medieval Germanic languages.

The sociolinguist, however, does see two clues here which suggest that contact can once again be invoked as an explanatory factor in gender loss. First, Jones (1998) disputes Lass's interpretation. According to him, texts from the relevant period show many instances of unetymological gender assignment which do *not* involve reassignment according to natural gender. What we see in the texts can be interpreted simply as increasing uncertainty about which noun has which gender – which reminds us of Kusmenko's (2000) argument about cross-linguistic gender confusion and gender simplification.

Second, Lass points out – and many other writers on this topic are agreed (see e.g., Bolze 2007) – that 'like many other structural simplifications in English, gender loss began in the north' (Lass 2000: 107). As we just noted, the gender-loss process can be seen to be under way in Old English in texts from the 900s in the north of the Old English-speaking area. Over the next three centuries, the loss gradually spread from the north to the south, and appears to have been complete by 1300 everywhere except in Kent in the far southeast of England, where grammatical gender lingered on somewhat longer, until about 1300.

White (2002, 2003) has argued that the general inflectional attrition which occurred as a consequence of Late British/Old English contact, especially in the north (see Chapter 3), was later reinforced there by contact with Old Norse (see

Chapter 4). This meant that the North experienced a double dose of language contact, a fact which explains, he suggests, why this part of England was by far the most innovating region generally in the late Old English/early Middle English period. White argues that the English southeast was the most conservative area because it experienced no significant contact with either Old Norse or Late British, while East Anglia and the southwest were intermediate in terms of degree of change because they experienced only one contact phase each: contact with Old Norse in East Anglia; and contact with Late British in Wessex.

III Contact and Diffusion: Bergen Again

The overall picture that we have painted here, then, is one where gender simplification has affected all of the western seaboard of the North Sea, as well as the eastern seaboard from the Rhine Delta up to Western Jutland and beyond. This geographical distribution suggests that the change was spread as a result of maritime, notably trading, contacts, especially when we recall that Bergen, Copenhagen and Stockholm have long histories as maritime trading ports.

The sociolinguistic pattern is a complex one, with long-term contact between geographically neighbouring communities leading to the diffusion of linguistic innovations gradually outwards from areas where they have already become established; but at the same time, long-distance contacts between urban centres, as a result of communication and trading patterns, leads to the development of exclaves such as Bergen, Copenhagen and Stockholm. Spatial diffusion, as already noted, takes two rather different forms. Long-term contact between geographically neighbouring communities leads, through face-to-face interaction and accommodation (Trudgill 1986), to the diffusion of linguistic innovations gradually outwards across neighbouring territories. But at the same time, long-distance contact between urban centres also occurs as a result of communication and trading patterns, with movements of speakers from one place to another leading to the jumping of innovations from one urban area to another (Chambers & Trudgill 1998).

This means that we can now conclude this chapter in the place where we began it, in Bergen. Gender simplification clearly took place in Bergen because of face-to-face contact-induced simplification in the town itself, as a result of the acquisition of Norwegian by non-native speakers, as argued for by Jahr, Nesse and others. But we can explain gender loss in Bergen Norwegian as resulting also from the fact that this was a town which received the long-term diffusion of the already established innovation *both* from the kernel area of northern Holland, *and* from the secondary focal area of western Jutland, which had been seeded with gender loss from the primary kernel area of Britain.

In the case of the West Jutlandic focal area, Hanseatic trade brought large numbers of northern Low German speakers to Bergen over a long period of time.

It is known (Rambø 2008) that traders from Lübeck played an especially important role. Lübeck itself is actually situated in the modern Holstein three-gender area, but the two-gender Schleswig- and Jutish-speaking areas were not far away – the distance from Lübeck to the Eckernförde-Tönning line is only about 50 miles/80 kilometres – and so it is not difficult to imagine that ships travelling out from Lübeck might well have been carrying a number of two-gender speakers. We also know that there were very many Danes in Bergen – Nesse (2002) cites figures showing that in the 200 years from 1550 more than a quarter of the foreigners resident in Bergen were from Denmark – and, especially in the earlier years, the West Jutland town of Ribe played a highly important part in North Sea trading activity (Rambø 2008).

Second, in the case of the north Holland kernel area, the long-term presence of a Dutch population in Bergen up until the late 1500s is made clear in Wubs-Mrozewicz (2008), who discusses the role in Bergen of the Dutch 'Hollanders', mostly from Amsterdam; and of 'Overijsselers', mostly from Kampen, Zwolle and Deventer. Notice that the former group were northern Low Franconian-speaking, while the latter group were speakers of Low German–western Low Saxon, both groups thus bringing a two-gender system to Bergen with them. The 'Dutch' presence probably also included actual Frisian speakers. A important role for Groningen in the linguistic history of Bergen also seems very likely: it was a semi-independent entity and a full member of the Hanseatic League which was situated in an originally Frisian and subsequently Low Saxon-speaking two-gender area.

In conclusion: Wubs-Mrozewicz (2008: 123) writes, referring to Helle (1982) and Nedkvitne (1983), that, during the 1500s, the Hanseatic population of Bergen could constitute as much as 30 per cent of the inhabitants in the summer months – and thus perhaps more than half of the entire adult male population. So, during the crucial decades when gender loss was taking place in Bergen, there were, walking around the streets of the town, such very large numbers of speakers of English, Scots (Rambø 2008: 329), Frisian, northern Dutch, western Low Saxon, Schleswig Low Saxon and Jutish-Danish – men who had actually brought their own zero- or two-gender systems with them – that we can readily consider contact between them and the indigenous Norwegian population as an important factor in the spread of the loss of the feminine gender. Given that Bergen received, not just non-native speakers of Norwegian as such, but also specifically immigrants – and thus linguistic influences – from both of the kernel areas where gender-simplification had originally been set in motion by earlier language contact events, it is really no surprise that the town lost the feminine gender so early on and so completely as it did.

In this respect, of course, Bergen Norwegian stands in total and dramatic contrast to most other dialects of Norwegian, as well as to Norwegian's various linguistic relatives such as High German, Icelandic and Faroese which still possess the ancient Indo-European three-gender system as they have faithfully preserved this across six millennia.

Sources

1. The uniformitarian hypothesis and prehistoric sociolinguistics. In (ed.), *Proceedings of the 20th Hungarian Sociolinguistics Conference*. Budapest. 2018
2. Sociolinguistic typology: social structure and linguistic complexity. In A. Y. Aikhenvald & R. M. W. Dixon (eds.), *The Cambridge handbook of linguistic typology*. Cambridge: Cambridge University Press, 124–50. 2017.
3. A tale of two copulas: language-contact speculations on first-millennium England. In Michael Schulte & Robert Nedoma (eds.), *Language and literacy in early Scandinavia and beyond = NOWELE 62/63*, 285–320. 2011.
4. Contact-related processes of change in the early history of English. In M. Kytö & P. Pahta (eds.), *English historical linguistics*. Cambridge: Cambridge University Press, 318–34. 2016.
5. English dialect 'default singulars', *was* vs. *were*, Verners Law, and Germanic dialects. *Journal of English Linguistics* 36, 341–53. 2008.
6. Linguistic and social typology: the Austronesian migrations and phoneme inventories. *Linguistic Typology*, 8, 305–20. 2004.
7. The Hellenistic koiné and what we can learn from it. Paper presented at the 1st International Conference on Koine, koines and the formation of Standard Modern Greek. Thessaloniki. 2017.
8. Gender reduction in Bergen Norwegian: a North-Sea perspective. In Ernst Håkon Jahr & Lennart Elmevik (eds.), *Contact between Low German and Scandinavian in the late Middle Ages – 25 years of research*. Uppsala: Royal Gustavus Academy, 57–74. 2012. Gender maintenance and loss in Totenmålet, English, and other major Germanic varieties. In Terje Lohndal (ed.), *In search of universal grammar: from old Norse to Zoque*. Amsterdam: Benjamins, 77–108. 2013.

References

Adams, James. 2003. *Bilingualism and the Latin language*. Cambridge: Cambridge University Press.

Adams, James. 2007. *The regional diversification of Latin 200 BC–AD 600*. Cambridge: Cambridge University Press.

Adger, David, & Jennifer Smith. 2005. Variation and the minimalist program. In Leonie Cornips & Karen Corrigan (eds.), *Syntax and variation: reconciling the biological and the social*. Amsterdam: Benjamins, 149–78.

Adrados, F. R. 2005. *A history of the Greek language: from its origins to the present*. Leiden: Brill.

Ahlqvist, Anders. 2010. Early Celtic and English. *Australian Celtic Journal* 9: 1–17.

Aikhenvald, Alexandra. 2003. *A grammar of Tariana, from Northwest Amazonia*. Cambridge: Cambridge University Press.

Aikhenvald, Aleksandra. 2004. *Evidentials*. Oxford: Oxford University Press.

Aikhenvald, Alexandra. 2007. Typological distinctions in word-formation. In T. Shopen (ed.), *Language typology and syntactic description*, 2nd ed. Cambridge: Cambridge University Press, 1–65.

Aikhenvald, Aleksandra. 2008. *The Manambu language of East Sepik, Papua New Guinea*. Oxford: Oxford University Press.

Aikhenvald, Aleksandra. 2011. Multiple marking of syntactic function and polysynthetic nouns in Tariana. In Aleksandra Aikenvald & R. M. W. Dixon (eds.), *Language at large*. Leiden: Brill, 377–93.

Alarcos, E. 1983. *Estudis lingüistics catalans*. 2nd ed. Barcelona.

Algeo, John. 2001. External history. In John Algeo (ed.), *The Cambridge history of the English language vol. VI: English in North America*. Cambridge: Cambridge University Press, 1–58.

Allen, W. S. 1987. *Vox Graeca*. 3rd ed. Cambridge: Cambridge University Press.

Andersen, Henning. 1988. Center and periphery: adoption, diffusion, and spread. In Jacek Fisiak (ed.), *Historical dialectology: regional and social*. Berlin: Mouton de Gruyter, 39–84.

Anderson, Stephen R. 1985. Inflectional morphology. In Tim Shopen (ed.), *Language typology and syntactic fieldwork III*. Cambridge: Cambridge University Press, 150–201.

Andersson, Lars Gunnar. 2011. Var lever bestämdhetsformer som *dörra* kvar? *Folia Scandinavica Posnaniensia* 12: 23–32.

Anderwald, Lieselotte. 2001. *Was/were*-variation in non-standard British English today. *English World-Wide* 22: 1–21.

Anderwald, Lieselotte. 2002. *Negation in nonstandard British English*. London: Routledge.

Anthony, David. 2007. *The horse, the wheel, and language*. Princeton: Princeton University Press.

Arboe, Torben. 2008. Pronominal repræsentation i danske dialekter. In Inger Schoonderbeek Hansen & Peter Widell (eds.), *12. møde om udforskningen af dansk sprog*. Århus: Nordisk Institut Aarhus Universitet, 29–38.

Aronoff, Mark. 1994. *Morphology by itself: stems and inflectional classes*. Cambridge: MIT Press.

Bailey, Charles, & Karl Maroldt. 1977. The French lineage of English. In Jürgen Meisel (ed.), *Langues en contact – pidgins – creoles*. Tübingen: Narr, 21–53.

Baldi, Philip, & Richard Page. 2006. Review of Vennemann Europa Vasconica – Europa Semitica (2003). *Lingua* 116: 2183–220.

Baldinger, Kurt. 1958. *Die Herausbildung der Sprachräume auf der Pyrenäenhalbinsel*. Berlin: Akademie.

Bammesberger, Alfred & Theo Vennemann (eds.). 2003. *Languages of prehistoric Europe*. Heidelberg: Winter.

Beal, Joan. 2004. English dialects in the North of England: morphology and syntax. In Bernd Kortmann & Edgar Schneider (eds.), *A handbook of varieties of English II: morphology and syntax*, Berlin: Mouton de Gruyter, 114–41.

Beauvoir, J. M. 1915. *Los Shelknam: indígenas de la Tierra del Fuego*. Buenos Aires: Talleres Gráficos de la Compañía General de Fósforos.

Bengtson, John (ed.). 2008. *In hot pursuit of language in prehistory*. Amsterdam: Benjamins.

Bergmann, Gunter. 1990. Upper Saxon. In Charles Russ (ed.), *The dialects of modern German: a linguistic survey*. London: Routledge, 290–312.

Bergsland, Knut. 1986. Comparative Eskimo-Aleut phonology and lexicon. *Aikakauskirja/ Journal de la Société finno-ougrienne* 80: 63–137.

Berman, Howard. 1996. The position of Molala in Plateau Penutian. *International Journal of American Linguistics*, 62(1): 1–30.

Bernard, John. 1981. Australian pronunciation. In *The Macquarie dictionary*. Sydney: Macquarie Library, 18–27.

Bethge, Richard. 1900. Konjugation des Urgermanischen. In F. Dieter (ed.), *Laut- und Formenlehre der altgermanischen Dialekte*. Leipzig: Reisland, 345–91.

Bickel, Balthasar, & Johanna Nichols. 2020. Linguistic typology and hunter-gatherer languages. In Tom Güldemann, Patrick McConvell & Richard Rhodes (eds.), *The language of hunter-gatherers*. Cambridge: Cambridge University Press.

Biggs, Bruce. 1978. The history of Polynesian phonology. In S. A. Wurm & L. Carrington (eds.), *Second international conference on Austronesian linguistics: proceedings*. Canberra: Australian National University, 691–716.

Biraben, Jean-Noël. 1979. Essai sur l'évolution du nombre des hommes. *Population* 1: 13–24.

Bishko, Charles Julian. 1975. The Spanish and Portuguese reconquest. In H. W. Hazard (ed.), *A history of the crusades*. vol. III. Madison: Wisconsin University Press.

Blomkvist, Nils. 1979. Kalmars uppkomst och äldsta tid. In I. Hammarström (ed.), *Kalmar stads historia I: Kalmarområdets forntid och stadens äldsta utveckling*. Kalmar: Kulturnämnden i Kalmar.

Blust, Robert. 1999. Subgrouping, circularity and extinction: some issues in Austronesian comparative linguistics. In Elizabeth Zeitoun & Paul Li (eds.), *Selected papers from the eighth international conference on Austronesian linguistics*, 31–94. Taipei: Academia Sinica.

Blust, Robert. 2005. Must sound change be linguistically motivated? *Diachronica* 22: 219–69.

Blust, Robert. 2009. *The Austronesian languages.* Canberra: Australian National University.

Blust, Robert. 2012. Hawu vowel metathesis. *Oceanic Linguistics* 51: 207–33.

Bock, Karl Nielsen. 1933. *Niederdeutsch auf dänischem Substrat: Studien zur Dialektgeographie Südostschleswigs.* Marburg: Levin & Munksgaard.

Bolze, Christine. 2007. *On the simplification of nominal and verbal inflections in Late Old Northumbrian in comparison to Late West Saxon.* University of Potsdam: MA thesis.

Bonnard, Henri, & Claude Régnier. 1997. *Petite grammaire de l'ancien français.* Paris: Magnard.

Bornkessel, Ina. 2002. The argument dependency model: a neurocognitive approach to incremental interpretation. Potsdam: Potsdam University PhD thesis.

Bradley, Henry. 1904. *The making of English.* London: Macmillan.

Branford, William. 1994. English in South Africa. In Robert Burchfield (ed.), *The Cambridge history of the English language vol. 5: English in Britain and overseas – origins and development.* Cambridge: Cambridge University Press, 182–429.

Braunmüller, Kurt. 2008. Das älteste Germanische: offene Fragen und mögliche Antworten. *Sprachwissenschaft* 33: 373–403.

Breivik, Leiv Egil, & Ernst Håkon Jahr (eds.). *Language change: contributions to the study of its causes.* Berlin: Mouton de Gruyter, 227–37.

Bremmer, Rolf. 2009. *An introduction to Old Frisian.* Amsterdam: Benjamins.

Britain, David. 2002. Diffusion, levelling, simplification and reallocation in past tense BE in the English Fens. *Journal of Sociolinguistics* 6: 16–43.

Britain, David. 2007. Grammatical variation in England. In David Britain (ed.), *Language in the British Isles.* 2nd ed. Cambridge: Cambridge University Press, 75–104.

Browning, Robert. 1969. *Medieval and Modern Greek.* Cambridge: Cambridge University Press.

Bruyne, Jacques de. 1995. *A comprehensive Spanish grammar.* Oxford: Blackwell.

Bynon, Theodora. 1977. *Historical linguistics.* Cambridge University Press.

Callebout, Bruno, & Hugo Ryckeboer. 1997. Contacts linguistiques français-néerlandais dans le Nord de la France. In P. Nelde, Z. Stary, W. Wölck & H. Goebl (eds.), *Contact linguistics II.* Berlin: Walter de Gruyter, 1240–52.

Campbell, Lyle. 1997. On the linguistic prehistory of Finno-Ugric. In R. Hickey & S. Puppel (eds.), *Language history and linguistic modelling: a festschrift for Jacek Fisiak on his 60th birthday.* Berlin: Mouton de Gruyter, 829–62.

Campbell, Lyle, & William Poser. 2008. *Language classification: history and method.* Cambridge: Cambridge University Press.

Capella, Joseph. 1997. The development of theory about automated patterns of face-to-face human interaction. In G. Philipsen & T. Albrecht (eds.), *Developing communication theories.* Albany: State University of New York Press, 57–83.

Carpenter, David. 2004. *The struggle for mastery: the Penguin history of Britain 1066–1284.* London: Penguin.

Carstairs-McCarthy, Andrew. 2010. *The evolution of morphology.* Oxford: Oxford University Press.

Chambers, J. K. 1995. *Sociolinguistic theory.* Oxford: Blackwell.

Chambers, J. K. 2000. Universal sources of the vernacular. In Ulrich Ammon, Peter Nelde, & Klaus Mattheier (eds.), *Sociolinguistica: international yearbook of European sociolinguistics*. Tübingen: Niemeyer, 11–15.

Chambers, J. K. 2001. Vernacular universals. In J. M. Fontana, L. McNally, M. T. Turell & E. Vallduví (eds.), *ICLaVE 1: proceedings of the First International Conference on Language Variation in Europe*. Barcelona: Universitat Pompeu Fabra.

Chambers, J. K. 2003. *Sociolinguistic theory: linguistic variation and its social implications,* Oxford: Blackwell.

Chambers, J. K. 2004. Dynamic typology and vernacular universals. In B. Kortmann (ed.), *Dialectology meets typology*. Berlin: Mouton de Gruyter.

Chambers, J. K., & Peter Trudgill. 1998. *Dialectology*. 2nd ed. Cambridge: Cambridge University Press.

Chapman, Kenneth. 1962. *Icelandic-Norwegian linguistic relationships*. Oslo: Universitetsforlaget.

Clackson, James, & Geoffrey Horrocks. 2007. *The Blackwell history of the Latin language*. Oxford: Blackwell.

Clark, Ross. 1976. *Aspects of proto-Polynesian syntax*. Auckland: Linguistic Society of New Zealand.

Clark, Ross. 1994. The Polynesian outliers as a locus of language contact. In T. Dutton & D. Tryon (eds.), *Language contact and change in the Austronesian world*. Berlin: Mouton, 109–40.

Coates, Richard. 2007. Invisible Britons: the view from linguistics. In N. J. Higham (ed.), *Britons in Anglo-Saxon England*. Manchester: Manchester University Press, 172–91.

Coates, Richard. 2009. A glimpse through a dirty window into an unlit house: names of some North-west European islands. In Wolfgang Ahrens, Sheila Embleton & André Lapierre (eds.), *Proceedings of the 23rd International Congress of Onomastic Sciences*. Toronto: York University, 228–42.

Combrink, Johan. 1978. Afrikaans: its origin and development. In L. Lanham & K. Prinsloo (eds.), *Language and communication studies in South Africa*. Cape Town: Oxford University Press, 69–95.

Comrie, Bernard. 1980. Morphology and word order reconstruction: problems and prospects. In J. Fisiak (ed.), *Historical morphology*. The Hague: Mouton, 83–96.

Comrie, Bernard. 1989. *Language universals and linguistic typology*. Oxford: Blackwell.

Comrie, Bernard. 1992. Before complexity. In J. Hawkins & M. Gell-Mann (eds.), *The evolution of human languages*. Santa Fe: Westview Press, 193–211.

Craig Christy, Thomas. 1983. *Uniformitarianism in linguistics*. Amsterdam: John Benjamins.

Cressman, Luther. 1956. Klamath prehistory: the prehistory of the culture of the Klamath Lake Area, Oregon. *Transactions of the American Philosophical Society* 46: 375–513.

Cubberley, Paul. 2002. *Russian: a linguistic introduction*. Cambridge: Cambridge University Press.

Curzan, Anne. 2003. *Gender shifts in the history of English*. Cambridge: Cambridge University Press.

Dahl, Östen. 2004. *The growth and maintenance of linguistic complexity*. Amsterdam: Benjamins.

Dahl, Östen. 2015. Linguistic mysteries around the North Sea. In P. Shaw, B. Erman & P. Sundkvist (eds.), *From clerks to corpora: essays on the English language yesterday and today*. Stockholm: Stockholm University Press, 17–34.

Dahlbäck, Göran. 1998. Invandring – särskilt tysk – till Sverige under medeltiden. In Lars Nilsson & Sven Lilja (eds.), *Invandrarna och lokalsamhället*. Stockholm: Stad- och Kommunhistoriska Institutet, 11–30.

Dalton-Puffer, Christiane. 1995. Middle English is a creole and its opposite: on the value of plausible speculation. In Jacek Fisiak (ed.), *Linguistic change under contact conditions*. Berlin: Mouton de Gruyter, 35–50.

Dalton-Puffer, Christiane. 1996. *The French influence on Middle English morphology: a corpus-based study of derivation*. Berlin: Mouton de Gruyter.

Danchev, Andrei. 1997. The Middle English creolisation hypothesis revisited. In Jacek Fisiak (ed.), *Studies in Middle English linguistics*. Berlin: Mouton de Gruyter, 79–108.

Darot, Mireille, & Christine Pauleau. 1993. Situation du français en Nouvelle-Calédonie. In D. Robillard & M. Benjamin (eds.), *Le français dans l'espace francophone*. Paris: Champion, 283–301.

Davidson, Herbert. 1990. *Han, hon, den: genusutvecklingen i svenskan under nysvensk tid*. Lund: Lund University Press.

de Reuse, Willem 2006. *A practical grammar of the San Carlos Apache language*. Munich: Lincom Europa.

De Vogelaer, Gunther. 2004. Person marking in Dutch dialects. In B. Kortmann (ed.), *Dialectology meets typology: dialect grammar from a cross-linguistic perspective*. Berlin: Mouton de Gruyter, 181–210.

De Vogelaer, Gunther. 2005. *Persoonsmarkering in de dialecten in het nederlandse taalgebied*. Ghent: Ghent University Press.

De Vogelaer, Gunther. 2009. Changing pronominal gender in Dutch; transmission or diffusion? In S. Tsipaklou, M. Karyolemou & P. Pavlou (eds.), *Language variation: European perspectives II*. Amsterdam: Benjamins, 71–80.

De Vogelaer, Gunther, & Johan van der Auwera. 2010. When typological rara generate rarissima: analogical extension of verbal agreement in Dutch dialects. In J. Wohlgemuth & M. Cysouw (eds.), *Rara and rarissima: documenting the fringes of linguistic diversity*. Berlin: De Gruyter, 47–72.

De Vogelaer, Gunther, & Gert De Sutter, 2011. The geography of gender change: pronominal and adnominal gender in Flemish dialects of Dutch. *Language Sciences* 33, 192–205.

Dediu, Dan, & Stephen Levinson. 2013. On the antiquity of language: the reinterpretation of Neandertal linguistic capacities and its consequences. *Frontiers in Psychology* 2013: 1–17.

DeLancey, Scott. 1991. Chronological strata of suffix classes in the Klamath verb. *International Journal of American Linguistics* 57: 426–45.

DeLancey, Scott, & Victor Golla. 1997. The Penutian hypothesis: retrospect and prospect. *International Journal of American Linguistics* 63, 1: 171–202.

Delsing, Lars-Olof. 2002. The morphology of Old Nordic II: Old Swedish and Old Danish. In O. Bandle et al. (eds.), *The Nordic Languages I*. Berlin: Mouton de Gruyter, 925–40.

Demiral, Sukru, Ina Bornkessel-Schlesewsky & Matthias Schleweski. 2008. On the universality of language comprehension strategies: evidence from Turkish. *Cognition* 106: 484–500.

Derbyshire, Desmond. 1977. Word order universals and the existence of OVS languages. *Linguistic Inquiry* 8: 590–9.

Dieter, Ferdinand (ed.). 1900. *Laut– und Formenlehre der altgermanischen Dialekte.* Leipzig: Reisland.

Dixon, R. M. W. 1972. *The Dyirbal language of North Queensland.* Cambridge: Cambridge University Press.

Dixon, R. M. W. 1997. *The rise and fall of languages.* Cambridge: Cambridge University Press.

Dixon, R. M. W. 2002. *Australian languages: their nature and development.* Cambridge: Cambridge University Press.

Dixon, R. M. W. 2010. *Basic linguistic theory 2: grammatical topics.* Oxford: Oxford University Press.

Donaldson, Bruce. 1993. *A grammar of Afrikaans.* Berlin: Mouton de Gruyter.

Donaldson, Bruce. 1994. Afrikaans. In E. König & J. Van der Auwera (eds.), *The Germanic languages.* London: Routledge, 478–504.

Dresher, B. Eland. 2000. Analogical levelling of vowel length in West Germanic. In Aditi Lahiri (ed.), *Analogy, levelling, markedness: principles of change in phonology and morphology.* Berlin: Mouton de Gruyter, 47–70.

Drinka, Bridget. 2003. The development of the perfect in Indo-European: stratigraphic evidence of prehistoric areal influence. In H. Andersen (ed.), *Language contacts in prehistory: studies in stratigraphy.* Amsterdam: Benjamins, 77–105.

Dryer, Matthew. 1989. Large linguistic areas and language sampling. *Studies in Language* 13: 257–292.

Dubé, Jaïmé. 2013. Reconsidering the 'isolating protolanguage hypothesis' in the evolution of morphology. In C. Cathcart, I.-H. Chen, G. Finley, S. Kang, C. Sandy & E. Stickles (eds). Proceedings of the 37th Annual Meeting of the Berkeley Linguistics Society, 76–90.

Duke, Janet. 2010, Gender reduction and loss in Germanic: three case studies. In D. Nübling, A. Dammel & S. Kürschner (eds.), *Kontrastive Germanistische Linguistik.* Hildesheim: Olms.

Dumond, Don. 1987. A reexamination of Aleut prehistory. *American Anthropologist* 89(1): 32–56.

Durrell, Martin. 1989. Westphalian and Eastphalian. In C. Russ (ed.), *The dialects of modern German.* London: Routledge, 59–90.

Durrell, Martin. 1999. Zum Ausgleich der Ablautalternanzen im Niederdeutschen. In Peter Wagener (ed.), *Sprachformen: Deutsch und Niederdeutsch in europäischen Bezügen.* Stuttgart: Steiner, 39–49.

Ebert, Wolfgang, Theodor Frings, Kathe Gleissner, Rudolf Kötzschke & Gerhart Streitberg. 1936. *Kulturräume und Kulturströmungen im mitteldeutschen Osten.* Halle: Niemeyer.

Eisikovits, Edina. 1991. Variation in subject-verb agreement in Inner Sydney English. In Jenny Cheshire (ed.), *English around the world: sociolinguistic perspectives.* Cambridge: Cambridge University Press, 235–55.

Ekwall, Eilert. 1960. *The concise Oxford dictionary of place-names,* 4th ed. Oxford: Oxford University Press.

Elcock, W. D. 1960. *The Romance languages.* London : Faber & Faber.

Emonds, Joseph, & Jan Terje Faarlund. 2014. *English: the language of the Vikings.* Olomouc: Palacký University Press.

Enger, Hans-Olav. 2010. Sound laws, inflectional change and the autonomy of morphology. In Angeliki Ralli et al. (eds.). *Morphology and diachrony*. Patras: Univeristy of Patras.

Etxepare, Ricardo. 2003. Valency and argument structure in the Basque Verb. In Jose Ignacio Hualde & Jon Ortiz de Urbina (eds.), *A grammar of Basque*. Berlin: Mouton de Gruyter, 363–426.

Evans, D. Simon. 1964. *A Grammar of Middle Welsh*. Dublin: Dublin Institute for Advanced Studies.

Evans, Nicholas. 2010. *Dying words: endangered languages and what they have to tell us*. Oxford: Wiley-Blackwell.

Evans, Nicholas, & Hans-Jürgen Sasse. 2002. Introduction: problems of polysynthesis. In N. Evans & H.-J. Sasse (eds.), *Problems of polysynthesis*. Berlin: Akademie Verlag, 1–13.

Faarlund, Jan Terje. 2005. Syntactic developments from Old Nordic to Early Modern Nordic. In Oskar Bandle, Kurt Braunmüller & Ernst Håkon Jahr (eds.), *The Nordic languages: an international handbook of the history of the North Germanic languages*. Berlin: de Gruyter, 1149–60.

Fairbanks, Gordon. 1977. Case inflections in Indo-European. *Journal of Indo-European Studies* 5: 1–31.

Feist, Sigmund. 1932. The origin of the Germanic languages and the Europeanization of North Europe. *Language* 8: 245–54.

Ferguson, Charles. 1959. The Arabic koiné. *Language* 25: 616–630.

Fernandes, Maria Alice. 2011. The diminutive suffixes of southern Portuguese: an example of new dialect formation by koineization. In *International Symposium on Limits and Areas in Dialectology*. Lisbon: University of Lisbon.

Ferrando, Antoni. 1989. La formació històrica del valencià. In A. Ferrando (ed.), *Segon Congrés Internacional de la Llengua Catalana. vol. VIII. Àrea 7. Història de la Llengua*. València: Institut de Filologia Valenciana, 399–428.

Filppula, Markku. 2003. More on the English progressive and the Celtic connection. In Hildegard Tristram (ed.), *The Celtic Englishes III*. Heidelberg: Winter, 150–68.

Filppula, Markku, Juhani Klemola & Heli Pitkänen (eds.). 2002. *The Celtic roots of English*. Joensuu: University Press.

Filppula, Markku, Juhani Klemola & Heli Paulasto (eds.). 2008. *Vernacular universals and language contacts: evidence from varieties of English and beyond*. London: Routledge.

Fischer, Steven. 2001. Mangarevan doublets: preliminary evidence for Proto-Southeastern Polynesian. *Oceanic Linguistics* 40: 112–24.

Foley, William. 1986. *The Papuan languages of New Guinea*. Cambridge: Cambridge University Press.

Foley, William. 1997. *Anthropological linguistics*. Oxford: Blackwell.

Forby, Robert. [1830] 1969. *The vocabulary of East Anglia*. [London: Nichols] New York: Kelly.

Fortescue, Michael. 1992. Morphophonemic complexity and typological stability in a polysynthetic language family. *International Journal of American Linguistics* 58: 242–8.

Fortescue, Michael. 1998. *Language relations across the Bering Strait: reappraising the archaeological and linguistic evidence*. London: Cassell.

Fortescue, Michael. 2002. The rise and fall of polysynthesis in the Eskimo-Aleut family. In N. Evans & H.-J. Sasse (eds.), *Problems of polysynthesis*. Berlin: Akademie Verlag. 282–97.

Fortescue, Michael, & Edward Vajda. forthcoming. *Mid-Holocene language connections between Asia and North America*.

Fortson, Benjamin. 2010. *Indo-European language and culture*. Oxford: Blackwell.

Fox, Cyril. 1932. *The personality of Britain: its influence on inhabitant and invader in prehistoric and early historic times*. Cardiff: National Museum of Wales.

Frings, Theodor. 1932. *Sprache und Siedlung im mitteldeutschen Osten*. Leipzig: Hirzel.

Gabelentz, Georg von der. 1901. *Die Sprachwissenschaft: ihre Aufgaben, Methoden und bisherigen Ergebnisse*. 2nd ed. Leipzig: Weigel.

Galmés de Fuentes, Álvaro. 1983. *Dialectología mozárabe*. Madrid: Gredos.

Gamble, Clive. 1986. *The palaeolithic settlement of Europe*. Cambridge: Cambridge University Press.

Garman, Michael. 1990. *Psycholinguistics*. Cambridge: Cambridge University.

Garrett, Andrew, & Michiel Weiss (eds.). *Handbook of Indo-European studies*. Oxford: Oxford University Press.

Geerts, Guido. 1966. *Genus en geslacht in de Gouden Eeuw*. Brussells: Belgisch Interuniversitair Centrum voor Neerlandistiek.

Gelling, Margaret. 1993. *Place-names in the landscape: the geographical roots of Britain's place-names*. London: Dent.

Georgiev, Vladimir. 1981. *Introduction to the history of the Indo-European languages*. Sofia: Bulgarian Academy of Sciences.

Geraghty, Paul. 1983. *The history of the Fijian languages*. Honolulu: University of Hawaii Press.

Geraghty, Paul. 1986. The sound system of Proto-Central-Pacific. In P. Geraghty, L. Carrington & S. A. Wurm (eds.), *FOCAL II: Papers from the fourth international conference on Austronesian linguistics*. Canberra: Pacific Linguistics C-94, 289–312.

Givón, Talmy, & Philip Young. 2002. Cooperation and interpersonal manipulation in the society of intimates. In M. Chibatani (ed.), *The grammar of causation and interpersonal manipulation*. Amsterdam: John Benjamins, 23–56.

Givón, Talmy. 1979. *On understanding grammar*. New York: Academic Press.

Givón, Talmy. 1984. *Syntax: a functional-typological introduction*. Amsterdam: Benjamins.

Goldinger, Stephen, Paul Luce & David Pisoni. 1989. Priming lexical neighbours of spoken words: effects of competition and inhibition. *Journal of Memory and Language* 28: 501–18.

Goltz, Reinhard, & Alastair Walker. 1989. North Saxon. In Charles Russ (ed.), *The dialects of Modern German*. London: Routledge, 31–58.

Gordon, E. V. 1957. *An introduction to Old Norse*. Oxford, UK: Clarendon.

Gordon, Elizabeth, Lyle Campbell, Jennifer Hay, Margaret Maclagan & Peter Trudgill. 2004. *New Zealand English: its origins and evolution*. Cambridge: Cambridge University Press.

Görlach, Manfred. 1986. Middle English: a creole? In Dieter Kastovsky & Aleksander Szwedek (eds.), *Linguistics across historical and geographical boundaries*. Berlin: Mouton de Gruyter, 329–44.

Grace, George. 1990. The 'aberrant' (vs. 'exemplary') Melanesian languages. In P. Baldi (ed.), *Linguistic change and reconstruction methodology*. Berlin: Mouton de Gruyter, 155–73.

Greenhill, Simon, Quentin Atkinson, Andrew Meade & Russell Gray. 2010. The shape and tempo of language evolution. *Proceedings of the Royal Society B: Biological Sciences* 277: 2443–50.

Güldemann, Tom, Patrick McConvell & Richard Rhodes. 2020. *The language of hunter-gatherers.* Cambridge: Cambridge University Press.

Hammarström, Göran. 1980. *Australian English: its origins and status.* Hamburg: Buske.

Härke, Heinrich. 2002. Kings and warriors: population and landscape from post-Roman to Norman Britain. In Paul Slack & Ryk Ward (eds.), *The peopling of Britain: the shaping of a human landscape.* Oxford: Oxford University Press, 145–75.

Harlow, Ray. 1987. *A word-list of South Island Maori.* 2nd ed. Auckland: Te Reo.

Harlow, Ray. 2001. *A Maori reference grammar.* Auckland: Longman.

Harris, Martin. 1988. The Romance languages. In Martin Harris & Nigel Vincent (eds.), *The Romance languages.* London: Routledge, 1–25.

Haspelmath, Martin. 2006. Against markedness (and what to replace it with). *Journal of Linguistics* 42: 25–70.

Hassan, Fekri. 1981. *Demographic archaeology.* New York: Academic.

Hatcher, John, & Mark Bailey. 2001. *Modelling the Middle Ages.* Oxford: Oxford University Press.

Haudricourt, André. 1954. De l'origine des tons en vietnamien. *Journal Asiatique* 242: 69–82.

Haudricourt, André. 1961. Richesse en phonèmes et richesse en locateurs. *L'Homme* 1: 5–10.

Haugen, Einar. 1976. *The Scandinavian languages: an introduction to their history.* London: Faber.

Hawkins, John. 1990 [1987]. Germanic languages. In Bernard Comrie (ed.), *The major languages of Western Europe.* London: Routledge, 58–66.

Hawkins, John. 2012. Patterns of asymmetry in argument structure across languages: some principles and puzzles. In Pirkho Suihkonen, Bernard Comrie & Valery Solovyev (eds.), *Argument structure and grammatical relations: a crosslinguistic typology.* Amsterdam: Benjamins.

Hedberg, Nancy, & David Potter. 2010. Equative and predicational copulas in Thai. *Proceedings of the 36th Annual Meeting of the Berkeley Linguistics Society.*

Heide, Eldar. 2003. Felleskjønnet i bergensk: resultat av mellomnedertysk kvantitetspåverknad? *Maal og Minne,* 2003: 23–35.

Helle, Knut. 1982. *Bergen bys historie I: kongssete og kjøpstad – fra opphave til 1536.* Oslo: Universitetsforlaget.

Hickey, Raymond. 2000. On the phonology of gender in Modern German. In R. Matti, T. Nevalainen & M. Saari (eds.), *Gender in grammar and cognition II: manifestations of gender.* Berlin: Mouton de Gruyter, 621–63.

Higham, Nick. (ed.). 2007. *The Britons in Anglo-Saxon England.* Woodbridge: Boydell

Hock, H. H., & Brian Joseph. 1996. *Language history, language change and language relationship.* Berlin: Mouton de Gruyter.

Hodge, Carleton. 1970. The linguistic cycle. *Language Sciences* 13: 1–7.

Hoekstra, Jarich. 1994. Preposition stranding and resumptivity in West Germanic. In Hubert Haider, Susan Olsen & Sten Vikner (eds.), *Studies in comparative Germanic syntax.* Dordrecht: Kluwer, 95–118.

Hoekstra, Jarich. 1996. Transitive pronouns and gender syncretism in Fering-Öömrang. *NOWELE* 27, 45–66.

Hoekstra, Jarich. 2001a. Comparative aspects of Frisian morphology and syntax. In Horst Haider Munske et al (ed.), *Handbook of Frisian studies.* Tübingen: Niemeyer, 775–86.

Hoekstra, Jarich. 2001b. Outline history of West Frisian. In Horst Haider Munske et al (ed.), *Handbook of Frisian studies*. Tübingen: Niemeyer, 722–34.

Hoekstra, Jarich. 2006. Uwz âde Friez'ne tonge, de Halbertsma's jonges en andere genitief-constructies in het Fries. *Taal & Tongval*, 2006: 96–114.

Hoekstra, Jarich. 2010. Die Kasusmarkierung von Eigennamen im Festlandnordfriesischen und in anderen westgermanischen Dialekten. In Antje Dammel, Sebastian Kürschner & Damaris Nübling (eds.), *Kontrastive germanistische Linguistik vol. 2: Germanische Linguistik.* Hildesheim: Olms, 749–79.

Hoijer, Harry 1945. Classificatory verb stems in the Apachean languages. *International Journal of American Linguistics* 11: 13–23.

Hollyman, Kenneth. 1979. Le français en Nouvelle-Calédonie. In A. Valdmann (ed.), *Le français hors de France*. Paris: Champion, 621–9.

Holman, Katherine. 2007. *The northern conquest: Vikings in Britain and Ireland.* Oxford: Signal Books.

Holmberg, Anders, & Jan Rijkhoff. 1998. Word order in the Germanic languages. In Anna Siewierska (ed.), *Constituent order in the languages of Europe*. Berlin: Mouton de Gruyter, 75–104.

Horrocks, Geoffrey. 1997. *Greek: a history of the language and its speakers*. London: Longman.

Hutterer, Claus Jürgen. 1975 [2008]. *Die germanischen Sprachen: ihre Geschichte in Grundzügen.* Budapest: Akadémiai Kiadó. [4th ed. Wiesbaden: VMA-Verlag].

Hymes, Dell. 1974. Speech and language: on the origins and foundations of inequality among speakers. In M. Bloomfield & E. Haugen (eds.), *Language as a human problem*. New York: Norton, 45–71.

Itkonen, Terho. 1983. Välikatsaus suomen kielen juuriin. *Virittäjä* 87: 190–229, 349–86.

Jackson, Kenneth 1953. *Language and history in early Britain*. Edinburgh: Edinburgh University Press.

Jahr, Ernst Håkon. 1995. Nedertysk og nordisk: språksamfunn og språkkontakt i Hansatida. In E. H. Jahr (ed.), *Nordisk og nedertysk: språkkontakt og språkutvilking i Norden i seinmellomalderen*. Oslo: Novus, 9–28.

Jahr, Ernst Håkon. 1998. Sociolinguistics in historical language contact: the Scandinavian languages and Low German during the Hanseatic period. In E. H. Jahr (ed.), *Language change: advances in historical sociolinguistics*. Berlin: Mouton de Gruyter, 119–13.

Jahr, Ernst Håkon. 2001. Historical sociolinguistics: the role of Low German language contact in the Scandinavian typological split of the late Middle Ages. *Lingua Posnaniensis* 43, 95–104.

Jakobson, Roman. 1929. Remarques sur l'évolution phonologique du Russe comparée à celle des autres langues Slaves =Travaux du Cercle Linguistique de Prague 2.

Janse, Mark. 2009. Greek-Turkish language contact in Asia Minor. *Études Helléniques/ Hellenic Studies* 17, 1: 37–54.

Jespersen, Otto. 1894. *Progress in language*. London: Swan Sonnenschein.

Jespersen, Otto. 1922. *Language: its nature, development and origin*. London: Allen and Unwin.

Jones, Bob Morris. 2010. *Tense and aspect in informal Welsh*. Berlin: Walter de Gruyter.

Jones, Charles. 1988. *Grammatical gender in English 950–1250*. New York: Croom Helm.

Jones, Michael. 1993. *Sardinian syntax*. London: Routledge.

Jørgensen, Peter. 1954. *Zum Schleswiger Niederdeutsch: Kritik und Forschung*. Copenhagen: Munksgaard.

Juneau, Marcel. 1972. *Contribution à l'histoire de la prononciation française au Québec: études des graphies des documents d'archives*. Sainte-Foy: Laval University Press.

Karabulatova, Irina, Flera Sayfulina & Bigaysha Akhmetova. 2013. Ethno-lingual aspect of modern functioning of Russian dialects in North Kazakhstan. *World Applied Sciences Journal* 27: 137–40.

Kari, James, & Ben Potter (eds.). 2010. *The Dene-Yenseian connection*. Fairbanks: University of Alaska Press.

Kastovsky, Dieter, & Arthur Mettinger (eds.). 2001. *Language contact in the history of English*. Bern: Peter Lang.

Kay, Paul. 1976. Discussion of papers by Kiparsky and Wescott. In S. R. Harnard, H. D. Steklis & J. Lancaster (eds.), *Origins and evolution of language and speech*. New York: New York Academy of Sciences, 17–19.

Keenan, Ed. 1976. Discussion. In S. R. Harnard, H. D. Steklis & J. Lancaster (eds.), *Origins and evolution of language and speech*. New York: New York Academy of Sciences, 92–6.

Keller, Rudi. 1994. *On language change: the invisible hand in language*. London: Routledge.

Keller, Wolfgang. 1925. Keltisches im englischen Verbum. In *Anglica: Untersuchungen zur englischen Philologie* 1. Leipzig: Mayer & Müller, 55–66.

King, Gareth. 2003. *Modern Welsh: a comprehensive grammar*. London: Routledge.

Kingston, John. 2011. Tonogenesis. In Marc van Oostendorp, Colin Ewen, Elizabeth Hume & Keren Rice (eds.), *The Blackwell companion to phonology*. Oxford: Blackwell, 2304–33.

Kiparsky, Paul. 2009. The Germanic weak preterite. In Patrick Steinkrüger & Manfred Krifka (eds.), *On Inflection*. Berlin: Mouton de Gruyter, 107–24.

Kirch, Patrick Vinton, & Roger Green. 2001. *Hawaiki, ancestral Polynesia: an essay in historical anthropology*. Cambridge: Cambridge University Press.

Kitson, Peter. 1996. British and European river names. *Transactions of the Philological Society* 94: 73–118.

Klemola, Juhani. 2006. *Was/were* variation in traditional dialects of England. *Paper given at ICEHL 14*, Bergamo, August 21–25.

Korotkova, Natalia, & Yury Lander. 2010. Deriving affix ordering in polysynthesis: evidence from Adyghe. *Morphology* 20: 299–319.

Kortmann, Bernd, & Benedikt Szmrecsanyi. 2004. Global synopsis: morphological and syntactic variation in English. In Bernd Kortmann & Edgar Schneider (eds.), *A handbook of varieties of English II: morphology and syntax*. Berlin: Mouton de Gruyter, 1142–202.

Kroch, Anthony, Ann Taylor & Donald Ringe. 1995. The Middle English verb-second constraint: a case study in language contact and language change. In Susan Herring, Pieter van Reenen & Lene Schøsler (eds.), *Textual Parameters*. Amsterdam: John Benjamins, 353–91.

Krupa, Victor. 1982. *The Polynesian languages*. London: Routledge.

Kurath, Hans. 1949. *A Word Geography of the Eastern United States*. Ann Arbor: University of Michigan Press.

Kusmenko, Jurij. 1996. Sprachkontakte und Sprachveränderungen in der süddänisch-nordfriesisch-niederdeutschen Kontaktzone. In Walter Baumgartner & Hans Fix (eds.), *Arbeiten zur Skandinavistik XII*. Vienna: Fassbänder, 65–83.

Kusmenko, Jurij. 2000. Entwicklung des Genussystems in den skandinavischen Sprachen. In Fritz Paul (ed.), *Arbeiten zur Skandinavistik XIII*. Frankfurt: Lang, 469–78.

Kusters, Wouter. 2003. *Linguistic complexity: the influence of social change on verbal inflection*. Leiden: Leiden University Press.

Labov, William. 1972. *Sociolinguistic patterns*. Philadelphia: University of Pennsylvania Press.

Labov, William. 1994. *Principles of linguistic change I: internal factors*. Oxford: Blackwell.

Laing, Lloyd, & Jennifer Laing. 1979. *Anglo-Saxon England*. London: Routledge.

Laing, Margaret. 2011. The reflexes of OE *beon* as a marker of futurity in Early Middle English. In Ursula Lenker, Judith Huber & Robert Mailhammer (eds.), *Verbal and nominal constructions in the history of English: variation and conventionalization*. Amsterdam: Benjamins.

Laker, Stephen. 2002. An explanation for the changes *kw-, hw-* > *χw-* in the English dialects. In Markku Filppula, Juhani Klemola & Heli Pitkänen (eds.), *The Celtic roots of English*. Joensuu: Joensuu University Press, 183–98.

Laker, Stephen. 2008. Changing views about Anglo-Saxons and Britons. In Henk Aertsen & Bart Veldhoen (eds.), *Six papers from the 28th Symposium on Medieval Studies*. Leiden: Leiden University Department, 1–38.

Lanham, Len. 1967. *The pronunciation of South African English*. Cape Town: Balkema.

Lass, Roger. 1997. *Historical linguistics and language change*. Cambridge: Cambridge University Press.

Lass, Roger. 1992. Phonology and morphology. In Norman Blake (ed.), *The Cambridge history of the English language vol. 2 1066–1476*. Cambridge: Cambridge University Press, 23–155.

Lass, Roger. 2000. Phonology and morphology. In R. Lass (ed.), *The Cambridge history of the English language: vol. III, 1476–1776*. Cambridge: Cambridge University Press, 56–186.

Lauttamus, Timo, Wybo Wiersma & John Nerbonne. 2008. Detecting syntactic substrate effects automatically in interlanguage corpora. In Muriel Norde, Bob de Jonge & Cornelius Hasselblatt (eds.), *Language contact in times of globalisation*. Amsterdam: Benjamins.

Laycock, Donald. 1982. Melanesian linguistic diversity: a Melanesian choice? In R. May & H. Nelson (eds.), *Melanesia: beyond diversity*. Canberra: Research School of Pacific Studies, 33–8.

Lehmann, Winfred P. 1961. A definition of Proto-Germanic: a study in the chronological delimitation of languages. *Language* 37: 67–74.

Lehmann, Winfred. 1993. *Theoretical bases of Indo-European linguistics*. London: Routledge.

Lenneberg, Eric. 1967. *Biological foundations of language*. New York: Wiley.

Lewis, Henry, & Holger Pedersen. 1937. *A concise comparative Celtic grammar*. Göttingen: Vandenhoeck & Ruprecht.

Lindow, Wolfgang, Dieter Möhn, Hermann Niebaum, Dieter Stellmacher, Hans Taubken & Jan Wirrer. 1998. *Niederdeutsche Grammatik*. Bremen: Schuster Leer.

Lipski, John. 1994. *Latin American Spanish*. London: Longman.

Lively, Scott, David Pisoni & Stephen Goldinger. 1994. Spoken word recognition: research and theory. In Morton Gernsbacher (ed.), *Handbook of psycholinguistics*. San Diego: Academic Press, 265–301.

Löfstedt, Ernst. 1968. *Beiträge zu einer nordfriesischen Grammatik. I. Das Substantiv und das Adjektiv, das Zahlwort und der bestimmte Artikel.* Uppsala: Uppsala University.

Luce, Paul. 1986. Neighbourhoods in the mental lexicon. In *Research on speech perception technical report No. 6.* Bloomington: Indiana University.

Luce, Paul, & David Pisoni. 1998. Recognizing spoken words: the neighborhood activation model. *Ear and Hearing* 19, 1–36.

Lupyan, Gary, & Rick Dale. 2010. Language structure is partly determined by social structure. *PLoS ONE* 5.1: e8559. doi:10.1371/journal.pone.0008559.

Luraghi, Silvia. 2009. The origin of the feminine gender in PIE: an old problem in a new perspective. In Vit Bubenik, John Hewson & Sarah Rose (eds.), *Grammatical change in Indo-European languages.* Amsterdam: Benjamin, 3–13.

Lutz, Angelika. 2009. Celtic influence on Old English and West Germanic. *English Language and Linguistics* 13: 227–49.

Lutz, Angelika. 2010. Why is West-Saxon English different from Old Saxon? In Hans Sauer & Joanna Story (eds.), *Anglo-Saxon England and the Continent.* Tempe: Arizona Center for Mediaeval and Renaissance Studies, 113–38.

Lynch, John, Malcolm Ross & Tony Crowley. 2002. *The Oceanic languages.* Richmond: Curzon.

Macaulay, Donald. 1992. *The Celtic languages.* Cambridge: Cambridge University Press.

Macaulay, R. K. S. 2002. I'm off to Philadelphia in the morning. *American Speech* 77: 227–41.

Mackridge, Peter. 1985. *The Modern Greek language.* Oxford: Oxford University Press.

Maddieson, Ian. 1984. *Patterns of sounds.* Cambridge: Cambridge University Press.

Madvig, Johan Nicolai. 1857. *De grammatische Betegnelser.* Copenhagen.

Mailhammer, Robert. 2011. The prehistory of European languages. In B. Kortmann & J. van der Auwera (eds.), *The languages and linguistics of Europe: a comprehensive guide.* Berlin: de Gruyter, 671–82.

Mailhammer, Robert. 2012. Diversity vs. uniformity: Europe before the arrival of the Indo-European languages: a comparison with prehistoric Australia. In Robert Mailhammer & Theo Vennemann (eds.), *Linguistic roots of Europe.* Copenhagen: Museum Tusculanum, 29–75.

Mallory, James. 1989. *In search of the Indo-Europeans: language, archaeology and myth.* London: Thames & Hudson.

Mallory, James. 2013. *The origins of the Irish.* London: Thames & Hudson.

Marck, Jeff. 1999. Revising Polynesian linguistic subgrouping and its culture history implications. In R. Blench & M. Spriggs (eds.), *Archaeology and language IV.* London: Routledge, 95–122.

Marck, Jeff. 2000. *Polynesian language and culture history.* Canberra: Pacific Linguistics.

Matras, Yaron, & Gertrud Reershemius. 2003. *Low German: East Frisian dialect.* Munich: Lincom.

Matthews, William. 1953. *The structure and development of Russian.* Cambridge: Cambridge University Press.

Mattoso Camara, Joaquim. 1972. *The Portuguese language.* Chicago: University of Chicago Press.

McDonough, Joyce, & Rachel Sussman. 2006. A methodology for the investigation of speaker's knowledge of structure in Athabaskan. *Proceedings of Berkeley Linguistic Society* 30: 102–13.

McMahon, April. 1994. *Understanding language change*. Cambridge: Cambridge University Press.

McMahon, Rob. 2011. Variation and populations. In Warren Maguire & April McMahon (eds.), *Analysing variation in English*. Cambridge: Cambridge University Press, 237–60.

McWhorter, John. 1997. *Towards a new model of creole genesis*. New York: Lang.

Melchert, Craig 2015. The position of Anatolian. In M. Weiss & A. Garrett (eds.), *Handbook of Indo-European studies*. Oxford: Oxford University Press.

Melchert, Craig, & Norbert Oettinger. 2009. Ablativ und Instrumental im Hethitischen und Indogermanischen: ein Beitrag zur relativen Chronologie. *Incontri Linguistici* 32: 53–73.

Miller, D. Gary. 2012. *External influences on English: from its beginnings to the Renaissance*. Oxford: Oxford University Press.

Milroy, James. 1992. Middle English dialectology. In N. Blake (ed.), *The history of the English language II: 1066–1476*. Cambridge: Cambridge University Press, 156–206.

Milroy, Lesley. 1980. *Language and social networks*. Oxford: Blackwell.

Mithun, Marianne. 1999. *The languages of Native North America*. Cambridge: Cambridge University Press.

Mittendorf, Ingo, & Erich Poppe. 2000. Celtic contacts of the English progressive? In Hildegard Tristram (ed.), *The Celtic Englishes II*. Heidelberg: Winter, 117–45.

Moore, Bruce. 1999. Australian English: Australian identity. *Lingua Franca*. www .abc.net.au/rn/arts/ling/stories/s68786.htm.

Moore, Emma. 2003. Learning style and identity: a sociolinguistic analysis of a Bolton high-school. Manchester: Manchester University PhD thesis.

Mørck, Endre. 2018. Seinmellomalderen (1350–1536). In Agnete Nesse (ed.), *Norsk språkhistorie IV: tidslinjer*. Oslo: Novus, 293–356.

Morin, Yves-Charles. 1994. Les sources historiques de la prononciation du français du Québec. In R. Mougeon & E. Beniak (eds.), *Les origines du français québécois*. Quebec: Laval University Press, 199–236.

Morris, John. 1973. *The age of Arthur: a history of the British Isles from 350 to 650*. London: Weidenfeld & Nicolson

Mortensen, David. 2012. The emergence of obstruents after high vowels. *Diachronica* 29: 434–470.

Mossé, Fernand. 1952. *A handbook of Middle English*. Baltimore: Johns Hopkins University Press.

Mougeon, Raymond, & Beniak, Édouard (eds.). 1994. *Les origines du français québécois*. Sainte-Foy: Laval University Press.

Mühlhäusler, Peter. 1977. *Pidginisation and simplification of language*. Canberra: Pacific Linguistics.

Munske, Horst Heine. (ed.). 2001. *Handbuch des Friesischen/Handbook of Frisian Studies*. Tübingen: Niemeyer.

Nedkvitne, Arnved. 1983. *Utenrikshandelen fra det vestafjelske Norge*. Bergen: Bergen University PhD thesis.

Nesse, Agnete. 2002. *Språkkontakt mellom norsk og tysk i hansatidens Bergen*. Oslo: Det Norske Videnskaps-Akademi.

Nesse, Agnete. 2005. Boken – han og kua – den: om endringer i norske genussystem. *Maal og minne*, 2005: 136–45.

Nesse, Agnete. 2009. Die Geschichte der Stadtmundart in Bergen (Norwegen) mit besonderem Augenmerk auf den Kontakt mit dem Mittelniederdeutschen. *Niederdeutsches Wort* 49: 31–40.

Nettle, Daniel. 1995. Segmental inventory size, word length, and communicative efficiency. *Linguistics* 33, 359–67.

Nettle, Daniel. 1999. *Linguistic diversity*. Oxford: Oxford University Press.

Nettle, Daniel, & Suzanne Romaine. 2000. *Vanishing voices: the extinction of the world's languages*. Oxford: Oxford University Press.

Nichols, Johanna. 1992. *Linguistic diversity in space and time*. Chicago: University of Chicago Press.

Nichols, Johanna. 1997. Modelling ancient population structures and movement in linguistics. *Annual Review of Anthropology* 26: 359–84.

Nichols, Johanna. 2007. Review of Ö. Dahl: The growth and maintenance of linguistic complexity. *Diachronica* 24: 171–8.

Nichols, Johanna, & David Peterson. 1996. The Amerind personal pronouns. *Language* 72.2: 336–71.

Nielsen, Gunhild. 1947. Glidning og lukning i Rømømaalets høje vokaler ('Klusilspring'). *Danske Folkemaal* 15: 41–65.

Nielsen, Hans Frede. 2007. English and the Jutland dialect; or, the demise of a romantic notion. In A. Wawn et al. (eds.), *Constructing nations, reconstructing myth: essays in honour of T. A. Shippey*. Turnhout: Brepols, 97–108

Nissen, Gunhild. 1945. Konsonaterne i Rømømålet i historisk belysning. *Danske Folkemål* 14: 97–119.

Noreen, Adolf. 1923. *Altnordische Grammatik*. Tübingen: Niemeyer.

Ó Siadhail, Mícheál. 1989. *Modern Irish: grammatical structure and dialectal variation*. Cambridge: Cambridge University Press.

Ojanen, Anna-Liisa. 1982. *A syntax of the Cambridgeshire dialect*. Helsinki: Helsinki University PhD thesis.

Pawley, Andrew. 1996a. On the position of Rotuman. In Bernd Nothofer (ed.), *Reconstruction, classification, description: Festschrift in honour of Isidore Dyen*, Hamburg: Abera Verlag Meyer & Co., 387–410.

Pawley, Andrew. 1996b. On the Polynesian subgroup as a problem for Irwin's continuous settlement hypothesis. In Janet Davidson, G. Irwin, F. Leach, A. Pawley & D. Brown (eds.), *Oceanic culture history: essays in honour of Roger Green*. Dunedin: New Zealand Journal of Archaeology, 387–410.

Pawley, Andrew. 1999. Chasing rainbows: implications of the rapid dispersal of Austronesian languages for subgrouping and reconstruction. In Elizabeth Zeitoun & Paul Li (eds.), *Selected papers from the eighth international conference on Austronesian linguistics*. Taipei: Academia Sinica, 95–138.

Pawley, Andrew, & Malcolm Ross. 1993. Austronesian historical linguistics and culture history. *Annual Review of Anthropology* 22: 425–59.

Pedersen, Karen Margrethe. 1999. Genusforenkling i Københavnsk. *Danske Folkemål* 41: 79–106.

Pedersen, Karen Margrethe. forthcoming. Genus: nominal- og adjektivbøjning. In Ebba Hjorth (ed.), *Dansk sproghistorie*. Copehhagen: Danske Sprog- og Litteraturselskab.

Pelech, William, 2002. Charting the interpersonal underworld: the application of cluster analysis to the study of interpersonal coordination in small groups. *Currents: New Scholarship in the Human Services* 1: 1–12.

Pelteret, David. 1995. *Slavery in early medieval England from the reign of Alfred until the twelfth century*. Woodbridge: Boydell Press.

Penny, Ralph. 1991. *A history of the Spanish language*. Cambridge: Cambridge University Press.

Penny, Ralph. 1998. Mozarabic. In G. Price (ed.), *Encyclopedia of the languages of Europe*. Oxford: Blackwell, 327.

Penny, Ralph. 2000. *Variation and change in Spanish*. Cambridge: Cambridge University Press.

Perkins, Revere. 1980. *The covariation of culture and grammar*. Ann Arbor: University of Michigan PhD thesis.

Perkins, Revere. 1995. *Deixis, grammar, and culture*. Amsterdam: Benjamins

Perridon, Harry. 1997. Is the definite article in Jutlandic a borrowing from Low German? *Multilingua* 16: 351–63.

Perridon, Harry. 2003. Language contact and grammatical change: the case of Bergen. *Tijdschrift voor Skandinavistiek* 24: 235–56.

Petyt, K. M. 1985. *Dialect and accent in industrial West Yorkshire*. Amsterdam: Benjamin.

Pietsch, Lukas. 2005. *The grammar of variation: verbal agreement in northern dialects of English*. Tübingen: Niemeyer.

Pittman, Christine. 2004. 'The key to the cabinets are rusty and unhinged': the conceptual and functional effects of the predicate on agreement error rates. *Toronto working papers in linguistics* 23: 115–46.

Pogatscher, Alois. 1888. *Zur Lautlehre der griechischen, lateinischen und romanischen Lehnworte im Altenglischen*. Strasbourg: Trübner.

Poirier, Claude. 1994. La langue parlée en Nouvelle-France: vers un convergence des explications. In R. Mougeon & E. Beniak (eds.), *Les origines du français québécois*. Sainte-Foy: Laval University Press, 237–74.

Pokorny, Julius. 1927–30. Das nicht-indogermanische Substrat im Irischen. *Zeitschrift für celtische Philologie* 16: 95–144, 231–66, 363–94; 17: 373–88; 18: 233–48.

Polomé, Edgar. 1990. Types of linguistic evidence for early contact: Indo-Europeans and non-Indo-Europeans. In John Greppin & Thomas Markey (eds.), *When worlds collide*. Ann Arbor: Karoma, 267–89.

Poulson, Laurie. 2011. Meta-modeling of tense and aspect in a cross-linguistic grammar engineering platform. *University of Washington Working Papers in Linguistics* 28.

Pountain, Christopher. 1982. *essere/stare as a Romance phenomenon. In Nigel Vincent & Martin Harris (eds.), *Studies in the Romance verb: essays offered to Joe Cremona on the occasion of his 60th Birthday*. London: Croom Helm, 139–60.

Poussa, Patricia. 1982. The evolution of Early Standard English: the creolisation hypothesis. *Studia Anglica Posnaniensia* 14: 69–85.

Priestly, Tom. 1983. On 'drift' in Indo-European gender systems. *Journal of Indo-European Studies* 11: 339–63.

Primus, Beatrice. 1999. *Cases and thematic roles: ergative, accusative and active*. Tübingen: Niemeyer.

Prokosch, Eduard. 1939. *A comparative Germanic grammar*. Philadelphia: University of Pennsylvania Press

Rambø, Gro-Renée. 2008. *Historiske og sosiale betingelser for språkkontakt mellom nedertysk og skandinavisk i seinmiddelalderen: et bidrag til historisk språksosiologi*. Kristiansand: Agder University PhD thesis.

Rice, Keren. 1999. Review of Leonard Faltz (1998): the Navajo verb: a grammar for students and scholars. *Linguistic Typology* 3: 393–400.

Ringe, Don. 2006. *From Proto-Indo-European to Proto-Germanic*. Oxford: Oxford University Press.

Ritt, Nikolaus. 1992. *Luick, the theoretician*. Vienna English Working Papers 1: 93–104.

Rivard, Adjutor. 1914. *Études sur les parlers de France au Canada*. Quebec: Garneau.

Roberge, Paul. 1995. The formation of Afrikaans. In Raj Mesthrie (ed.), *Language and social history: studies in South African sociolinguistics*. Cape Town: Philip, 68–88.

Roberge, Paul. 2010. Contact and the history of Germanic Languages. In Raymond Hickey (ed.), *The Handbook of Language Contact*. Oxford: Blackwell, 406–31.

Roma, Elisa. 2007. Relativisation strategies in insular Celtic languages: history and contacts with English. In Paolo Ramat & Elisa Roma (eds.), *Europe and the Mediterranean as linguistic areas: convergencies from a historical and typological perspective*. Amsterdam: Benjamins, 245–88.

Ross, Malcolm. 1992. The sound of Proto-Austronesian: an outsider's view of the Formosan evidence. *Oceanic Linguistics* 31: 23–64.

Ross, Malcolm. 1997. Social networks and kinds of speech community events. In R. Blench & M. Spriggs (eds.), *Archaeology and language*. London: Routledge, 209–61.

Rothwell, William. 1998. Arrivals and departures: the adoption of French terminology into Middle English. *English Studies* 79: 144–65.

Russ, Charles (ed.). 1989. *The dialects of Modern German*. London: Routledge.

Russ, Charles. 1982. Die Vereinfachung der Nominalflexion im Englischen und Jutisch-Dänischen: ein Fall der gegenseitigen Beeinflussung? *Orbis* 29: 120–29.

Ryckeboer, Hugo. 2002. Dutch/Flemish in the North of France. *Journal of Multilingual and Multicultural Development* 23: 22–35.

Sadock, Jerrold. 2003. *A grammar of Kalaallisut*. Munich: Lincom.

Sammallahti, Pekka. 1977. Suomalaisten esihistorian kysymyksiä. *Virittäjä* 81: 119–36.

Samuels, Michael. 1972. *Linguistic evolution: with special reference to English*. Cambridge: Cambridge University Press.

Sapir, Edward. 1912. Language and environment. *American Anthropologist* 14: 226–42.

Sapir, Edward. 1921. *Language*. New York: Harcourt Brace.

Schadeberg, Thilo. 1981. Die Geschichte der Nominalklassen des Laru (Kordofanisch). *Berliner Afrikanistische Vorträge* 21: 203–12.

Schlegel, August Wilhelm von. 1846. *Œuvres de M. Auguste-Guillaume de Schlegel*. Leipzig: Weidmann.

Schönfeld, Helmut. 1989. East Low German. In Charles Russ (ed.), *The dialects of Modern German*. London: Routledge, 91–135.

Schrijver, Peter. 1995. *Studies in British Celtic Phonology*. Amsterdam: Rodopi.

Schrijver, Peter. 2002. The rise and fall of British Latin: evidence from English and Brittonic. In Markku Filppula, Juhani Klemola & Heli Pitkänen (eds.), *The Celtic roots of English*. Joensuu: University Press, 87–110.

Schrijver, Peter. 2003. Early developments of the vowel systems of Northwest Germanic and Saami. In Alfred Bammesberger & Theo Vennemann (eds.), *Languages of prehistoric Europe*. Heidelberg: Winter, 195–226.

Schrijver, Peter. 2007. What Britons spoke around 400 AD. In Nicholas Higham (ed.), *Britons in Anglo-Saxon England*. Woodbridge: Boydell and Brewer, 165–71.

Schrijver, Peter. 2009. Celtic influence on Old English: phonological and phonetic evidence. *English Language and Linguistics*, 13: 193–211.

Schumacher, Stefan. 2009. Lexical and structural language-contact phenomena along the Germano-Celtic transition zone. In Stefan Zimmer (ed.), *Kelten am Rhein II: Philologie. Sprachen und Literaturen*. Mainz: von Zabern, 247–66.

Shetter, William. 1991. *Dutch: an essential grammar*. London: Routledge.

Sheynin, Hayim. 2004. Review of T. Vennemann: *Europa Vasconica – Europa Semitica*. http://linguistlist.org/issues/15/15-1878.html#1.

Shields, Kenneth. 2010. Linguistic typology and the reconstruction of the Indo-European accusative plural. *Emerita: Revista de Lingüística y Filología Clásica* 78: 33–42.

Shorrocks, Graham. 1999. *A grammar of the dialect of the Bolton area II: morphology and syntax*. Frankfurt: Lang.

Sibata, Takeshi. 1999. The evolution of the Common Language in Hokkaido. In Takeshi Shibata, Tetsuya Kunihiro, Fumio Inoue & Daniel Long (eds.), *Sociolinguistics in Japanese contexts*. Berlin: de Gruyter, 229–248.

Siemund, Peter. 2008. *Pronominal gender in English: a study of English varieties from a cross-linguistic perspective*. London: Routledge.

Siewierska, Anna. 2004. *Person*. Cambridge: Cambridge University Press.

Sinnemäki, Kaius. 2009. Complexity in core argument marking and population size. In G. Sampson, D. Gil & P. Trudgill (eds.), *Language complexity as an evolving variable*. Oxford: Oxford University Press, 125–40.

Skard, Vemund. 1967. *Norskspråkhistorie I: til 1523*. Oslo: Universitetsforlaget.

Skard, Vemund. 1972. *Norskspråkhistorie II: 1523–1814*. Oslo: Universitetsforlaget.

Skautrup, Peter. 1944. *Det Danske Sprogs Historie I*. Copenhagen: Gyldendal.

Skjekkeland, Martin. 1997. *Dei norske dialektane: tradisjonelle særdrag i jamføring me skriftmåla*. Kristiansand: Høyskoleforlaget.

Skrzypek, Dominika. 2010. Interactions of grammatical categories: how three genders became two. *Skandinavistik: European Journal of Scandinavian Studies* 38: 91–106.

Smith, Aaron. 2001. The role of frequency in the specialisation of the English anterior. In Joan Bybee & Paul Hopper (eds.), *Frequency and the emergence of linguistic structure*. Amsterdam: Benjamins, 361–82.

Smitherman, Thomas, & Jóhanna Barðdal. 2009. Typological changes in the evolution of Indo-European syntax? *Diachronica* 26(2): 253–73.

Sneddon, J. N. 2006. *Colloquial Jakartan Indonesian*. Canberra: Australian National University.

Søndergaard, Bent. 1970. Den såkaldte klusilspring, specielt i morsingmål. *Sprog og kultur* 26: 61–8.

Song, Jae Jung. 2001. *Linguistic typology: morphology and syntax*. London: Longman.

Spalinger, Edeltraut. 1955. *Absterben von jacere im Galloromanischen*. Berne: Francke.

Stassen, Leon. 2008. Zero copula for predicate nominals. In Martin Haspelmath, Matthew S. Dryer, David Gil & Bernard Comrie (eds.), *World atlas of linguistic structures online*. Munich: Max Planck Digital Library, nr. 120.

Stevenson, Roland C. 1956. A survey of the phonetics and grammatical structure of the Nuba Mountain languages. *Afrika und Übersee* 40: 93–115.

Sutton, Douglas (ed.). 1994. *The origins of the first New Zealanders*. Auckland: Auckland University Press.

Szemerényi, Oswald. 1996. *Introduction to Indo-European linguistics*. Oxford: Clarendon Press.

Tadmor, Uri. 2015. When culture grammaticalises: the pronominal system of Onya Darat. In Rik De Busser & Randy J. LaPolla (eds.), *Language structure and environment: social, cultural, and natural factors*. Amsterdam: John Benjamins, 77–98.

Taeldeman, Johan. 2005. *Oost-Vlaams*. Tielt: Lannoo.

Tagliamonte, Sali. 2008. There was universals; then there weren't: a comparative sociolinguistic perspective on 'default singulars'. In Markku Fillpula, Heli Paulasto & Juhani Klemola (eds.), *Vernacular universals versus contact induced change*. London: Routledge.

Thomas, Mark, Michael Stumpf & Heinrich Härke. 2008. Integration versus apartheid in post-Roman Britain. *Proceedings of the Royal Society B*. 275: 2419–21.

Thomason, Sarah, & Terrence Kaufman. 1988. *Language contact, creolization, and genetic linguistics*. Berkeley: University of California Press.

Thráinsson, Höskuldur. 1994. Icelandic. In E. König & J. van der Auwera (eds.), *The Germanic languages*. London: Routledge.

Thurston, William 1989. How exoteric languages build a lexicon: esoterogeny in West New Britain. In R. Harlow & R. Hooper (eds.), *VICAL I: Papers in Oceanic linguistics*. Auckland: Linguistic Society of New Zealand, 555–79.

Tiersma, Pieter Meijes. 1985. *Frisian reference grammar*. Dordrecht: Foris.

Tolkien, J. R. R. 1963. English and Welsh. In Henry Lewis (ed.), *Angles and Britons: O'Donnell Lectures*. Cardiff: University of Wales Press, 1–41.

Tolkien, J. R. R. 1983. English and Welsh. In J. R. R. Tolkien (ed.), *The monsters and the critics and other essays*. London: Allen & Unwin, 162–97.

Tomlin, Roger. 1988. The curse tablets. In B. Cunliffe (ed.), *The temple of Sulis Minerva at Bath II: the finds from the Sacred Spring*. Oxford: Oxford University Press, 59–277.

Townend, Matthew. 2002. *Language and history in Viking Age England: linguistic relations between speakers of Old Norse and Old English*. Turnhout: Brepols.

Trask, Larry. 1997. *The history of Basque*. London: Routledge.

Trask, Larry.1995. Origin and relatives of the Basque language: review of the evidence. In José Ignacio Hualde, Joseba Lakarra & Larry Trask (eds.), *Towards a history of the Basque language*. Amsterdam: Benjamins, 65–77.

Tristram, Hildegard (ed.). 2003. *The Celtic Englishes III*. Heidelberg: Winter.

Tristram, Hildegard. 2004. Diglossia in Anglo-Saxon England, or what was spoken Old English like? *Studia Anglica Posnaniensia* 40: 87–110.

Tristram, Hildegard. 2006. Why don't the English speak Welsh? In N. J. Higham (ed.), *Britons in Anglo-Saxon England*. Woodbridge: Boydell, 192–214.

Trotter, David. 2000. Anglo-Norman. In Glanville Price (ed.), *Languages of the British Isles*. Oxford: Blackwell, 197–206.

Trudgill, Peter. 1973. Linguistic change and diffusion: description and explanation in sociolinguistic dialect geography. *Language in Society* 3: 215–46.

Trudgill, Peter. 1983. *On dialect: social and geographical perspectives*. Oxford: Blackwell.

Trudgill, Peter. 1986. *Dialects in contact*. Oxford: Blackwell.

Trudgill, Peter. 1998. Typology and sociolinguistics: linguistic structure, social structure and explanatory comparative dialectology. *Folia Linguistica* 31: 349–60.

Trudgill, Peter. 2000. On locating the boundary between language contact and dialect contact: Low German and continental Scandinavian. In E. H. Jahr (ed.), *Språkkontakt: innverknaden frå nedertysk på andre nordeuropeiske språk*. Copenhagen: Nordisk Ministerråd, 71–86.

Trudgill, Peter. 2002. Linguistic and social typology. In J. K. Chambers, N. Schilling-Estes & P. Trudgill (eds.), *Handbook of Linguistic Variation and Change*. Oxford: Blackwell, 707–28.

Trudgill, Peter. 2003. *The Norfolk dialect*. Cromer: Poppyland.

Trudgill, Peter. 2004. *New-dialect formation: the inevitability of colonial Englishes*. Edinburgh: Edinburgh University Press.

Trudgill, Peter. 2008. Colonial dialect contact in the history of European languages: on the irrelevance of identity to new-dialect formation. *Language in Society* 37(2): 241–54.

Trudgill, Peter. 2010. Contact and sociolinguistic typology. In R. Hickey (ed.), *Handbook of language contact*. Oxford: Blackwell, 299–319.

Trudgill, Peter. 2011. *Sociolinguistic typology: social determinants of linguistic complexity*. Oxford: Oxford University Press.

Trudgill, Peter. 2012. The history of dialect contact in English. In Alexander Bergs & Laurel Brinton (eds.), *Historical Linguistics of English*. Berlin: Mouton de Gruyter.

Trudgill, Peter. 2013. Gender maintenance and loss in Totenmålet, English, and other major Germanic varieties. In Terje Lohndal (ed.), *In search of Universal Grammar: from Old Norse to Zoque*. Amsterdam: Benjamins, 77–108.

Trudgill, Peter. 2020. Sociolinguistic typology and the uniformitarian hypothesis. In Mily Crevels, Jean-Marie Hombert & Pieter Muysken (eds.), *Language dispersal, diversification, and contact: a global perspective*. Oxford: Oxford University Press.

Tryon, Darrell. 1993. *Comparative Austronesian dictionary*. Berlin: Mouton.

Tuten, Donald. 2003. *Koineization in medieval Spanish*. Berlin: de Gruyter.

Urbańczyk, Stanisław. 1976. *Zarys dialektologii polskiej* [An outline of Polish dialectology]. Warsaw: PWN.

Väänänen, Veikko. 1967. *Introduction au latin vulgaire*. Paris: Klincksieck.

Vajda, Edward. 2010a. A Siberian link with the Na-Dene. *Anthropological Papers of the University of Alaska* 5: 31–99.

Vajda, Edward. 2010b. Yeniseian, Na-Dene, and historical Linguistics. *Anthropological Papers of the University of Alaska* 5: 100–18.

Van Loey, Adolphe. 1973. *Middelnederlandse spraakkunst I: vormleer*. 7th ed. Groningen: Tjeenk Willink.

van Riemsdijk, Henk. 1978. *A case study in syntactic markedness: the binding nature of prepositional phrases*. Dordrecht: De Ridder.

Vennemann, Theo. 2000. English as a 'Celtic' language: Atlantic influences from above and below. In Hildegard Tristram (ed.), *The Celtic Englishes II*. Heidelberg: Winter, 399–406.

Vennemann, Theo. 2001. *Atlantis Semitica*: structural contact features in Celtic and English. In Laurel Brinton (ed.), *Historical linguistics 1999: selected papers from the 14th International Conference on Historical Linguistics*. Amsterdam: Benjamins, 351–69.

Vennemann, Theo. 2002. Semitic → Celtic → English: the transitivity of language contact. In Markku Filppula, Juhani Klemola & Heli Pitkänen (eds.), *The Celtic roots of English*. Joensuu: Joensuu University Press, 295–330.

Vennemann, Theo. 2003a. Languages in prehistoric Europe north of the Alps. In Alfred Bammesberger & Theo Vennemann (eds.), *Languages in prehistoric Europe*. Heidelberg: Winter, 319–32.

Vennemann, Theo. 2003b. *Europa Vasconica – Europa Semitica*. Edited by Patrizia Noel Aziz Hanna. Berlin: Mouton de Gruyter.

Vennemann, Theo. 2010a. Contact and prehistory: the Indo-European Northwest. In Raymond Hickey (ed.), *The handbook of language contact*. Oxford: Blackwell, 380–405.

Vennemann, Theo. 2010b. Contact and prehistory in the Indo-European Northwest: lexical influences. *Sprachwissenschaft* 35: 247–90.

Vennemann, Theo. 2011. English as a contact language: typology and comparison. *Anglia* 129: 217–57.

Visser, Willem. 2011. Historical gender change in West Frisian. *Morphology* 21: 31–56.

Vogt, Hans. 1948. Dans quelles conditions et dans quelles limites peut s'exercer sur le système morphologique d'une langue l'action du système morphologique d'une autre langue? In M. Lejeune (ed.), *Actes du Sixième Congrès International des Linguistes*. Paris: Klincksieck, 31–45.

Wagner, Heinrich. 1959. *Das Verbum in den Sprachen der Britischen Inseln*. Tübingen: Niemeyer.

Wagner, Max. 1920. Amerikansich-Spanisch und Vulgärlatein. *Zeitschrift für romanische Philologie* 40: 286–312, 385–404.

Wagner, Susanne. 2005. Gender in English pronouns: Southwest England. In Bernd Kortmann, Tanja Herrmann, Lukas Pietsch & Susanne Wagner (eds.), *Comparative grammar of English dialects: agreement, gender, relative clauses*. Berlin: Mouton de Gruyter, 211–367.

Wahrig-Burfeind, Renate. 1989. *Nominales und pronominales Genus im südlichen Nordseegebiet: eine areallinguistische Untersuchung*. Bremen: Tuduv.

Walker, Alastair. 1980. *Die nordfriesische Mundart der Bökingharde*. Stuttgart: Steiner.

Walker, James. 2007. 'There's bears back there': plural existentials and vernacular universals in (Quebec) English. *English World-Wide* 28: 147–66.

Wall, Arnold. 1938. *New Zealand English: how it should be spoken*. Auckland: Whitcombe & Tombs.

Wandruszka, Mario. 1965. *Stare* in den romanischen Sprachen. *Zeitschrift für romanische Philologie* 81: 423–40.

Wang, Luming, Matthias Schlesewsky, Balthasar Bickel & Ina Bornkessel-Schlesewsky. 2009. Exploring the nature of the 'subject'-preference: evidence from the online comprehension of simple sentences in Mandarin Chinese. *Language and Cognitive Processes* 24: 1180–226.

Watkins, Calvert. 1998. Proto-Indo-European: comparison and reconstruction. In A. Giacalone Ramat & P. Ramat (eds.), *The Indo-European Languages*. London: Routledge, 25–73.

Weijnen, Anton. 2000. *Nederlandse dialectkunde*. 2nd ed. Assen: Van Gorcum.

Weiss, Helmut. 2015. The Wackernagel position and complementizer agreement: the emergence of a syntactic particularity at the left edge of the middle field. In R. Hinterhölzl, K. Bentzen, A. Speyer & L. Szucsuch (eds.). *The German Middle Field in a comparative and diachronic perspective*. Berlin: Mouton de Gruyter.

Wessén, Elias. 1970. *Schwedische Sprachgeschichte*. Berlin: De Gruyter.

White, David. 2002. Explaining the innovations of Middle English: what, where, and why? In Markku Filppula, Juhani Klemola & Heli Pitkänen (eds.), *The Celtic roots of English*. Joensuu: Joensuu University Press, 153–74.

White, David. 2003. Brittonic influence in the reductions of Middle English nominal morphology. In H. Tristram (ed.), *The Celtic Englishes II*. Heidelberg: Winter, 29–45.

Whitelock, Dorothy. 1952. *The beginnings of English society*. Harmondsworth: Penguin.

Whorf, Benjamin Lee. 1956. *Language, thought, and reality: selected writings of Benjamin Lee Whorf* [edited by John B. Carroll]. Cambridge, MA: MIT Press.

Wier, Thomas. 2006. Review of J. Sadock: a Grammar of Kalaallisut. *Language* 82: 221–2.

Wiesenhann, Tjabe. 1977. *Einführung in das ostfriesische Niederdeutsch*. Leer: Schuster.

Wiik, Kalevi. 2003. Finnic-type pronunciation in the Germanic languages. *Mankind Quarterly* 44: 43–90.

Willemyns, Roland. 2002. The Dutch-French language border in Belgium. *Journal of Multilingual and Multicultural Development* 23: 36–49.

Wischer, Ilse. 2011. On the use of *beon* and *wesan* in Old English. In Ursula Lenker, Judith Huber & Robert Mailhammer (eds.), *Verbal and nominal constructions in the history of English: variation and conventionalisation*. Amsterdam: Benjamins, 217–36.

Wohlgemuth, Jan. 2010. Language endangerment, community size, and typological rarity. In Jan Wohlgemuth & Michael Cysouw (eds.), *Rethinking universals: how rarities affect linguistic theory*. Berlin: De Gruyter, 255–77.

Wohlgemuth, Jan, & Michael Cysouw (eds.). 2010. *Rara and rarissima: documenting the fringes of linguistic diversity*. Berlin: De Gruyter.

Woolf, Alex. 2007. Apartheid and economics in Anglo-Saxon England. In N. Higham (ed.), *The Britons in Anglo-Saxon England*. Woodbridge: Boydell, 113–29.

Wray, Alison, & George Grace. 2007. The consequences of talking to strangers: evolutionary corollaries of socio-cultural influences on linguistic form. *Lingua* 117: 543–78.

Wright, Roger. 1982. *Late Latin and Early Romance in Spain and Carolingian France*. Liverpool: University of Liverpool.

Wubs-Mrozewicz, Justyna. 2008. *Traders, ties and tensions: the interactions of Lübeckers, Overijsslers and Hollanders in Late Medieval Bergen*. Hilversum: Verloren.

Index